T0128421

SHAPING OF A SERVANT

The Odyssey of a Family

CARL E. HANSEN

WESTBOW
PRESS®
A DIVISION OF THOMAS NELSON
& ZONDERVAN

Copyright © 2023 Carl E. Hansen.

All rights reserved. No part of this book may be used or reproduced by any means, graphic, electronic, or mechanical, including photocopying, recording, taping or by any information storage retrieval system without the written permission of the author except in the case of brief quotations embodied in critical articles and reviews.

WestBow Press books may be ordered through booksellers or by contacting:

WestBow Press
A Division of Thomas Nelson & Zondervan
1663 Liberty Drive
Bloomington, IN 47403
www.westbowpress.com
844-714-3454

Because of the dynamic nature of the Internet, any web addresses or links contained in this book may have changed since publication and may no longer be valid. The views expressed in this work are solely those of the author and do not necessarily reflect the views of the publisher, and the publisher hereby disclaims any responsibility for them.

Any people depicted in stock imagery provided by Getty Images are models, and such images are being used for illustrative purposes only.
Certain stock imagery © Getty Images.

Cover designed by Destiny Joy Gomez-Kreider of "Destiny Designs," a granddaughter of the author, using a photo of the Hansen brothers standing in front of their much-loved Jeep

Scripture quotations marked (JB) are taken from the JERUSALEM BIBLE Copyright© 1966, 1967, 1968 by Darton, Longmand & Todd LTD and Doubleday and Co. Inc. All rights reserved.

Scripture quotations marked (NIV) are taken from the Holy Bible, New International Version®, NIV®. Copyright © 1973, 1978, 1984, 2011 by Biblica, Inc.® Used by permission of Zondervan. All rights reserved worldwide. www.zondervan.com The "NIV" and "New International Version" are trademarks registered in the United States Patent and Trademark Office by Biblica, Inc.®

Scripture marked (KJV) taken from the King James Version of the Bible.

ISBN: 978-1-6642-8396-1 (sc)
ISBN: 978-1-6642-8398-5 (hc)
ISBN: 978-1-6642-8397-8 (e)

Library of Congress Control Number: 2022921338

Print information available on the last page.

WestBow Press rev. date: 01/06/2023

To God, the Architect and Builder:

It was you who created my inmost self,
and put me together in my mother's womb;
for all these mysteries I thank you:
for the wonder of myself, for the wonder of your works.

You know me through and through,
from having watched my bones take shape
when I was being formed in secret,
knitted together in the limbo of the womb.

You had scrutinized my every action
All were recorded in your book,
my days listed and determined,
even before the first of them occurred.

God, how hard it is to grasp your thoughts!
How impossible to count them!
I could no more count them than I could the sand,
And suppose I could, you would still be with me.
-- Psalms 139:13-18 The Jerusalem Bible

DEDICATION

I dedicate this book to the memory of my mother and father, Elizabeth Winnifred (Friesen) and Jens Peter Hansen, who brought me into this world and taught me the most important essential, the key to life: "In all your ways acknowledge him, and he will make your paths straight." (Proverbs 3:6 – NIV). They modeled for me and taught me the importance of aligning my spiritual life and what we can know about God, with the physical realities, including the value of hard work, of honesty and integrity, of stewardship and bearing responsibility, of being dependable and trustworthy, of being co-creators with God in caring for his "garden" planet Earth, and of being generous and self-giving for the good of others – all of these, the key to a life well-lived.

> *Since my youth, O God, you have taught me,*
> *and to this day I declare your marvelous deeds.*
> *Even when I am old and grey, do not forsake me, O God,*
> *till I declare your power to the next generation,*
> *your might to all who come.*
> -- Psalms 71:17, 18 NIV

CONTENTS

PREFACE

Since I was a youth in high school, I had a desire to write a book about our growing years as a family. Although I recognized that we were just ordinary people, I also realized that every family has a unique story. A life worth living should be worth reading about. I knew my father's story and my mother's story were interesting, and I believed the story of growing up with my four brothers and two sisters was interesting enough to warrant a book.

My resolve was rekindled while taking a course in 1985 called Leadership Perspectives ML 530 under Professor J. Robert Clinton at the School of World Missions, Fuller Theological Seminary. One of our assignments was to write a "Personal Leadership Selection Process Paper" in which we were to reflect upon our whole life, and even that of our progenitors, those who have gone before us, to see how God used so many different people, influences, circumstances, and events, both good and seemingly bad, to mold and shape us into the kinds of persons we are today.

It was exciting and sobering to see how God, the expert craftsman, builds people who will later fill the roles of service for which they have been uniquely fitted. The work accomplished on my paper gave me courage and confidence that my story would be worth writing.

Today, reflecting again on this assignment from the perspective of thirty-seven years later, I can see so much clearer how this life process has worked out in my life. In the words of Ulysses as quoted by Alfred, Lord Tennyson, "*I am a part of all I have met!*" All of those seemingly unrelated events, influences, experiences, and circumstances that I faced since my birth, and even those of my forebearers, have shaped and equipped me and have come into convergence in my later years, enabling me to undertake and accomplish the more difficult and profound level of service that I would not have been able to succeed in doing, even in my mid years. Each of these process items has worked together to make me the kind of person I have become and enabled me to undertake the kinds of challenges that I have now completed.

During one of our furlough years, those precious times when we could reconnect with family and friends and supporters, our sponsoring mission asked me to spend time with a counselor. One thing I took away was the counselor's question: "What is driving you?" I do not think he ever got to an answer, and I did not either, but the question did make me think. Am I a "driven person"?

I reflected for a long time and finally admitted to myself that I am a driven person. Throughout my adult life, I have been approaching whatever I do with determination and tenacity and a sense of purpose. But what is that purpose that has been driving me? Is it comfort, security, money, possessions, success, popularity, fame, power and respect, or leisure and enjoyment? What is driving me?

The question is too introspective, too shallow. Should we not also take into consideration an often-overlooked dimension, the role of our Creator and Sustainer, the one so intimately connected in our lives, the One by whom "we live and move and have our being?" When we ask, "What is driving me?" should we not also ask, "Who is driving me?" Recently, I came across a quotation that reminded me again of this synergistic relationship we humans can have with the Almighty:

> *It is Jesus who stirs in you the desire to do something great with your lives, the will to follow an ideal, the refusal to allow yourselves to be ground down by mediocrity, the courage to commit yourselves humbly and patiently to improve yourselves and society, making the world more human and more fraternal.*
> -- Karol Wojtyla (who became Pope John Paul II)

Looking back from the perspective of advancing age, I think the answer may be that from my youth on, I have been driven to make my life count, in some way, to make the world a better place for my having been here, to leave a legacy of having made a difference, of contributing some good that would be of benefit to others and all future generations.

It is that purpose that now drives me to devote many days and months of my declining years to reflect upon my life and write my memoirs so future generations, and particularly my descendants, can get a glimpse of lessons I have learned. This exercise is taking the form of a series of books on different phases of my life. Together, this series expresses *The Odyssey of a Family*.

In 1991, at the age of fifty, I began to write a rough draft of my story. It began with a review of all the information I could collect about my paternal and maternal ancestors. It continued with the years from earliest family memories up to September 28, 1967, the day my wife and daughter and I boarded a plane on our way to begin a term of missionary service in Ethiopia.

From the first part of this material, I developed the book, *Jacob and Justina: Pilgrims, The Odyssey of a Family* that was printed by Masthof Press in 1998 and reprinted as *Pilgrims Searching for a Home: The Odyssey of a Family,* by Westbow Press in 2022. This is the story of my maternal grandparents who grew up in Russia and immigrated to western Canada in 1924 and raised their family of fourteen children through the severe hardships of the Great Depression.

The later part of that material I am incorporating into this second book, *Shaping of a Servant: The Odyssey of a Family,* recording the story of my birth family and my growing years. As in every story of a family, there must be overlap between the generations. While the subject of my first book was that of my grandparents, it of necessity included the early lives of my parents and subsequently the appearance of their grandchildren, my siblings and myself.

In the early part of this book, I ran the risk of including too much detail in giving names and dates of various of our ancestor families. While I apologize for the boredom this will cause some of my readers, I did this intentionally, knowing that a few of the descendants will appreciate finding the detailed information that would otherwise be lost to them forever.

In this volume, the subject includes my biographical interest in the story of my parents and siblings as the milieu in which I took shape and grew to maturity. The later part of this story is more completely autobiographical, focusing on those formation factors which shaped me into the person I have become.

In addition to these two books, I am working on publishing three more books in this "*The Odyssey of a Family*" series. "*Into Abyssinia*" covers eight years of our lives as a family living and working in Ethiopia from 1967 to 1975. The fourth manuscript, "*Reconciliation in Trans Mara*" is the story of our family working at a community development project among the Maasai and Luo people in the Trans Mara region of Kenya in the years, 1985-1991. The fifth and last book will be "*A Legacy in Bishoftu: The Odyssey of a Family*" which is an autobiographical history of founding the Meserete Kristos College in Ethiopia, 1996-2020.

I also realize that the signs pointing towards my own mortality are much more obvious as memory begins to fade, skin wrinkles, joints ach, and energy levels decrease. The compulsion to put our story on record is most urgent. Yes, I am still being driven!

I want to write this story as I would tell it to my grandchildren and great grandchildren. Although they may still be too young to understand, the time will come when they, as adults, will want to know about their roots. This is my gift to them, a link between their ancestors and all generations to come. They will live or survive in a world that will be vastly different from the one I was born into, just as my world then was hugely different from the one my grandparents were born into.

It is my hope that the writing of this story will be honoring and bring glory to God to whom I belong and whose kingdom I have been privileged to represent. He thought of me before I was formed me in my mother's womb. He placed me in a godly family who loved me and nurtured me. He shaped me with thousands of influences through the years and called me to a father-son relationship with himself. All I am, and all I have, come from him, and belong to him, because I belong to him.

I am not writing this to glorify myself or members of our family, but that others who, upon reading it, may also learn to trust him without reservations and find life to be more complete and fulfilling in relating to him, as I have found.

In this story there are no heroes and no villains, although there is bit of hero material and a particle of villain material in each of the characters. It is good to remember the words of Robert Louis Stevenson who once said: "*There is so much good in the worst of us, and so much bad in the best of us, that it behooves us all not to talk about the rest of us.*"

I am first a Christian, and view life historically and theologically from the Judeo-Christian tradition. That is, I see God as the source of all life, as personal, and as interested in entering a covenantal relationship with each of us, inviting each human being into a community of fellow believers, an alternate community within, but different from, the general society in which we all live.

My view of what it means to be a Christian is shaped by my Anabaptist-Mennonite heritage. To become a Christian is to become a follower of Jesus. Nothing more, and nothing less. It is not enough to just be born into a Christian family or to hold citizenship in a "Christian" nation. To use patriotic terms, to be a Christian is to "pledge allegiance" to Jesus Christ as "Lord" or "King" of one's entire life. To have no other "Lords." To become a Christian, one must recognize that Jesus is Lord, and make a concrete decision to follow him on a lifelong odyssey together in a Jesus-following community.

Following Jesus is an exciting and sometimes costly journey. One can never predict when he will lead one to make an abrupt turn on the way, nor will one always know where the journey will lead, nor what the journey may cost in terms of self-denial or suffering, nor what will be the outcome of the journey. But the Christian goes in abandonment and loyalty because that is where his Master is leading.

It is that basic seriousness about their journey with Jesus that led our ancestors to leave the security and comforts of Holland, along with its intolerant dogmas, and flee to the swamps of northern Prussia to establish their own Christian communities. It was that same seriousness that drove them on to the steppes of southern Russia 200 years later, and on to Canada 150 years after that. And it is that same call to journey with Jesus that has moved our immediate family on its journey to Ethiopia, Kenya, and Peru. May our descendants join us on this odyssey as we continue in faithfulness "until our journey ends eternally."

> *Oh, may all who come behind us find us faithful*
> *May the fire of our devotion light their way*
> *May the footprints that we leave, lead them to believe*
> *And the lives we live inspire them to obey.*
> -- "Find Us Faithful" -- by Jon Mohr, Publisher, Birdwing Music, 1987

ACKNOWLEDGMENTS

First, I want to express my gratitude to God for a good heritage, for godly ancestors that shaped my life and made it a story worth writing. Also, I am thankful for the gifts of time, opportunity, ability, and stamina to write it.

For the early part of the material in this book, I am most indebted to several individuals whose contribution I must mention. Without their assistance, I would never have uncovered the many details recorded in this book.

Of primary importance, I owe a debt of gratitude to my late mother, Elizabeth Winnifred (Friesen) Hansen, who was an eyewitness and participant in much of the drama that occurred in this story. It is mostly through her that I gained the detailed information about my late father, Jens Peter Hansen's early life and his family roots in Denmark. Throughout her life she had been recording information, and in her later years learned to type and recorded about forty single-spaced pages of her memories and products of her research. This provided me with a good starting point. She also provided for me her collection of early family photos, several of which I have included in this book.

I am also indebted to my late aunt Tena Friesen who gave me a copy of her unpublished memories, a book of about 284 double-spaced typed pages illustrated with her own sketches. This provided me with a second witness, a set of younger eyes through which to evaluate my mother's perceptions.

With these two witnesses I added insights given by my aunts, Helen Biehn, Esther Visser, Susan Friesen, and Annie Roth, and my uncle, Jake Friesen, now all deceased.

For the autobiographical parts of this story, I relied on my memory and the many letters I had written to my mother after I left home. She lovingly saved them all and returned them to me when I was ready to peruse them.

I would also express my appreciation for the assistance of my two daughters, Cindy Kreider and Karen Hansen who have both read my manuscript, made grammatical corrections, and offered advice. I also must thank my niece, Trinda Cole, a professional proofreader, for her willingness to read my manuscript and make helpful observations, corrections, and suggestions.

A special thanks goes to my granddaughter Destiny Kreider for carefully and artfully arranging the cover by imposing an old 1949 photo of my brothers and I posing in front of our 1948 Willis Jeep upon a simple landscape photo.

I must mention deep gratitude for my wife, Vera, my faithful companion of fifty-eight years, who patiently spent many lonely evenings by herself and often went to "our" cold bed alone while I pecked away at my keyboard. She was always supportive and read my manuscript with helpful suggestions. And she still loves me.

Carl Edward Hansen
1523 Park Road
Harrisonburg, VA 22802
July 12, 2022

ACRONYMS

CPR   Canadian Pacific Railroad
CO   Conscientious Objector
EID   Eastern Irrigation District
EMC   Eastern Mennonite College
EMBMC   Eastern Mennonite Board of Missions and Charities
EMM   Eastern Mennonite Mission
MCC   Mennonite Central Committee
RCMP   Royal Canadian Mounted Police
USSR   Union of Soviet Socialist Republics

ONE

"THE DANE": SEARCHING FOR A HOME

A New Neighbor

The young Elizabeth saw him first and called her mother, Justina, to the window of their isolated little farmhouse in the West Duchess District, Alberta. Curiosity, accentuated by their lonely existence in their sparsely populated rural community, drew them to watch this unsuspecting stranger's every step.

The man was walking alongside a team of horses pulling a wagon heaped with several farm implements and a few boxes of personal effects, followed by a few more horses, a cow, and a calf tied up behind.

Could this be the new neighbor rumor had predicted would be coming to occupy the vacant farmhouse two miles north?

Seventeen-year-old Elizabeth felt a certain excitement. Life was lonely in rural Alberta in the spring of 1938. Neighbors were valued. "Would this man's wife become a friend?" Elizabeth watched. The man seemed tired, as if he had walked a long way. Then he and his entourage turned north at the corner and trudged on in the direction of the vacated farm. This must be the man from Saskatchewan.

Rumor had it that this man would come to seed his crop and prepare the home and then return to Saskatchewan to bring his wife and children.

Sometime later, Elizabeth was helping a neighbor lady who was not feeling well. While she was scrubbing the woman's floor, her two excited little girls came into the room, exclaiming, "There is a man at the door!"

She went out to see if she could help the stranger. Here was the Dane, wanting to know where he could find "the boss." She could not understand him at first because of his heavy accent. A strange feeling of determination came over her. "I am going to understand this man."

She still thought he was a married man. The girls told her that he was a bachelor. She argued with them, but in the end, she found out that the girls were right.

Family Ancestry

The paternal ancestors of "The Dane," Jens Peter Hansen, lived and died in Denmark. They were common folk, descendants of the dreaded Norsemen, the notorious Vikings, the fearless Danes, who in their barbarous days in the ninth and tenth centuries terrorized the Atlantic coastal villages of Europe as far south as Spain and into the Mediterranean as far as Marseilles and Pisa. They conquered and ruled England and Normandy and penetrated Central Europe, sailing their slick warships up the Vistula River and down the Dnieper River to reach as far south as Constantinople on the Black Sea. They traded with the Mediterranean world.

They also traveled east to the Caspian Sea, reaching north, penetrating the whole Volga River basin, and south by camel caravan, reaching Baghdad in the interests of trade. Known sometimes as the "Rus," they founded Kiev and left their influence and their name on the Ukrainian and Russian cultures of the region in the eighth to tenth centuries.

They moved as far west as Greenland and temporarily established a settlement in Vineland in North America six hundred years before Christopher Columbus "discovered" it.

In the late tenth century AD, these people were Christianized and "civilized" through the influence of Western missionary priests and monks. At the time of the Protestant Reformation, they joined the Lutheran schism against Roman Catholic domination.

In recent centuries, the Danes have been known as industrious, hardworking, and dependable people. They keep neat and well-organized homes and communities. Politically, they are quiet, peaceful, socially liberal, and deeply concerned with issues of justice and fairness to all.

Hansen is a Scandinavian patronymic surname meaning "son of Hans." It is the third most common surname in Denmark, representing 4.3 percent of Danish surnames. It is also common in Norway and occurs with the spelling *Hanson* among the Swedish people.

Jens's paternal grandfather, also named Jens Peter Hansen, was commonly known as "big Peter" because he was very tall, although not very heavy. He was a fisherman living with his wife, Kristine, at Hojby, a small village on the northwest coast of Zealand. He had two sons and three daughters. One son, Christian, died at thirty-five years of age.

The other son, Jens's father, Hans Peter Hansen, was born on May 21, 1870. After completing the compulsory military training, he met a girl from Bur, a small farming village close to the northwest coast of Jutland. Else Marie Nielsen Ragborg (born at Bur on October 1, 1872) was a tailor. She had come to Hojby to work for a while.

Hans Peter found Else Marie incredibly attractive and won her hand in marriage. The life of a fisherman held little promise for the couple, so they moved to her home in Jutland. Bur is situated on the north bank of the Stora River between Holstebro and Vemb in the township of Hjerm in the district of Ringkobing. It is sixteen kilometers inland from the North Sea and six kilometers from the Nissum Fjord. A railroad runs through the village.

Niels Christensen, Else Marie's father (my other paternal great-grandfather), a blacksmith and sometimes farmer, gave his nineteen-acre farm to the couple to try their hand at farming.

Else Marie's mother was Fredrika Schleiner. She had been previously married to a Ragborg who had died. Besides their one daughter, Else Marie, Niels and Fredrika Christensen had three or four sons, two of whom were Marinus and Christian. Fredrika died in the late 1910s or early 1920s. Niels lived into the 1930s.

Hans Peter and Else Marie Hansen worked hard at farming near Bur. It was not easy in those days. There were neither engines nor electricity, so all the farmwork had to be done by hand or oxen or horses.

Then the babies started coming. In those days, babies were born on a regular annual or biannual basis and were normally born at home. Many did not live to reach adulthood.

Hans Peter and Else Marie had twelve offspring. Katherine was born on July 24, 1898, Jensine ("Sina") followed on January 20, 1899, and Anna arrived on March 26, 1901. Then Niels appeared on May 30, 1902, followed by Kristine on July 8, 1903. My father, Jens Peter, was born on February 17, 1904. Then there came Karl, two Ottos, and Marie. Christian, the youngest, was born on April 20,1913. The first Otto was found dead in his crib when he was a few months old. Another baby, Ejner, died in infancy. Karl died of tuberculosis when he was twenty-two years of age. The second Otto died of tuberculosis in 1921 when he was eight or nine years old. All twelve children were born in the space of about fifteen years. Eight survived to adulthood.

Is it any surprise that mother Else Marie's health went bad? For seventeen years, she suffered from what was thought to be rheumatism or arthritis. But she continued her domestic duties with determination. Even when she was so crippled that she had to be assisted to get on and off the milking stool, she insisted that she must keep on milking the cows. In the kitchen, she did the cooking while her daughters did the cleaning. The last winter, she was utterly unable to walk. The doctors diagnosed her ailment as "tuberculosis of the spine." Today they probably would have diagnosed it as multiple sclerosis (MS). She finally passed away on January 7, 1922, at fifty years of age. Jens was almost eighteen years old.

Hans Peter Hansen moved several times during his lifetime. When the boys were big enough to work, he sold the farm and moved to a bigger one. It was important that the boys learn the value of hard work. Then after the boys had grown, he sold that farm and bought a smaller one.

Being from Zealand, he spoke a Zealand dialect of Danish. His children learned it from him and spoke like their father until they went to school. There the other children made fun of them, so they switched to the Jutland dialect.

The children were all born in their home one kilometer from Bur. They were all baptized at the village church at Vemb, and they all went to the district school in Bur.

It was a one-room schoolhouse with one teacher for all the primary grades. Jens often referred to his teacher, an older male, with deep respect and awe. He taught the seven classes in one room with strict discipline, and the students learned.

Jens told the story of the time some of the older boys got rowdy. One of them jumped out the window. Just as fast, the teacher jumped out the window after him, grabbed the boy, and shoved him back in through the window. There was no fooling around allowed.

The teacher was exceptional at playing the violin. Jens was impressed that the man could make the violin "talk."

Denmark is a Lutheran country. The Lutheran Church is still the established state church. Maintenance of churches and pastors' salaries are provided by the state from tax money. Every village had one church. But where the villages were small, a pastor was frequently required to serve more than one congregation.

All babies were baptized there. Religious people came to the services every Sunday. Others came for the special events, such as Christmas, Easter, weddings, baptisms, christenings, confirmations, and funerals. Others did not come at all. The dead were buried in the churchyard.

The system had its own beauty in its simplicity and harmony. No rival churches confused the people. The assumption was that everybody was a Christian by virtue of baptism and having been the recipient of God's grace.

In the case of the village of Bur, the pastor was responsible for the neighboring congregations at Vemb and Corrin as well. The central congregation was at Vemb, and special services like baptisms and confirmations were held there. Although Bur was the Hansens' home church, at age fourteen, Jens was confirmed in the Lutheran Church at Vemb.

There was an evangelical element underlying the ancient formality. Jens recalls his pastor having evangelistic meetings in the church and being concerned about the members' personal salvation as they prepared for confirmation. He and his sister Sina both came to express having a personal assurance of salvation.

The church at Bur is a small chapel built of dressed stone about 500 years ago. Its walls are about five feet thick, and it has a sharp spire that rises above the village. Inside the church door, there is a register that lists all the pastors that served the church and community since its founding in the 16th century. A pipe organ was installed at the front sometime near the beginning of the twentieth century. Outside is a rather large burial ground where Hans Peter and Else Marie Hansen are both buried in unmarked graves, as are those children who died young, as well as Else's parents and ancestors.

There is a legend concerning the building of this church. It is said that those concerned could not agree where the new church should be built. They were holding their deliberations in a castle some fifteen or more miles away. The builder, standing there with them, picked up a four-foot cube of hewn stone, held it with three fingers, and flung it out saying, "Where this stone falls, the church will be built." And so, it was. That stone was used in the building, being placed in the east end where the three fingerprints are plainly visible to any who may be plagued with the weakness of doubt!

In earlier years, people took their religion very seriously, and any perceived lack of devotion in others was simply not tolerated. People were compelled to attend church. There were stocks outside the church door. If anyone missed even one service, without good reason, he was liable, and could find himself locked in the stocks the next Sunday for all to see, and to be spit upon, by those who perceived themselves to be more devout or holy than he, as they filed past into the sanctuary. One can only imagine attendance was quite exemplary.

Entering Early Adulthood

After finishing seven years of school, Jens Peter Hansen, then almost fifteen years of age, helped at home for one year. His father gave him a new bicycle, which his older brother soon wrecked. According to Jens, the relationship between the two brothers was a rocky one. Niels was portrayed as the rough, aggressive and maybe selfish type, while Jens was of a more conciliatory and peaceful nature.

When Jens reached sixteen years of age, he started working out on a neighbor's farm. Those were hard times for a young person to start out on his/her own. World War I had just ended, and the economies of Europe were in a shambles. Jens worked for a year and a half and never got paid. All he received for his efforts was his food and lodging and enough money to buy some work clothes.

He left that job and found work at another farm. The farmer promised him 900 krone per year plus room and board. He worked at this place for five years. But here, also, he was unable to collect all his wages. He had to beg and show need before he would be given a portion of what was owed to him.

There were rarely days off. Sunday afternoons were free, but, because of the livestock, there was the morning and evening chores. Usually, he would go home then or visit the neighbor boys where he would check out their sisters. If the field was favorable, he would come back the next Sunday. Sometimes he would go to church. Occasionally he would be given a few days off. Then he would visit his home, or on rare occasions, travel to Hojby to visit his grandparents.

Despite difficult circumstances, a young man will always find a way to court a girl he favors. Jens would persuade her to go bicycle riding with him or take her to one of the popular silent movies. He did not like to dance, and besides, most decent self-respecting girls did not go to dances. It was a questionable activity.

Jens measured five feet seven inches tall and was of sturdy build, weighing about 190 pounds. He had brown hair and very blue eyes. With a straight nose and square chin, all his features suggested strength and sturdiness. He had learned to work hard at an early age and never shirked responsibility; Jens was honest and upright in all his ways. He was friendly, gentle, kind, and patient and was well-liked by people.

Passport photo of Jens Peter Hansen in 1927

Setting Out To See the World

After devoting the strength of his youth for almost seven years, laboring faithfully on his neighbors' farms and not being able to collect most of the wages due him, Jens decided it was time to seek his fortune elsewhere. At twenty-three years of age, he decided he would like to see the world.

Apparently, an added stimulating factor in this brash decision was a disappointment in love. He had been engaged to a charming, dark-haired maiden who led him to believe she wanted to center her life on his. Then, one day he came unannounced for a visit, and saw her under a tree being kissed by her boss's son. When she was confronted about it, she denied it.

Deeply hurt, he decided that, if that is the way it is with women, he wouldn't have any further dealings with them. He would get as far away from them as he could.

At first, he wanted to go to Australia but did not have enough money to go that far. His second choice was to go to the U.S.A., but he found that they were closed to immigration at that time. Then he saw an advertisement put in the local paper by the Canadian Pacific Railroad (CPR) offering to assist people who would like to immigrate to western Canada. He wrote for an application. He thought he could always cross the border into the U.S.A. at a later time. The CPR accepted his application and promised to help him find a job.

At 4 o'clock, p.m. on March 1, 1927, Jens Peter Hansen left Denmark by the Espier Port. His boat arrived in London, England in the afternoon of the next day. He stayed in London, walking around and seeing the sights for two days. He did not like London. For a Danish country boy, the city was too dirty and crowded, and no one could speak his language. Then he took a train to Liverpool. He felt much better passing through the green fields of the English countryside.

At Liverpool, he boarded the ship S.S. Montnairn of the Canadian Pacific Line. It took the ship ten days to cross the Atlantic. Jens was a bit disappointed in the trip. He had hoped to see a big storm, but all they were able to find was a small one in which the waves washed across the deck of the ship.

Jens first stepped on Canadian soil at Ft. St. John, New Brunswick, on March 13, 1927. The CPR workers put him on a train along with other immigrants and sent him west.

While traveling on the train, Jens developed a very bad case of nose bleeding. In fact, he lost so much blood that he passed out. The railroad people took him off and left him at a hospital at Smith's Falls, Ontario.

It was a trying experience for this young stranger to be helpless in a strange hospital in a strange land where everybody spoke a strange language. There were no family or friends to cheer him up or to comfort him. What if he were to die there? Who would care, and how would his family find out?

The Canadian nurses would come and sit in the room with this strange, handsome young man and put him to work helping with folding napkins or other small chores.

After three days, Jens was discharged from the hospital and continued his journey on to Winnipeg. The CPR office had a job lined up for him with a rancher in Maple Creek in southwestern Saskatchewan. They put him back on the train and sent him to Maple Creek. There he met his new boss, Mr. Fenwick Martin, at the local restaurant.

Finding a Home in Maple Creek

Fenwick Martin was an Ontario-born Irish Canadian. He was one of the early settlers who came to Maple Creek in 1881. At that time, he, his wife, his mother, two brothers, and a sister each took out a "homestead."

A "homestead" was 160 acres, or a quarter section of land given to each settler by the government for ten dollars based upon a commitment to build a house on it and live in it at least six months of each year for six years and to plow at least twenty acres. In the end, Fen and his wife inherited all those six homesteads.

At one time Fen had leased 10,000 acres of pastureland from the government. On it he had kept up to 10,000 sheep. But he thought that rent at two cents per acre per year was too much, so he cancelled the lease agreement. He thought he would be able to use the land for free. Later, he found he was wrong and tried to get the lease back, but only got 3,000 acres.

When Jens arrived, the Martins were both about sixty years of age. They cropped about fifty acres with horses and kept over one hundred beef cattle. They had no children of their own. They were glad to have this young Dane come and live with them and help them with the work. They promised to teach him English, which they did in a haphazard way.

Jens always spoke with a very heavy Danish accent and mixed Danish words with his English. The Martins apparently either gave up or never tried to correct him. To the end of his life, strangers found it difficult to understand him.

Maple Creek was a small ranchers' town, snuggled among gently rolling treeless hills in southwestern Saskatchewan. The roads at that time were just trails across the grassy prairie. The railroad was the main link with the outside world of supplies, markets, news, and politics. Radios, only having been invented in 1920, were not yet in common use in 1927. It was a wild, unbroken, empty country.

Jens fell in love with the prairies immediately. He loved the vast clear blue empty sky, the wide-open grassy spaces, the warm dry spring winds, and the bright and warm spring sunshine. Most of all, he was enthralled by the promise of the soil, its virgin richness untouched and un-exploited by man. This was truly the land of challenge and opportunity, the right place for strong and ambitious young men to struggle and rise above the poverty that kept them bound back in Europe. This was the place to settle.

He cancelled his plan to go on to the U.S.A. He forgot any idea of ever returning to his crowded little homeland of Denmark, where one could slave forever in the tiny fields or the stuffy little barns of others and never rise above servitude. Having once breathed the air of freedom and opportunity, it would be impossible to return to the regimentation and predictability of the old order in the old world. Jens Peter Hansen was convinced and converted. He was now, and for the rest of his days, a Canadian!

Jens swung into the routine of his new job with gusto. Besides a new language, there were so many things for a young Danish peasant farmer to learn in becoming a western Canadian pioneer rancher. Cattle were to be kept outside year around, even when the temperatures fell to an unbelievable -40- or -50-degrees F. In Denmark, such temperatures were unheard of, yet the cattle were kept in hot, humid, little barns.

On the prairies, the cattle grazed all winter like the bison they replaced. If the snow lay too deep, the farmer simply fed them hay out on the pure clean snow. There were no stables to clean. Sheds were constructed of fence wire and poles and covered with straw to give the cattle and pigs shelter from the fierce, cold north winds, if needed. Water for the livestock could be had by simply cutting a hole through the ice, sometimes up to four feet thick, on the pond or nearby slough. The clean cold water would come bubbling up to fill the bowl-like excavation in the ice. and the animals would come and sip as much as they needed.

The cowboy's use of the horse for herding cattle was different from riding horses in Denmark. Horses were used for watching, herding, rounding up, and tying cattle. Jens had to learn how to use the lariat to rope the wild calves, how to throw them down, tie them, and brand them. Good saddle horses had to be "broken" or trained. A good prospect would be selected, either a young colt or a wild horse captured from the many roving bands of wild horses that still could be found on the western plains.

This horse, when properly trained, would become the cattleman's best friend. It could do the work of herding with very little guidance from the rider.

Plowing and seeding was done with horse-drawn equipment. Hay was cut with a horse-drawn mowing machine from a dried slough bottom or a section of prairie that was reserved for hay production and not grazing.

After cutting, the hay would be gathered in windrows with a dump rake. Then it would be collected with a horse drawn buck rake and taken to a stack. There it was placed on top of the stack with the help of a contrivance called a "stacker." The farmer would level or arrange the hay on the stack.

Later, on a nice day, maybe in the winter, the farmer would come with the horses and wagon and take a load of the hay home to the feedlot where it would be stacked again or fed to the animals.

The Martin's farm was about sixteen miles west of Maple Creek. The yard was in a depression along a creek bed surrounded by higher ground so that no one could see the buildings until he reached the edge of the escarpment overlooking it.

The house was a rectangular solid little frame structure that had a roof covered with cedar shingles. It was one and one-half stories high and was unpainted.

There was a small barn or milking shed, a few pigpens, a chicken house, and a few trees in the yard. Mrs. Martin had a small vegetable garden that grew mostly Russian thistles and other prairie weeds. Fences were poorly organized and carelessly kept. Old farm machinery lay scattered around the yard among the weeds that seemed to thrive everywhere. This was a great contrast to the neat, orderly little yards in Denmark.

Jens worked for the Martins for three years, from 1927-29. Those were good years in which the land lived up to its promise. Grain crops yielded twenty-five to thirty bushels per acre. But Jens got restless. He wanted his own place, but he still had no money. He heard that the CPR was offering to sell cheap land at Hussar in Alberta.

Homesteading in Hussar

In the spring of 1930, Fen and Jens, in company, bought a section of prairie land at Hussar in Alberta, from the CPR. Jens moved there to establish a farm. He built a small shack and broke a large field of virgin prairie sod.

They broke the sod with a special one-bottom sulky breaking plow. This contraption had a metal seat for the driver that was shaped to approximately fit the natural contours of the typical male's posterior dorsal side. The seat was fastened in such a way as to stick out behind the plow, perched nicely on the end of a three-and-one-half-foot piece of three-inch wide spring steel. This was to give the occupant of the seat a little comfort for the extremely uncomfortable job of breaking rough sod.

One day as Jens was plowing, dangling along at the end of his usual perch on a typical dry hot day, no doubt half-awake or half asleep, the plow suddenly struck an unmovable rock, while the four huge Belgian horses continued moving ahead with irresistible force. The plow became an instant catapult, and the spring-loaded seat projected its unwary occupant in a forward trajectory that landed him on the doubletree between the two foremost horses.

The horses were a bit surprised at their unexpected company, but they had the courtesy to stop until Jens was able to regain his senses and extricate himself from his new perch. When he surveyed the situation, he was grateful for a few minor bruises in an accident that could have been fatal. After all, out alone on that desolate prairie, there was no "911" to call!

There was no rain at Hussar that year, so there was no crop. Consequently, there was no money to pay for the land. The land went back to the CPR, and Jens returned to Maple Creek in time to harvest. The land of promise was not keeping all its promises.

Ranching in Maple Creek

Back in Saskatchewan, Jens rented the Martin ranch for the next six years, and the Martins retired to town. But after one year in town, the Martins felt they could not afford to stay there, so they returned to live in their farmhouse, and Jens boarded with them. It was a mutually satisfying arrangement for the old folks and for the bachelor.

We might wonder what kind of social life this single young man had, living with this elderly couple out on a ranch, surrounded by the empty prairie of southwestern Saskatchewan in the 1930's?

There were neighbors, but they were far apart. Many of his neighbors were men like himself: Scots, Irish, Norwegians, Russians and Ukrainians, poor men who were lured west by the promise of cheap farmland and the hope of prosperity. Some of them came with their wives and families. Others, like Jens, came alone, hoping to make a good start and then return and bring a wife later.

Though the farms were far apart, it was possible, with the help of a good saddle horse, to visit one's neighbors on a Sunday or a holiday. Often, they would arrange to help each other with their work, or one would come over to borrow some needed item. Such occasions always called for putting on the kettle for a "spot of tea" or a cup of coffee. The conversation would often carry on for several hours, which usually prompted an invitation to "join us for a bit of lunch." Such an invitation was seldom turned down, especially if the visitor was a bachelor.

Jens told a story about one of his bachelor friends who got tired of the all-too-frequent visits of another bachelor neighbor who always timed his visits to include the lunch hour. Therefore, one day when his neighbor made his customary long visit, the host graciously invited his guest, as usual, to share lunch with him.

After they ate, he took the dirty dishes off the table, set them on the floor, called in the dog to lick them, and when they were licked clean, he stacked them away in his cupboard, and made some joke about doing it the easy way. Needless to say, the friend never stayed around for mealtime again.

Jens often kept a hired hand around to help with the farm work. Sometimes he had a young Russian while one year he had an indigenous Canadian. These men helped to diminish the loneliness somewhat.

One of his Russian hired hands was an expert shot with the rifle. One day, a neighbor man in a rather altered state of mind came over to see Jens over an issue that concerned them both. In the discussion, the man became very angry, and harsh words were exchanged. Jens was not immune to enjoying a lively debate or a hot argument, so we can imagine that he was not altogether innocent of provoking the man to higher levels of rage.

Finally, the man went storming out of the house and jumped in his buggy and whipped his horse into action. Jens said to his hired hand, "Shoot over his head." The Russian pulled up his rifle and shot off the man's hat. That neighbor did not come back!

Jens was of medium height and compact with broad shoulders and barrel-chested with a substantial abdomen. He had a reputation for being strong. Someone from Denmark reported seeing the young Jens leaving a blacksmith shop, slinging the walking plow he had brought for repairs across his shoulder and mounting his bicycle and heading for home. No big deal!

Sometimes, the young cowboys and ranchers would get together on a Sunday afternoon and entertain themselves with storytelling, gossiping, bragging, or competing in feats of strength such as target practice, wrestling, or weightlifting. One Sunday, Jens and his Russian hired hand were the only ones who were able together, by each grabbing a back wheel, to lift the rear end of a 15-30 McCormick Deering tractor off the ground.

There was a certain Russian neighbor with two grown sons with whom Jens found it a bit difficult to live at peace. At one time they cut his barbed wire fence and chased their cows to graze on his oats crop and posted a young girl to shepherd them. To say the least, Jens was not happy about it and went on his horse and drove the cattle out. He asked the girl why she was keeping them there. She was very shy and felt guilty and started to cry, so he went out to find his neighbor. He found the three of them nearby and began to ask them the meaning of their action.

One of the sons grabbed at the horse's bridle, so Jens dismounted to face him on equal footing. While Jens confronted two of them, the third sneaked up behind him and hit him on the head with his shovel, knocking him unconscious.

When he came to, he found himself tied up with barbed wire and a terrible wound on the head. His neighbors were gone. It took him a bit of time to untangle himself from the wire and regain his senses, but after getting free, he set out to find his neighbors and settle the score. He never told us how that was accomplished.

Those were still "frontier days" on the prairies. The ranchers, especially the young bachelors, and particularly the Russians, were noted for being a bit wild. Those were the days of "prohibition" when it was illegal to buy or trade or make alcoholic beverages. But it was very much a part of the Russian culture to make and drink vodka or "home-brew."

A Russian neighbor was planning a wedding for a member of his family. They must have the proper drinks for the festive occasion. Several weeks ahead of time, the brewing got underway.

A few days before the wedding, an R.C.M.P. (Royal Canadian Mounted Police) officer was passing by on an errand. He stopped at the house to ask directions to a certain place. (There was no GPS nor even road maps in those days!) The family members were horrified to see this embodiment of the king's law come strolling into the yard and up to the door.

While the man went, in fear and trepidation, to answer the front door, the wife poured the entire precious brew out the back door (destroy the evidence). The smell was almost overpowering.

When the officer finished his business and was taking leave, he commented, "You wouldn't have had to pour it all out!" Although it was an uncustomarily dry wedding, to our limited knowledge, the groom and bride were married and lived reasonably "happily ever after" anyway.

The members of the community banded together to form a "telephone company." They linked all their homes together with a wire fastened to their fence posts. Each home had a receiver/sender box with a switch that could be turned off or on, not unlike a modern intercom system.

Since there was only one line, everybody was on it and had to patiently, or not so patiently, wait their turn. If you left the switch on, you could hear the conversation of your neighbors, but they could also hear whatever was being said in your house. Needless to say, the telephone system provided many hours of entertainment and relief from boredom, not to mention how it increased the general level of community awareness and correspondingly decreased the number of secrets kept.

It was especially interesting when a family forgot to turn their set off and got into the normal lively discussions that families do. Many a neighbor found out what others really thought about them in this way.

The prairies had no trees, so fence posts, corral rails, and logs for building sheds were brought in from the Cypress Hills which were about forty miles to the west.

In the winter, when the ground was frozen and covered with a layer of snow and the weather was calm, Jens would take a team of horses and a bobsled to the hills for wood. The trip took a full day to get there, another day to cut the trees and load the sleigh, and a third day to return home. He would camp out overnight. This was a bit risky because a storm could arise and cut him off before reaching home.

A south Saskatchewan blizzard could be completely deadly. One day a Russian neighbor was out hauling feed for his cattle. The temperature was about forty below zero, and there was a wind blowing which picked off his cap and blew it away across the prairie. He tried to go home without his cap but froze to death on the way.

Surviving the Great Depression

Those six years that Jens rented the Martin farm were harsh, disappointing years, marred with a double curse of drought and the great economic depression. For three of those six years, he planted but never harvested at all. In the worst years, the seed did not even sprout. Some years the grasshoppers ate every bit of the little that was there. Those years that he did harvest, the parched soil yielded only six bushels per acre.

When it came to selling the products of their labor, the price of wheat dropped to five or six cents per bushel, and they could not even sell oats. Butter sold for five to seven cents per pound, and eggs for five or six cents per dozen. The best cattle sold, delivered in Moose Jaw, for five dollars a head. It was not enough to pay the rail transportation charges. Farmers who sent their cattle to market received bills for remaining unpaid transport instead of checks. The land of promise turned out to be a land of deception.

The drought worsened until there was not enough grass for the cattle. Russian thistles were cut in the green stage and put up for hay.

When Jens realized there would not be enough fodder to keep all the cattle through the winter, and since there was no market for the weaker skinny animals, he felt obligated to shoot seventy-five of the cattle so that the remainder would have enough food to survive the winter.

He took their skins and left their skeletal carcasses for the coyotes. What else could he do? Those who did not do likewise found that in the spring the major portion of their cattle had starved to death, and those which survived were unable to nurse their spring calves, which also died.

Because of the prolonged drought, Jens undertook to build a dam across the creek with the intention of irrigating crop or hay land. He loosened the soil with a plow and then used a slip scraper drawn by four horses to move the soil to the dam site. He worked at it alone in his spare time between seeding and harvesting. The season was extremely hot and dry. The work went slowly. Sometimes he had to stop the work for a while because the horses did not have the sufficient food to do such hard work, and Mr. Martin wouldn't buy them any oats.

After several summers of intermittent work, the dam was a couple of hundred feet long and wide enough for two cars to pass on top. It held enough water to irrigate two hundred acres.

Jens did irrigate five or six acres once. But because Fen did not want to spend any money on the materials needed or feed for the horses, the head gate was never built, and the head ditches were never dug. Becoming discouraged, Jens decided to quit.

When visiting the Martin homestead in 1971, we noticed that the dam was in use for irrigation purposes, so though Jens never received a cent for his sweat, his efforts were not in vain. His labor had borne fruit and had been a blessing to others. The dam stands as a silent monument to the strength of the man (and the horses) who built it.

One of Jens P. Hansen's virtues as well as vices was his tenacity. After being frustrated by Fen Martin's unwillingness to invest in the dam and experiencing another crop failure in 1937, Jens finally came to face reality. There was no future for him in Maple Creek; the bounty of the harvest he had experienced back in 1928 was an anomaly that nature would never repeat. He had better part company with the Martins and seek his fortune elsewhere.

Starting Over in West Duchess

During those years of drought, many dry land farmers and ranchers turned their eyes towards the irrigation schemes that sprang up across Alberta and Saskatchewan. The Eastern Irrigation District (EID) was one of those schemes. The CPR started it in 1909 with the building of a dam across the Bow River near Bassano. A system of canals, aqueducts, reservoirs, and head gates eventually made it possible to bring about one-half million acres under irrigation. The EID later became a farmer-owned and operated co-operative. It has brought prosperity and progress for thousands of people in a land that would otherwise be desolate ranching country. It was to this land that Jens Hansen now turned his attention.

In the spring of 1938, Jens loaded a team of horses, a cow and a calf, some farm implements, and a few boxes of personal effects onto the train and headed for Brooks.

There, he contacted the EID land agent, Mr. McFarlane, and made an agreement to rent a one-half section of irrigated land northeast of Rosemary. It was an abandoned farm with a five-room house and a small barn on it. The land was very sandy and rough, which made it exceedingly difficult to irrigate.

But it was the only place the land agent had available at the time, so Jens signed an agreement and moved onto the place. He planted the crop and returned to Maple Creek to bring his 1927 Model A Ford Coupe. After completing harvest in November, he went once more and brought the remainder of his ten horses and his other belongings.

Jens soon learned the farm had been abandoned for a reason. The soil was very sandy and uneven. Since the only method of irrigating was by flooding, one had to be careful, or the crops on the high places would dry out, and those in the low places would drown out.

The water came to the highest point of the farm through a main canal. From there, the farmer had to dig a system of ditches that would take the water to all the parts of his farm. If he did not make the ditches right, he would have difficulty in getting the water distributed evenly.

Jens had no experience in designing this ditch system. He found it difficult the first year. The high spots dried out, and the low spots drowned out. Some ditches eroded into cavernous gullies so huge that one could have buried a car in them.

Despite this problem, the soil was very fertile, and the crop was a success. Hope was restored. Jens bought the farm for $1200. At last, he had a farm of his own. It may not have been much to boast about, but it belonged to him, and he was happy.

T W O

THE DUTCH MENNONITE MAIDEN

Those were tumultuous times in Russia when Elizabeth Winnifred Friesen was born on August 24, 1920. The Revolution of 1917 had replaced the ancient imperial regime, and a bloody civil war was still in progress, with the White army and the Red army vying for control of the various regions of this vast land.

And various marauding bands of bandits roamed about terrorizing the unarmed inhabitants in between, wreaking murder and pillage, enriching themselves and impoverishing the people. Of course, little Elizabeth did not remember much of that, but she did remember the famine that followed, and how she valued even a crust of bread.

Further, in the aftermath of losing a devastating war with Germany, in the face of rising nationalism, patriotism, and now atheistic communism, sentiments turned against the Mennonites. The locals viewed them as unreliable foreigners, Germans, unpatriotic, religious believers, and capitalists, enemies of the Revolution and of the people's Communist Socialist state. The atheistic revolutionary government began immediately to take repressive actions against the Mennonites and all other dissenting groups.

It was in answer to the cries and prayers of these desperate people that God moved the hearts and minds of seven different Mennonite denominations in North America to organize a "Mennonite Central

Committee" (MCC) to send food shipments all the way to Russia to relieve their hunger in 1920-23.

Thousands of Jesus Christ's followers poured out a torrent of generosity, contributing food and clothing and other relief goods that saved the lives of thousands of starving Mennonites and other Russians. And it saved the lives of the Jacob Friesen family, including the little girl, Elizabeth, who was to become my mother.

With the ascendancy to power of the Bolshevik Party led by Lenin and the consolidation of that power under Joseph Stalin and his communist followers, Jacob and Justina Friesen discerned that there was no bright future for their little religious community in Russia.

They uprooted their family of three children, Elizabeth, age four, Jake, age two, and Agnetha, nine months old, along with Justina's younger brother, John Warkentin, and left their home in Ischalka and joined a major exodus of over 21-22,000 Mennonites from Russia to Canada between 1923 and 1929. Their family arrived in Quebec, Canada, on November 16, 1924. From there they travelled by train to Rosthern, Saskatchewan.

Challenge of Becoming Canadians

Now they were in Canada, strangers in a strange land, among a strange people with a strange language and strange customs. However, they were met at the railroad station by Mennonites who had come before, their own kind of people to welcome them, comfort them, and help them make the adjustments to this new land.

Elizabeth, at age four, had memories of their journey and the welcome they received. The community gave them shelter in a church until they could all be placed with families for the winter.

That was no small undertaking for the poor Mennonite community, as they themselves were recent immigrants, and this train brought four hundred new people for their small houses to accommodate, all while facing a cold Saskatchewan winter!

The Jacob Friesen family moved in with the Bernhard Friesen family (no relation) in Eigenheim. Jacob helped Bernhard with his chores. They were given some used clothing from a clothing department organized for that purpose.

Canada had been portrayed to the immigrants as a "land of promise." But immigrants had to discover the economic opportunities for themselves, and it took time for this to happen. They tended to move around during those first few years, while also learning the new customs and a new language.

For the Friesen family, the next thirteen years were difficult. First, they moved wherever Jacob could find work. Some of the places in which they lived and worked were Hague, Aberdeen, and near Saskatoon in Saskatchewan, and in Oyen in Alberta. Then in the fall of 1926, they bought their first farm at New Brigden, north of Oyen. Two years after leaving their old home in Ischalka, the wandering family was finally able to settle into their own home once again, and this time they were landowners. Yes, there was a heavy mortgage, but it felt good. The new country was good to them and held a lot of promise.

That was where, in April of 1928, Elizabeth and Jake enrolled in the McConnell School, a one-roomed country schoolhouse two-and one-half miles away. The children were terrified as they did not know a word of English. However, the teacher was most helpful, and it was not long before they felt at home in using English and playing with the other children.

Farming was good those first years. The crops of 1928 were exceptionally good, and 1929 was not bad either, but by 1931, the good years were over. The stock market crashed in 1929, and the "Great Depression" was on, strangling the economic world. With it, a "climate change," a long drought set in, turning the prairies into a "dustbowl" and the decade into what is known as the "dirty thirties." The hopes and dreams of farmers changed into nightmares. Each spring, the farmer would "seed his fields in hope, only to reap in despair." Each year got worse. Hot, dry winds and vicious storms worked against the struggling pioneer farmers.

For the Friesen family farm, there was no exception. In the fall of 1931, they managed to harvest only a meager two hundred bushels of grain. That could not pay the mortgage and feed the family. They lost the farm.

When Jacob learned that the crops were better that year a few miles away at Chinook, he loaded all their belongings on a truck and moved there in November. The next spring, he rented an 800-acre farm. Again, the weather was so dry that they got very little harvest.

After one season, he let that farm go and rented another nearby that had a five-room house. That summer was also hot and dry that even the well dried up. They gave up and allowed the horses to graze on what little crop remained in the grain fields. They had dried out completely -- no crop, no garden, no money, no nothing, and nothing to do.

Jacob Friesen went west to investigate the opportunities for finding a better life in the Eastern Irrigation District (EID) in Alberta. He returned and announced to his family that they would be moving to the Rosemary or Duchess community.

Trek Away from Disaster

On hearing the news, Elizabeth, now thirteen years old, was devastated. She was tired of moving, of leaving all her friends and school and church and all that was familiar. But Jacob was the head of the home and knew best.

Therefore, with the heavy work horses hooked to a hay wagon that held all their earthly possessions, this family with nine children started out on an eight-day trek west and south to Rosemary, Alberta.

A cow with a calf and a yearling were tied behind, along with a spare team of horses. Crates holding a small pig and thirty chickens served as the "box springs" for a straw mattress for the family to sleep on. A cook stove stood in the middle. Elizabeth and Jake rode their two saddle horses following the "happy campers" as they headed out across the dry, barren prairie, hoping to start a new life, once again, at a better destination.

This primitive version of the modern "recreation vehicle," covering 120 miles in eight days, arrived at the family's destination on September 1, 1933. Theirs was a half section of good farmland with a small, weather-beaten, three-bedroom cottage and a couple other buildings. There was a small gray chicken coop, a straw barn, and a gray outhouse. It was located off, what was then, the Trans-Canada highway, about five miles northwest of the village of Duchess and about five miles southeast of Rosemary. It was in a community to which other Russian Mennonite families had also moved.

Beginning Once Again in West Duchess

Life was hard for the pioneers, especially for the women. Through those years this family moved fifteen times or on an average of once every eighteen months.

Each time they moved, Justina and her growing children would have to clean up a dirty abandoned house, fix it up, and make it into a home. They would always make large, wonderful gardens, tend them, and, when they did not dry out, harvest them, and preserve the produce. Besides that, they helped with fieldwork whenever needed.

Justina, as mother, was responsible to manage all the affairs of the home. Together with the older children, there were the daily chores of milking cows, feeding pigs and chickens, collecting eggs, etc., not to mention cooking three meals a day, baking bread for the large family every day, cleaning house, making clothes, washing clothes by hand, hanging them out to dry, bringing them in when dry, mending clothes and ironing them with the old "sad irons" that had to be heated and reheated on the hot stove before wash-and-wear was ever heard of. They also had to darn socks, knit sweaters, carry fresh water in and wastewater out, collect cow chips or chop wood for fuel, tend the fire when cooking or baking or when it was cold, churn cream until it became butter and sell the butter along with the eggs.

Besides all this, Justina took time to be a real mother to each of her children, feed them, bathe them, dress them, listen to them, teach them, tell them stories, tend to their hurts, comfort them, care for them when they were sick, solve their problems, answer their questions, and give them the guidance they needed.

While performing all these duties, she managed to produce another new healthy baby to raise every nineteen months on the average!

Now at West Duchess, once again, the family had to make all the adjustments to a new home, a new community, a new school, a new church, and new friends. Irrigation demanded a total new way of farming. By this time, they had made so many moves that they were quite adaptable.

Farming, under irrigated conditions, was much more productive. In the next three years, three more children, Susan, Edward, and Martha were born respectively in March 1935, April 1936, and October 1937.

The Friesen children attended the one-roomed West Duchess School, two-and one-half miles away, on foot or by horse. Elizabeth completed her sixth and seventh grades there, thus ending her academic career.

At age fifteen, she started to work outside the home, not steady, just here and there for a month or so at a time. She worked for people who were expecting babies, or to pay off her dad's bills. In between, she worked at home.

Sometimes Elizabeth would entertain the younger ones with her story telling in the evenings. They would often gather around her outside, and she would start her story, making it up as she went along. The story would go on until bedtime and sometimes would continue for weeks.

At first, the Friesen family attended the Russian immigrant General Conference Mennonite Church in Rosemary. Besides a Sunday school, there was a Saturday school during the winter where the young people studied the German language. Elizabeth enjoyed her teachers and the Sunday school. The Christian young folks often got together Sunday afternoons or evenings, especially in winter, for choir practice, Bible study, or social events with singing, music, and recitations.

As Elizabeth grew older, she had a fervent desire for these good things. She reminisced:

> *It was so far and transportation so meager I seldom got to go … It was seven miles and I walked and sometimes it was cold. When I would get back late at night mom would be up, and Jake sometimes, and we'd have a cup of hot postum and talk. … Later in life I asked mom how she felt when I would just walk off seven or eight miles by myself to church or choir practice. She said, "I could see you wanted the good things, and I could not say anything."*

Elizabeth became disillusioned with the church at Rosemary. The young folks engaged in activities of which she did not enjoy nor approve. One of the wealthier German men jokingly made insensitive, disparaging comments about the large Friesen family that insulted her feelings. Further, since the German Mennonites used the High German in their worship and Sunday school services, the younger Friesen children did not really understand and had little incentive to go to church or Sunday school.

When, in 1937, Mervin Stanton invited them to attend the Duchess Mennonite Church's Summer Bible school, the Friesen children were willing to go. Mervin brought them faithfully every day for the two weeks. They enjoyed the experience. Elizabeth started to attend the Duchess Mennonite Church where everything was in English. The younger children were more than glad to go along.

The Friesen parents taught their children that God loved them, and they were not burdened by the thought of their sin and guilt. Elizabeth, at the age of twelve, was carefree as to her spiritual destiny. "When we die, we go to heaven. God is love, and He loves us."

When she attended some meetings in the Duchess Church, she heard for the first time in an understandable way, that we need to consciously accept Jesus as our savior in our hearts. At the age of sixteen, she made a public commitment and accepted baptism on October 28, 1937, at age seventeen.

THREE

PUSHING THE BOUNDARIES
IN ROMANCE

Then in the spring of 1938, "the Dane" showed up. Elizabeth had left home to work for the Corny Siemens family for the summer months, so she was not at home when her dad met the new neighbor and began collaborating with him, sharing machinery and labor. Of her coming home on weekends, she recalls, "Any time I came home, my sisters were full of 'the Dane.' He was all they could talk about; he was just it!"

Then one Sunday afternoon, Cornys took Elizabeth home for a visit. She remembers:

> *While we were there, 'The Dane' came to discuss plans for some machine the next day. My siblings were so excited. Snack time the men were called in and for the first time, I really met 'The Dane'. I poured him tea and he looked so pleased. Strange things went through my heart and thoughts."*

Later she admitted it was "love at first sight." It was the mysterious work of God in the heart of a barely eighteen-year-old maiden reaching out for love to a thirty-four-year-old lonely man.

That fall, this Dane, Jens Peter Hansen, was on the threshing crew when it was Friesen's turn to thresh their grain. Elizabeth found herself admiring him. He seemed to notice this young girl as well and later found excuses to visit in the Friesen home. Gradually they got acquainted.

Another Economic Defeat

Things did not go well on the Friesen farm. The Depression continued its stranglehold on their economic throats. Irrigation produced crops all right, and there were harvests and good gardens, but there was no market for the produce. The whole family worked, scrimped, saved, and pulled together, but they were fighting a losing battle. The Great Depression relentlessly wore them down and defeated them.

There was no money to pay their obligations, including their mortgage. Once again Jacob Friesen lost his farm. In November 1938, he was forced to move his big family out of their home. This time, besides having no money, they had no place to go, and a harsh Alberta winter was upon them.

Their new neighbor, Jens Hansen, was living in his five-room house all by himself. Jacob went over to see him and asked if it would be possible to find shelter there for his family. Jens agreed to give the family shelter "for the winter" if they "would cook" for him.

There was little choice, so the Friesen family, with twelve children, moved in. Needless to say, the lonely bachelor's private lifestyle was drastically altered. He reserved one room with a single cot for himself and took his meals with the Friesen family, who occupied the other four rooms.

In the spring they decided to continue the arrangement with Friesens farming half of Jens's land.

Jens and Elizabeth were obviously interested in each other before making this arrangement. That raised many eyebrows and brought some complications.

Jacob's well-meaning German Mennonite friends at Rosemary warned him of the most terrible consequences that would likely result if he allowed "The Dane" to marry his daughter. Then he would stir up his wife's fears. In those days it was unthinkable for a Mennonite to marry a person of another denomination, and it was equally unthinkable for a German to marry a person of another ethnic origin.

Therefore, the parents did what all concerned parents feel they should do. They tried to stop this romance in the bud stage.

Jacob called his daughter aside and informed her, "You can't get married without my permission!" To this declaration, Elizabeth defiantly replied, "Then I'll wait until I'm twenty-one!" The law required parental consent for a girl to marry under the age of twenty-one.

One day while Jacob was driving to town with Jens, he very correctly and courageously did the fatherly thing and informed Jens that there was no way that he could marry his daughter.

Jens replied calmly, "If she wants to, I'm not going to ask you!" So much for the protocol. What leverage did the destitute Jacob have when his whole family was beholden to the Dane's generous hospitality?

Jens declared his love to the sweet Elizabeth, and she responded in the appropriate positive manner, and their engagement was sealed on March 13th, 1939. They set their wedding date tentatively as "after harvest" (if there was to be a harvest). By this time, Mother Justina, convinced by the many virtues of this candidate for a son-in-law, agreed to sign the legally required parental consent document.

Jens Peter Hansen, the Danish Lutheran, began to attend the Duchess Mennonite Church. Bishop J. B. Stauffer baptized Jens and Jake on October 15th, 1939, in that church. Jens Hansen became a true "Anabaptist." And "Hansen" became a "Mennonite name."

Jens's place was four miles straight north of the West Duchess School, so the Friesen children had even further to go. They missed a lot of school. Going to church was also more difficult. Sometimes Jens would hook up his team and wagon and take Mother Friesen and all the children to church in Duchess.

The Friesen family moved in to live with Jens Hansen in November 1938

The End of the Great Depression

For almost ten years, the "Great Depression" held a chokehold on the economies of Canada and the western world. Slowly, conditions began to improve by 1938.

Then, on September 9th, 1939, Canada declared war on Nazi Germany. Suddenly, there were jobs for everybody as the nation geared up to support the war effort. The best young men were needed to compose the huge army. Factories were needed to produce the war materials. Workers were needed to run the factories. Everybody looked to the farmers to produce the food that would keep all the rest strong and healthy as they each played their part in the war effort.

Since Jens was a little above the draft age, he was not inducted into the military. He was a farmer, and as such, he would make his contribution through food production.

The war effort took priority over everything. Certain consumer goods such as gasoline and spare parts and certain food items were rationed among the civilian population. Each family was issued ration cards, according to the number of its members. This limited the amount anyone could buy. Other items simply were not available.

Merging the Danish With the Dutch

The wedding date had been set for "after harvest." In 1939, harvest time came with wet weather, so it went slowly. The eager couple's anxiety level went up another notch with each passing cold, wet, useless day in October. They would have to complete the harvest and sell some grain before there could possibly be a wedding. It was not just their crop that needed to be threshed; they also had to meet their obligations to their neighbors who shared the threshing work.

Finally, the bad weather broke, and a nice late "Indian Summer" set in, and the threshing went ahead full steam.

As soon as they completed the harvest, the couple set a date. There was little time left for a "fall" wedding. It needed the services of a pastor. Clarence Ramer, their pastor, was heading for Tofield on Sunday afternoon,

November 26ᵗʰ to start Winter Bible school. It would suit to have the marriage ceremony that morning. There were no other options.

The few remaining days were filled with the necessary preparations that inevitably accompany even the simplest wedding. Once Jens sold the grain, he took the Greyhound bus to Calgary to buy the necessary black suit and new shoes.

Elizabeth found a suitable white dress with the lavish price tag of three dollars and matching white shoes for a pricey one dollar and ninety-eight cents.

Jens, now baptized, was a bonafide Mennonite, and no further obstacles remained for this Dane to marry this Dutch German-Russian-Canadian-Mennonite girl.

The couple made a trip to Moore's Furniture Store in Brooks and bought a bed and a drop-leaf table. They returned along with the furniture delivery truck, bringing a marriage permit for Mother Friesen to sign. They did not ask the father to sign it.

With the permit signed, they returned to Brooks with the delivery person, procured the marriage license, and returned home.

The big day finally came. The wedding was to be a part of the Sunday morning service at the Duchess Mennonite Church. There would be Sunday school first and then the wedding. Bennet Torkelson and Neta Friesen were to be groomsman and bridesmaid. Since Jens no longer had a car after trading it for livestock, Corny and Lois Siemens were to bring the couple to the service after Sunday school. Depending upon a faulty clock, Corny managed to bring the happy couple late to their own wedding! The congregation was running low on extra songs to sing while they waited.

They walked up the aisle together, unaccompanied, and sat on the front bench. Clarence Ramer preached a real wedding sermon for a whole hour. He based his sermon on the story of Abraham finding a wife for his son Isaac. "He that findeth a wife findeth a good thing." Proverbs 18:22 KJV.

Then Henry B. Ramer led the couple through the marriage vows and pronounced them "man and wife."

There was a surprise wedding reception at their home in the afternoon. Members of the congregation came and brought food and gifts. Although it was November 26ᵗʰ, and it was in Alberta, Canada, and there was snow on the ground, the weather was so sunny and warm that people were comfortable to come without coats.

They spent the afternoon singing and visiting. For their honeymoon night, the newlyweds caught the bus to Brooks and found a hotel there. They returned the next day. There simply was not money for a more romantic and adventurous getaway.

*On November 26, 1939, Jens & Elizabeth merged the
Danish and the Dutch to become "one flesh"*

FOUR

JOINING ON THE JOURNEY

Beginning a New Journey Together

After the one-night honeymoon, the newlyweds set about serious housekeeping. They had a coal/wood burning cookstove, a bed, table, chairs, buffet, and washstand, all in one room. They had a cardboard wardrobe for their good clothes. They built a closet over the cellar stairway with shelves that served as a pantry.

They had forty dollars left to see them through spring seeding time and up to the next harvest. Also, they milked a few cows and sold cream, which helped them survive. To heat their home, they got their free winter supply of coal from the John Ware Coulee on a "dig your own" basis.

When there was not any cash, they often resorted to barter. Earlier Jens had traded his Model A Ford car for a horse, a cow, and a gilt pig. Each was worth about forty dollars, but a horse could go without having to buy gasoline. Also, the horse, the cow, and the pig would reproduce themselves. A car never would, so it was a good deal.

Their assets at the beginning of 1940 were nine horses, four cows, two heifers, seven sows, thirteen piglets, four geese, two turkeys, a dozen hens, and some old horse-drawn machinery. Theirs was truly a "mixed farm" operation. They were young, happy, and felt that life was good.

The next year the crops were good, so Jens bought his first tractor, an old Fordson Major, for $200. It was a noisy machine, and when its exhaust pipe broke off at the manifold, it was exceedingly so. Jens plowed with it in that condition, not knowing the long-term effects of such loud noises on one's hearing. When he tried to sleep, his ears would roar all night. He blamed this tractor for the permanent damage to his hearing that plagued him for the rest of his life. Eventually, it led to his becoming half deaf in his old age.

Since the Friesen family was still sharing the same house with Jens, the marriage did not impact the living arrangements that much. Of course, Elizabeth moved into the one room with her new husband. They also shared the yard with Jens and Elizabeth and worked together to do the daily chores. Elizabeth planted, harvested a successful garden, and preserved many vegetables for the next winter. She was digging potatoes when her mother warned her, "You shouldn't be digging potatoes. People will say, 'Yesterday, she was digging potatoes and today her baby was born.'"

And that is exactly what happened. The next day, September 13, 1940, Elizabeth was rushed to the hospital in Rosemary where a little baby boy, Peter Jens Hansen, made his appearance. He added much joy, and congestion, in the little house! His grandmother, Justina, insisted that the couple take a second room of the shared house. Therefore, his presence was felt by all. Four months later, on January 30, 1941, Esther Ruth Friesen was born. The walls of the house bulged a few more inches!

Baby Peter, Elizabeth, & Jens Hansen, Feb. 16, 1941

About thirteen months later, in the pre-dawn darkness of a frosty October morning, Elizabeth awoke to the now familiar discomfort of labor pains. She promptly informed her husband, who shook off his drowsy sleep, dressed, and saddling his favorite white horse, galloped over to awaken his neighbor, Carl Liebert, to beg him to assist with his car. It would be awfully slow, uncomfortable, and cold for the lady in labor to ride the seven miles of bumpy, frozen, rutted roads to the hospital with the horses and wagon in the chilly darkness of a wintry dawn.

The kind neighbor, anticipating this pre-arranged rendezvous, quickly dressed and went out into the moonlit yard and scrapped the frost from the windshield of his fine jalopy. His breath came in little white puffs of steam on the frosty air, as he, hunching over the front of the car, his mittened hand grasping the cold steel crank and turned it down, and around, down, and around, down, and around. The engine was cold, and the oil was thick. It would take time to start.

Anxiety mounted with each futile round. But, finally, mustering every resource in his well-muscled body, Carl drove the crank down and around once more in that jerky clockwise fashion. His anxious face lightened as the motor gave a loud pop and then a hissing, chugging, coughing sound that broke the agonizing silence. Then the motor roared to life.

Carl quickly dropped the crank and ran to the dashboard. After skillfully adjusting the choke until the jalopy puttered smoothly, he deposited the crank in its customary place under the back seat where the jack and tire irons lay. Immediately, he got in and drove over to the Hansen homestead where the anxious Elizabeth was, all bundled up and waiting by the door.

The nurses at the little Rosemary Hospital were just waking up and getting themselves ready for the day's duties when the Liebert "ambulance" came clattering and chuffing to a halt at the entrance. They quickly brought the patient inside and immediately prepared her for the ordeal. In half an hour, I made my appearance, all nine pounds and twelve ounces of me. I was off to a great start "in half an hour!" What would the story have been if the Liebert jalopy would not have started that cold frosty morning?

Not many took notice of this momentous, historical, earth-changing event on that quiet Sunday morning, 7:00 a.m., October 26th of 1941. However, over the past eighty years, I have been regularly reminded of the importance of this date. Every time I make an appointment at a doctor's office or fill out an application form for anything, October 26, 1941, is the magical password that opens all the secret files and records that pertain to my medical, mental, emotional, economic, legal, and physical wellbeing. About spiritual? I trust St. Peter will not be requiring the same information!

Attending doctor, G. F. Enns, and nurse, Olga Keeling, expedited my safe arrival. I am forever grateful to these two dedicated health workers for their successfully launching me to a healthy vigorous start.

In those days they kept maternity patients in the hospital for ten days. Mom recalls:

> *My roommate was a former neighbor girl and schoolmate. One day both our husbands were to come to see us. We woke up to a snowstorm. As the day progressed, she said her man wouldn't come out in that kind of weather. In the afternoon all at once Miss Keeling, our nurse, came in and said quite loudly, "Mrs. Hansen. See how much you're worth!" And there was my husband. He had said he'd come, and he came, blizzard or not!*

Although I do not remember all the details, I received the impression that my first act in this life was to disappoint my mother. She wanted me to be a girl. I was ill prepared to please her on that issue. Although born with that "original sin," I have always been secretly unrepentant that I managed to disappoint her. Also, since I was a male, my mother could not name me "Susie." I am also grateful for that. Her second choice was to name me "Paul," but my dad intervened, wanting to name me after his favorite brother, Karl who had died at age twenty-two. Obviously, Dad's argument held more sway, so I became known as "Carl Edward Hansen." I am forever grateful.

A Population Crisis

I, being person number eighteen, put additional stress on the living conditions in that little five-room "two-family dwelling." The grossly over-populated house was ready to start popping nails. Grandmother Friesen was still also giving birth. With a sustained growth of two new souls per year, there loomed a real population problem just ahead. Something had to be done to dissipate the looming crisis. And in those days, in that cultural setting, planned parenthood or contraception was not on the radar.

That fall Jake and Neta, with some help from their church, purchased a good simple four-roomed CPR house to be moved. Clarence Ramer gave an acre of rent-free land on the corner of his property. Someone brought a caterpillar and moved the house onto the land.

After cleaning and painting this new house, the Friesen family vacated our house, and moved their precious belongings by hay wagon to their new home in December 1941. Thanks to the loyalty of the grown children, their mother would never need to live in other people's houses again!

In 1942, continued prosperity allowed our family to add to our asset list a new McCormick cream separator, a used sewing machine, a better heater, and a used Model A Ford car.

The progressive couple undertook to help a farrowing sow give birth in the dead of winter. Jens closed off a stall in the barn, made a shelter of straw, and, when it was ready to deliver, sat with the sow through the lengthy process late into the night. Elizabeth had prepared jars of warm water in a cardboard box. Whenever a piglet came out, it was quickly put into the box with the warm jars. Thus, the whole litter survived this precarious business of being born out of season in an unheated, drafty barn on a cold Alberta winter night.

In February of 1943, Neta started to work for my parents. Then on March 25, 1943, a third son, Paul Hans Hansen, was born in the Rosemary Hospital. Then, my youngest and last uncle, David James Friesen, was born in the new hospital at Bassano on September 14, 1943. His arrival completed the "Friesen Fourteen," making it eleven daughters and three sons. Now, for each of us three brothers there were ten aunts and three uncles. A sizable family!

A Move to Clancy

Early in 1943, our parents sold our first farm and bought another one from the EID. It was located about seven miles south of Duchess, halfway towards Brooks in the Clancy District and one-mile due west of the Clancy School. It was located on the west side of the road. It was a half section of good land for which Dad paid $2,500. One quarter was dryland. The rest was irrigated. A creek flowed through the farm from Rocky Lake in the west along the north side of the property where it crossed the road under a small bridge and continued east past the Clancy School.

Our parents moved to this new farm with all their belongings in April 1943, a few weeks after Paul was born. This move is probably my earliest memory. I can distinctly remember our cook stove and Peter's little wagon being unloaded off a truck at our new place. I was all of eighteen months old. It seems I was quite concerned about the wagon.

The farmstead was about 1500 feet up the hill from the creek that spanned the northern edge of our farm. A very thick shelterbelt of poplar and willow trees to the north offered some protection from the harsh north winds for the house and for an enclosed garden area. South of the garden was a big yard surrounded with one row of poplar trees that sheltered a small one and one-half storied frame house.

Hansen Home on Clancy Area Farm March 1943 – 48

The house had a cedar-shingled roof with gabled ends. There was an upstairs window in each gable end that gave light to one little bedroom that we used for hired help and storage space under the eaves. On the front, the house had a central door flanked by two windows and a roofed porch with steps coming down. At the back of the house was one kitchen window and a door with a small stoop and one step. Each side of the house had two windows.

Entering the kitchen from the back door to one's left, in front of the window, was a washstand with basin and soap and towel and a bucket of water with an enameled dipper floating in it. Anybody who was thirsty, whether family or visitor, drank from that dipper. Also along that wall to the corner was a cupboard. Straight ahead was a large, black coal or wood-fired kitchen range with chrome and ivory enamel trimmings. Somewhere in between, in that crowded little room, stood the folk's new cream separator, the butter churn, and Mom's galvanized Renfrew washing machine.

To the right, a door opened to a rickety set of steps that led down into a small excavation called a "cellar" where vegetables and canned goods were stored. We boys did not like to go down there. It was too dark, spooky, and stale smelling. Besides, we saw something like a lizard slithering around down there somewhere.

From the kitchen, straight ahead was a doorway that led into the living room. Off the living room, to the right was the parent's bedroom and another bedroom where we kids slept. In front of the north window stood the dining table with six chairs and a highchair. There was a heater in the living room that was used on freezing days.

I remember, on cold mornings, awaking to the sound of mom building a fire in the heater. After it was roaring for a while, my brothers and I would get up and rush over to the warm heater and dress ourselves there.

We joked that, at our house, we had "running water"! If you wanted it, you had to run for it! Dad would run down to the creek to bring water in a wooden barrel with a horse and a "stone boat" or skid. There was no such thing as "indoor plumbing." In the summer, the barrel was left outside the back door for everyone's convenience. You had to "run" for it, dip it out, and bring it in.

In winter with the sub-zero temperatures, the barrel had to be brought inside, or it would freeze solid. This made our kitchen even more crowded. I remember licking the ice off the steel rim of the frozen barrel when it was brought in. After my tongue stuck to the frozen metal once, I learned that it was a very foolish thing to do.

It was a good little house, and my mom was very pleased with it, except it was drafty in winter. One fall, Dad and Mom took all the siding off the house and covered it with black tar paper and put the siding back on and painted it. They found honey in the north wall. After that it was a very warm, cozy house for our little family.

Northwest of the house, in the shelter of the trees, stood a small barn where the few cows were milked. It had a small hayloft above it. Beside that was a corral and straw shed where the pigs, cattle, and horses could find shelter from the coldest weather.

North of the barn was a small "outhouse," "biffy," "john," or "outdoor toilet." This was a small wooden structure made of shiplap and "two by fours," that sat over a shallow hole in the ground. Ours was a deluxe model, for it was a three-seater with holes designed to meet the individual needs of the "three bares," a big one for daddy bare, a middle-sized one for mommy bare, and a wee tiny one for baby bare.

This outhouse was connected to the big house by a very long path. In winter, this path seemed very long indeed for a small boy. When one got there, one had to bare a certain part of his anatomy and sit on the icy, cold, and often frosty, or ice-covered rim for a nature-determined number of seconds. I can assure you that we were as efficient as possible in the winter.

But the summer use was a different story. Although we never liked the odors surrounding the place, nor the flies and mosquitoes, we were fascinated by the old T. Eaton catalogues that served as wiping tissue. I am afraid many an hour was squandered in absorbing the educative value of the tissue before using it for its final hygienic function.

Years later, we asked Dad why he moved from the good farm at West Duchess. He replied, "I was getting all boys, and my Mormon neighbors were raising all girls, and I did not want them to be crossed." He did not really appreciate living among the Mormons all that much.

Hansen brothers: Carl, Peter & Paul, 1944

Friends and Neighbors

In our new community, we had good neighbors. To the south lived the Alfred Olsets, a Norwegian family. Mrs. Olset was a staunch member of the Jehovah's Witness group, so my folks had some lively discussions with them. I remember my dad bringing his Bible outside in a shady place and entering an argument that was beyond my little head. Apparently, no one was convinced by the other, for they remained in their faith, and we remained in ours, and most importantly, we all remained friends. They had a daughter, Marie, about Peter's age, and a boy called Melvin who had Down's syndrome.

To the north was the Kool family. They had several children of late teen to early adult age, so we did not associate much with them.

Across the road and across the creek lived the Hjalmar Hanson family. They had three grown sons, Herman, Sylvan, and Norman, a couple of whom were soldiers in the war, and three daughters who were younger. Helen was in her teens. Edith was about a year older than Peter, and Carol was about a year older than me. Their grandmother lived with them. She was blind, and their mother was almost blind as well.

The girls were our main playmates during those years. They taught us a few of the children's games that children must learn from somewhere if they are to play them. Mostly, we played around in our yard, as we were seldom allowed to go to their place unless Mom accompanied us on one of her friendly visits to their mother and grandmother.

One time Peter and I sneaked off, unbeknownst to our mother, to our neighbor's place. We were having a fun time until we spied our mother striding down the road at a determined pace carrying a switch in her hand. It sure did not take long for us to reach home, but we were not fast enough to avoid getting our bottoms warmed a bit. I cannot recall ever making any more unauthorized friendly playtime visits.

Edith and Carol gave us our first taste of soda pop. I must have been about six years old. It was a bottle of orange crush. I had never tasted anything like it in my life, and I'll never forget the impression it made on me. It was, to me, the best possible thing on earth to drink! Why did our parents never buy soft drinks?

Another neighbor worthy of mention was the John Nielsen family. They were an older Danish couple that lived about three miles northwest of us. We used to visit with them on occasion. The lady was very hospitable to us children. Dad had a chance to talk Danish for a change. We would listen but could not understand.

They built a new house, which was of great interest to us boys. It seemed so big and nice and new in comparison with the pioneer hovel they had been living in. Yet today, that "mansion" stands empty, just a small, abandoned shack.

It was at Nielsen's that I heard a radio for the first time. They had a large floor model with a big battery. We were sure that a small man was hiding in the box, but then, how could there also be singers and other people in there beside him? The mysteries of this world!

Farm Life

One of my earliest memories is of lying on my back and looking up at the underbelly of a horse and noticing how absolutely huge the bottom of the horse's foot was. In my mind's eye that foot was as big around as a large sized pizza. How did I get in that unique position to have a worm's eye view of the horse? I do not remember.

Dad told me years later that he was making hay on a bright summer day. He was up on the rack busy building a large load of hay, and the team of horses was moving ahead to the next pile of hay to be loaded. As he worked, Dad noticed me, a less than two-year-old toddler coming by myself to the field. Then in his work, he lost sight of me.

When he realized I had disappeared, he immediately stopped the team. They found me under the wagon unhurt. Apparently, I had wondered in front of the horses as they were pulling the heavy load, and they knocked me down and pulled the wagon over me. Does God have guardian angels to watch over carefree little boys?

We had a sheep that gave birth to a lamb. One Sunday, we came home from church and found the ewe had drowned herself in the irrigation ditch, so we had to raise the lamb ourselves. We called him "Charlie," and he became a beloved pet. He went to pasture with the calves. When we wanted to know where the calves were, we just needed to call "Charlie," and he would answer us. Then we would know where the calves were.

House help, Aunt Helen Friesen feeding the calves behind the house while Carl, Paul, and Peter clown around, 1947

One day in 1943, Dad was working in the field with the Fordson tractor when a large chunk of cast iron blew out of the side of the engine into the field. The engine gave one noisy "clunk" and died on the spot. It had pushed a broken rod through the block. He traded it to Dan Burkholder, the International Harvester dealer in Duchess, for a McCormick Deering 15-30. This was a good tractor which he used until 1945, when he traded it for a Massey-Harris Pacemaker for $600. The Pacemaker was the first tractor to show off rubber tires in the community.

In 1944, as Dad wanted to become a dairy farmer, my folks bought a new milking machine driven by a gasoline engine. They were milking about eight cows that year. They carried the whole milk from the barn to the kitchen to be separated, the cream from the skim milk. The cream separator had a hand-cranked centrifuge through which the milk poured and separated. We small boys were fascinated by this devise and took turns cranking it. They stored the cream in a cream can until it could be taken to the creamery in Brooks and sold. They carried the skim milk back out to the barn and fed it to the calves and pigs.

Our parents tried growing potatoes as a cash crop in 1944 and in 1945. It was a lot of work, and the potatoes did well, but the marketing company had problems, and they did not get paid for many of their potatoes.

Another baby boy made his appearance at the Bassano Hospital on August 16, 1945. I remember the excitement in that old Model A when we drove to Bassano to retrieve our mother and to bring home our new brother. We repeated over and over again: "George Marinus! George Marinus!" from the back seat as we drove him home. At that stage it did not matter to us that we did not have a sister. George Marinus would make a fine brother, a necessary addition to our team, and he did not disappoint us.

Mom had an old Renfrew washing machine that had a galvanized steel tub that moved back and forth in a rocking fashion as one pulled and pushed on the handle. This agitated the water, making it swish back and forth with the clothes. One hoped that eventually the clothes would get clean. After being swished back and forth for an appropriate time, the clothes were taken out and put through a hand-turned wringer to squeeze out as much of the water as possible, then rinsed by hand and put through the wringer again, and then hung out to dry. The water, of course, was carried from the ditch in summer or from the water barrel in winter.

In the year 1947, Dad bought Mom a brand new, gasoline-powered Maytag washing machine, which served her for more than twenty years. She was happy and proud of that machine. Compared to the old hand-powered Renfrew washer, it was something out of this world.

That year, Sylvan Hanson, one of our neighbor's sons, and Helen, my mom's sister, worked for us. Helen began to work for us in the summer of 1947 and again in the summer of 1948. She helped with milking cows, feeding pigs, putting up hay, cutting grain, doing housework, and taking care of us four boys. Helen was always happy and had a good sense of humor. She remembered some of the laughable incidents:

> *Sometimes I got to put the boys to bed. I told them a Bible story and had them say their prayers. The first time Carl says, "You forgot something." I did not know what I forgot. Well, I had not given them a kiss! They thought that the prayer and kiss went together. So, I gave them each a kiss, and every time after that, when I put them to bed, they got their kiss after they prayed.*
>
> *Jens and Elizabeth disciplined their boys. ... Sometimes they had to stand in a corner for being naughty. One evening*

their aunts came over. Carl was standing in a corner. One of them, not thinking, asked, "What are you doing?" "None of your business." came the reply. Sometimes their mother sent them outside to fetch a stick to be punished with. One time Carl was sent, and he came in bringing a short piece of 2" x 4" and said that was all he could find. I do not think he got his spanking that time; his mother could not keep a straight face.

Sometimes the boys had to wash their own feet before going to bed. They would just sit there and not wash them. "Wash your feet!" their mother commanded. "I can't reach them!" came the reply.

What I remember most of George was the way he wore his cap. He pulled it down to his eyes and walked around with his nose in the air. He was just under three years. If you adjusted it for him, he would rearrange it his way and look at you from under his cap with his blue eyes.

Mervin Biehn became an interested visitor at the Hansen home. He met Helen in November 1946 at the Fall Conference of the Mennonite Church at Carstairs, Alberta. His interest made sure he was present for the next Summer Conference at Duchess in 1948. Of course, he stayed at our place where Helen was working. He made some observations:

Hansens had four very active young boys. Peter at eight years of age was the obvious leader of the group. Carl was his faithful follower. There was Paul, whose adventures kept his guardian angel very busy, and George, the little gaffer with the bright blue eyes, which he kept covered with the peak of his cap. He could not always see too well where he was going, but it kept the sun out of his eyes.

Helen recalls that there was a baptismal service at church one Sunday. After dinner, Peter became busy baptizing his brothers. Peter was always the leader and preacher when we played church.

Carl E. Hansen

German Prisoners of War

I was born during the second world war. As I grew older, I gradually became aware that a war was going on. The Canadian Government made certain German prisoners of war available to farmers for help because there was a great shortage of labor due to the demands for men in the armed forces and in the factories. Following the requirements or rules of law concerning these prisoners of war, they wore stripped uniforms with a red patch on the back.

I was about three years old when we got our first German prisoner, Fritz Wiseman, to live with us and work for us as a hired hand. He was very homesick and only stayed with us for a few months. He said he quit because Neta, who was also working for us, laughed at him when he told us he had eaten three pounds of wieners at a party one night. I am sure that young German men have a healthy capacity to eat wieners, but there seems to have been a language problem in this case.

Later, we got another prisoner, Heinz Stadthaus, a twenty-two-year-old who had been a member of the Hitler Youth and then served in the merchant marine when his ship was captured by the Allies in the war. Heinz had a good attitude and adjusted well to his situation. He was fun to have around. He stayed with us for eleven months, from late 1944 to the fall of 1945.

We kids enjoyed him because he played with us. I remember going out to the field to tell him it was dinnertime, and he gave me a ride on his shoulders. There was one problem. I had wet my pants earlier. I was soaking wet. Heinz did not object, but for the first time in my life I became embarrassed about wetting my pants. I believe that was the last time I wet my pants.

Dad was sort of nasty to Heinz. He would tease him by telling him that Hitler was going to lose the war. Heinz would become very agitated and would almost cry. The poor prisoner must have been very lonely and homesick, for he had no way of knowing how things were really going at home. Should one believe the Allied version of the news? He was too far from home to hear the German side of the story. He got to be good friends with the young people in the community. Then he decided to leave our place because he said he was getting too involved with our neighbor young people and he did not want to spoil his life.

Aircraft

Airplanes fascinated me. I longed for a chance to get up close to one, to admire it, to touch it, maybe to look inside it and perhaps even to ride in one. Most of all, I dreamed of someday learning to fly one of those marvelous contraptions.

Many times, during the war, my brothers and I would rush out of the house when we heard the approaching sound of a plane. We would stand in the yard gaping up at the little one-engine planes on war-training maneuvers as they swooped down low in a pretend dive-bombing mission, just skimming the tops of our trees and sending the chickens, sheep, and cattle scattering in terror in a wake of wind and leaves and swirling dust. If we were lucky, we could see the pilot, and I would wave to him with as big a sweep as my short arm could manage. A few times he waved back, or he would tip the plane's wing in recognition.

I will never forget the Sunday afternoon my mother called us boys to come in and clean up. We were going for a little drive. Paul and I were busy playing under a tree, and as we often did, we delayed our response to her commands. Then, all at once we saw our parents with our brothers come out of the house, climb into the old Model A Ford, start up the engine and drive out the lane without us. Oh well, so what? They probably just went out to look at the crops or something. We were having fun anyway, so let them go.

A little while later, they arrived back home. My brothers came running over to us spilling over with excitement. They had driven to the local airport, and they had seen some of those planes up close, and they even could touch them!

How cheated I felt! I wanted to see the airplanes more than anything else! Yet I had missed this golden opportunity! My parents had always taught us the importance of obedience; now they had driven the lesson home in a way I would never forget. Ultimately, the cost of disobedience is that one will miss the best in life.

The Dam

In 1944, Dad and his next-door neighbors built a dam across the creek, close to the road. The resulting pond was about twelve feet deep in the middle and made a nice little lake for community swimming and fishing in the summer and for skating in the winter. It was also nice to have a reservoir of water for the livestock in case of need. Dad and one of the neighbor boys bought a canoe together to play with on the lake. He took us for a boat ride.

One day in the late fall of that year, after an exceptionally light snow had fallen, we boys disappeared. Dad went looking for us. He traced our steps in the snow down to the pond. He was shocked. The tracks of his three little boys went out on the thin ice just so far, and then back again. He could not believe the ice was strong enough to hold even one little boy, let alone three of them. Mom said, "God kept them!"

During the winter when the ice was thick, the cattle became accustomed to going on the ice to drink from a hole Dad chopped in it. In spring, the ice got soft. One evening one cow came home bawling and all wet. Dad noticed it, but soon put it out of mind. The next day he found another cow floating dead in the pond. That was the end of the pond. He and his hired hand dug it open and drained it.

Creek water was not the most appealing water for human consumption. Sometimes we would fish out little minnows or bugs from the barrel that Dad brought home. There were all kinds of little wiggly things and algae swimming in it, not to mention the invisible microbes. We also became aware that the neighbors upstream dumped their garbage in the creek, and their cattle walked through and defecated in its waters, so Dad decided to dig a well down near the creek, just east of the dam, to get safe water.

One chilly November day, my brothers and I decided to inspect the digging site. We walked down to where Dad and Heinz, our hired hand, were digging. Heinz was down in the hole digging and placing the mud and water into a bucket attached to a rope. Dad was up on top of the hole using the rope to lift the bucket with its contents to the surface. They must have reached a depth of about fourteen feet. A little water was beginning to seep in.

We boys came in a hurry, full of excitement and curiosity, and while greeting Dad, we moved close to the hole to get a glimpse of the work going on down there. I must have moved too close, for the next thing I knew, I was down there in the cold wet mud!

I had fallen behind Heinz, and at first, he did not even notice I was there. Dad had to holler to him to turn around and pick me up. Somehow, they got me out of there in a hurry, put me on a wagon to which a team of horses was hitched, and rushed me up the hill to the warmth of the house. I remember how the horses galloped and the wagon rattled as the steel wheels bounced over the frozen earth. I was wet, cold, and muddy, so I got a nice hot bath. It could have been a bad accident, but all is well that ends well. It was another reason to believe that God's guardian angel was watching over a little boy!

A Trip to Eagle Hill

Corny and Lois Siemens had moved with their family to a place called "Eagle Hill" near Westward Ho northwest of Calgary. Since they were my parents' best friends, we decided to pay them a visit. It was a lovely summer day, on August 16, 1946, that our parents packed their four boys, some clothes, and a picnic lunch into our old Model "A" Ford and struck out west across the prairie. It was the first of the very few vacations that our family ever made together. I remember driving across prairie trails and opening and closing gates as we took a shortcut before we got on the main road, the Trans-Canada Highway, that took us towards Calgary. In those days, the highway was still a gravel road.

The road was long and rough, and the weather turned rainy, and we boys were impatient. When we were not sleeping, we quarreled and kept asking, "Is that Calgary?" or "Are we almost there?"

Finally, after what seemed a long ten-hour day, we arrived at the Siemens' home at around 8:30 p.m. and did we ever get a good welcome! We boys were shy and did not remember the Siemens' children, so it took a while for us to get acquainted, but when we did, we had such a fun time playing with them.

After supper, they put us to bed. We boys all slept crosswise on a big bed in a big open room. The Siemens family lived in a log house that was still under construction. In the morning we could see out through the cracks in the walls and roof. The house was in a very bushy place up on a hill. It seems to me they were trying to be pioneers or something. I was not yet five years old, so I did not understand everything and can remember less. We were there for a weekend. I do not remember much about the trip home.

Celestial Sensitivity

My earliest recollections of going to church involve travelling by horse and wagon in the snow in wintertime. As weather and road conditions allowed, we usually went to church in our Model "A" Ford car. My folks were faithful in attending church even though it was a major struggle to get there.

I remember sitting beside my dad in the sanctuary and smelling the sweat of the men. Deodorant was not yet a known entity in our circles. My two brothers and I would sit on the "men's side" to the right, with Dad halfway up to the front, and baby George would be on the left with Mom on the "women's side" of the meetinghouse. We had to sit quietly in church. Dad would tolerate no nonsense during the service. We understood that and got along well although it was tiresome at times. The sermons were long, and there was little in them that could hold a child's attention.

I remember thinking about God. I would look up at the ceiling to perhaps catch a glimpse of Him. I never saw Him. Then I noticed Fred Martin, maybe a Sunday school superintendent or something, walking with an expression of solemn determination, and I wondered if maybe he was God? But I had my doubts. Then I noticed this young man, Paul Martin, preaching maybe his first sermon, with his left hand in his pocket jingling coins, and I wondered, "Does this man know God? Does God tell him what to say?"

I was too young to notice clothing styles but found out later that many of the men wore regulation "plain suits," and of those that did not, none wore neckties. I remember hearing the words "cape dress" in sermons several times. First, I thought it was a special kind of material, so finally I asked Mom. She tried to explain that it was a certain style some church members thought especially important. Mom did not wear the cape though.

At home on a warm summer day, I would often lay on the soft grass on my back and look up at the blue heavens and wonder about God. I would see the hawks soaring at great heights, watch the white clouds move across the sky, ever changing their shape and size, until I felt as if I was the one moving under them. I would think of Jesus riding on a cloud and wonder what that would be like. What if he came on that cloud over there? That would be a nice surprise!

I learned more about God at home from my mother than I learned in all the churches I ever attended put together. My parents had Bible reading and prayer with the family every morning before breakfast and again every evening before retiring to bed at night. For us children, bedtime always included story time, often from the Bible Story Book, with plenty of time for discussion.

Church was an important part of our lives. I can remember playing church at home. We would line up some chairs. Then we would agree who was the chorister, deacon, preacher, or even missionary. Their degree of importance was definitely in the reverse order. We continued doing all the functions of church, including communion and foot washing.

The first funeral I remember was when Bennet and Ruth Torkelsons' little girl, Anna Mae, died. We followed them to the graveyard and watched the burial. After leaving the cemetery and driving away, I remember looking back through the rear window of our Model "A," hoping I just might get a glimpse of an angel carrying the little girl home to heaven! We went further and further away until I could not see the cemetery anymore. I was disappointed.

Starting School

By September 1947, Peter was old enough to enter the strange new world of school. Mom took him the first day and registered him in the Clancy School. After that, he would walk the one mile east across the field, following the creek. He made sure he reached the Hanson girls' place in time to walk with them. We younger brothers would wait eagerly all day for him to return. We wanted to hear him tell of his adventures in that big world out there.

The Clancy School was a two-roomed schoolhouse with about forty to forty-five students from grades one to nine. Each room had a teacher. Peter was quite impressed by the bullies in the school. There was Billy Harstead, a grade three boy who took Peter into the outhouse and showed him his fist and said, "Show me your stockings or I will punch you with this." We knew that Billy would be a boy we would have to beat someday. Unfortunately, he later got polio, and we had to forgive him and even felt sorry for him. Many years later we were happy to learn that Bill Harstead became a successful hockey player.

The next year was my turn to start school. It was a great comfort to me to have an older brother to go with me to that big, strange place. He gave me advice and clued me in on who were the bullies and how to avoid trouble and survive. We walked with the Hanson girls and often with the Pierson children who came from further west. We soon made friends. My teacher was Ms. Jones. She struck me as a kind and competent teacher. I soon was learning to read and count.

I developed a crush on a certain little pretty girl named "Vicky." Different than my brothers, she had long, pretty curls and a vivacious smile, so I thought it would be nice to be friends with her. She had a new balloon-tired bicycle that fascinated me. I had never seen a bicycle up close before, so when it was lying there by itself, I went over and lifted it up and looked at it. I did not try to ride it.

Several hours later, Vicky's big brother who was in grade eight called me aside and scolded me for touching Vicky's bicycle and warned me to never touch it again. I was very scared of this big hostile fellow and decided then and there that, since my brother was no match for Vicky's brother, I better steer clear of Vicky and her wonderful bicycle. Thus ended my first fantasy of romance.

Uncle Chris

My Dad had been writing to his youngest brother, Christian Hansen, in Denmark, about his interest in coming to Canada. Dad had agreed to sponsor him and give him a job if he came. We had never seen any of our dad's family and were extremely excited about seeing this brother of his.

Finally, the day came. He had flown by airplane from Iceland to New York and would be coming on the train. It was a cold, snowy, early morning in April 1948 when Dad went to the train station in Brooks to meet our uncle, Chris.

Chris was a bit shorter and smaller than our dad. He wore funny European clothes. He had a short, pointed nose that curved out, and a cleft chin that supported an overly broad smile that revealed a set of decaying teeth. He and Dad sat talking in Danish for many hours. This was the first time Dad had seen a member of his family for more than twenty years. Certainly, there was a lot of catching up to do. Chris had been in Germany for three years during the war, so he could speak some German. Therefore, Mom could communicate with him in that language.

Since Germany had invaded Denmark during the war, they drafted young Danish men to be laborers for Germany. Chris had been working under the Third Reich for three years as a laborer in construction, building concrete bunkers, pillboxes, and other fortifications. For the past year, he had been working on a farm in Iceland. He had very interesting stories to tell. Now he had migrated to Canada and would live with us and work for us; we were glad to finally have a Hansen uncle of our very own.

Chris did not like the irrigating and the billions of mosquitoes that tried to taste him while he was doing it. He did not like the cold weather that he experienced the next winter either, so when we decided to move to Ontario later that year, he decided to follow us.

Jens & his brother, Christian Hansen who immigrated to Canada, April 1948

Researching the Reproduction Question

Our parents did not tell us much about reproduction of the species in those days. We boys pondered much about where babies came from or how they suddenly appeared in our home. We tried to ask questions of our parents but were diverted with evasive answers. I must give credit, at least they did not resort to the "fake" answers of their ancestors. In Denmark, babies were brought by "the stork." Russian Mennonite babies were brought by "the coyote." Our parents would not deceive us; they only resorted to evasive promises like, "We will tell you when you get older." How much older did we need to be? We felt left in the dark. A sex education opportunity missed.

In the meantime, we boys noticed that our mother was getting to look mighty "fat" around her middle. We began conducting our own private investigations, making observations, holding consultations, making hypotheses, and testing them with further observations that led inevitably to conclusions. We concluded that our mother was about to bring us another baby. But "How?" and "Why?" was still a mystery.

Sure enough, one quiet, clear, warm October evening, Mom dressed up and went with Dad to Brooks. They left us boys home in the care of our aunt, Neta, who was working for us. It seemed rather strange for our parents to go to town in the evening when all the businesses were closed. It was a further mystery why they were going away when our grandparents, along with Esther and David, came to visit that evening.

There was a full harvest moon that night, and no one made us go to bed, so we played hide-and-seek outside in the yard. It was a glorious evening. Then Dad came home without Mom and informed us that Mom was going to have another baby. We were not surprised. It was obvious that Mom had something big inside, but how did it get there? It would require more research and detective work.

The next day, October 18, 1948, our mom's fifth son, Charles Robert Hansen, was born. He weighed nine pounds and fifteen ounces. Of course, we were very happy to welcome our new brother ten days later when Dad brought him and our mother home. He was a lovely specimen of a baby: blond hair, brown eyes, and a perfectly shaped face. What a marvelous little fellow. But where did he come from? Mom's stomach was a bit smaller, but how did he get in there in the first place, and how did he get out? His origin and presence were surrounded in mystery.

Looking to Ontario

Things were going quite well for us in 1948. Our dad traded the Model A Ford for a new Willys Jeep that had a metal covered cab instead of the usual canvas cover typical of the Jeeps of that era. Since the Jeep had four-wheel drive and a low range gear, we used it for fieldwork, especially harrowing and seeding, as well as for family transportation. We were proud of our dad and of our new vehicle.

During those days it was not easy to buy a new vehicle because during the war all manufacturing was geared towards war production, and consumer goods just had to wait. Now the factories were converting to the production of consumer goods, but the demand was very high, so there was a very long waiting list. Dad was fortunate to get the new Jeep without waiting very long.

Farming was going better, but Dad was restless. Irrigating was hard labor; there were other parts of Canada where rainfall was abundant, and crops flourished without irrigation. An article appeared in the *Monitor*, our church paper, telling of a church-planting mission near Alma, Ontario. It portrayed glorious farming opportunities in the community there and urged Mennonites to move to the area to help the new mission. Our parents' best friends, the Dave and Levoy Roth families, both moved to that area in search of a better life in Ontario. Mom and Dad became interested. They decided to sell the farm and follow them.

My favorite aunt, Helen, married Mervin Biehn on November 14th at the Duchess Mennonite Church. There was a reception for them in the Friesen home. I remember how full the house was. She went with Mervin to live with him on his farm near Guernsey, Saskatchewan.

Shortly after Helen's wedding in the fall of 1948, our parents sold our farm to Malcom Dowling, and our family prepared to move. Dad took the train to Ontario to look for a place for us to live. After he returned, we got ready for an auction sale in late November.

Dad had to part with his favorite white saddle horse, Nancy. A certain man offered him $100 for her. Dad did not trust the man to treat the horse right, so he took his gun, jumped on Nancy, and rode her out to the far end of the pasture. Later, he returned on foot carrying his gun and the horse's bridle. He preferred to put his faithful old friend to permanent rest rather than to betray her for money to anyone who might abuse her.

That was a powerful lesson in loyalty, fairness, and justice to me as a little seven-year-old. (Today, I wonder what my dad's opinion would be about the current controversies surrounding the question of euthanasia for suffering loved ones?)

After our trip to Eagle Hill, Dad had experienced some problem with his ear and nasal drainage that would not go away. Eventually, the doctor sent him to a specialist in Calgary where he stayed from November 22 to 25, 1948. They did an operation up his nasal cavity and cut out a piece of bone. That was supposed to help his drainage. When he came home, he had a little device that fascinated me the most, an atomizer, to spray medicine up his nose. He seemed to get better after that healed.

My folks had decided to keep mom's best dishes, her sewing machine, and the Maytag washing machine. These, they crated and sent on the train to Ontario. The Jeep would follow us when John Grove, a young man from Ontario, would drive it there several weeks later. Everything else was listed to be sold at auction.

Since the trip to Calgary took longer than expected, Dad was not even present when the day of the sale came. All our possessions were taken out of the house and arranged on the lawn. Mom's wedding gifts, her jars of preserved fruit, our toys, furniture, farm machinery, livestock, everything was to be sold to the highest bidder.

Then the auctioneer and the people came. In a few hours, the happy people carried all our things out the gate, and our house and yard were empty. This was no longer our home, so we might as well go.

In November 1948, we sold household goods, farm machinery, and livestock by auction before departing from Alberta

We, now a family of seven, stayed with Grandpa and Grandma Friesen's until the business was all cleared. Then, on the night of November 29th, our grandparents, aunts, and uncles escorted us to the railroad station at Brooks. They came along to say goodbye and to send us off.

I remember the awful feeling. It was about eight o'clock on this dark, cold, wintry night. The huge CPR steam locomotive came clanging and puffing and hissing into the station from the west, and behind it followed a long line of rumbling passenger cars. The regular clackity clack of their wheels slowed as they passed, slower and slower until finally, there was a mighty screeching of brakes and a bumping of all the cars down the line, then a final hiss, and the train was dead still.

Grandmother and the others hugged and kissed us goodbye. My new aunt Wilma, Jake's wife, kissed me goodbye. It made me feel I was special. I liked her.

Then we all hurried and climbed up the steps into this dark, unfamiliar monster. Strange black people hurried us to our seats. Mom carried the six-week-old baby Charles and saw that we got in place, and Dad saw to it that the suitcases and boxes were all on board. Our aunt, Anita, helped him. She was coming with us to help us get settled into our new home. There were whistles and shouts in the darkness outside, and soon the monster was slowly chuffing forward, at first very slowly, then faster and faster, and we were on our way.

There were dim electric lights in the train, so we could see to settle ourselves into our seats. Soon the conductor came by to punch our tickets, and his assistant came to see that we were comfortable.

They were both black people. This was my first time to see a real live black person. Mom had read *Uncle Tom's Cabin* to us and had told us all about the times when people were captured in Africa and stolen away to America where they were sold as slaves, and how they were abused and cruelly mistreated, and how some of them escaped to Canada and freedom.

I just stared and stared at these men, thinking they or their fathers may have been slaves once. Africa must be a vastly different place if all the people looked like these two!

Soon the steward came by and announced he was ready to make up our beds. We were amazed as he took the cushions off the seats, pushed, and lifted and shoved, and suddenly, the seats turned into beds, and a compartment was pulled down from the ceiling making another bed. Soon we were all in beds, Dad and Peter and I in the upper bunk, Mom and Paul and Charles in a lower bunk, and Anita and George in a third bed.

The steam whistle screamed outside at every railroad crossing as we sped eastward through the dark, empty prairies in that lonely, wintry night. Its mournful wail found its echo in the depths of my empty, lonely heart. It was, somehow, incredibly sad to be riding on this train, away from all that was home and familiar, into the darkness of an unknown world ahead in this strange chuffing monster. But my dad was beside me, and my mother was below me, so there was nothing to fear. I was soon fast asleep.

The morning sunshine took away the sad feeling, and we began to look forward with excitement. What would our new home in Ontario be like? The first night and the first day we crossed the Great Plains, the next two days we snaked our way through the rocks and mountains and lakes of the Great Canadian Shield. We had never imagined there could be so many rocks and trees and lakes in the entire world.

That train took three nights and three days to reach our destination in southern Ontario. Finally, we came to Union Station in Toronto where we had to get off the train and find another train to take us to Drayton.

Union Station was a huge, strange place for us little "prairie chickens." We wondered in awe as we crossed through a vast underground basement with huge pillars and were told that the trains were overhead. We went up the stairs and sure enough, there were the trains, many of them. We found our train and reached Drayton later that day. The date was December 2nd, 1948.

FIVE

GROWING A FAMILY IN ONTARIO

Lavoy Roth met us at the Drayton train station. We moved in with his family for about a week until my folks could find a place for us to live. Lavoy and Lula Roth were farming near Drayton. They had four children: June, a year older than Peter, James, about my age, Faith, about George's age, and Ruth, a baby girl, about Charles's age. Dave and Emma Roth were the grandparents and lived in their own small house on the farm.

When our Hansen family moved in with our five children, the Roth house was really full. If we could still be friends after a week of living together in such conditions, then it was true friendship indeed! The oldest children went to school during the day, so it was not too bad.

But one evening the Amos Brubaker family dropped in for a visit. They brought two big girls and an older boy. That was too many for one house. We soon were taking sides and getting into a fight. Our friendship was strained that night.

Finding a Home in Ontario

When Dad came earlier in search for a home, he found that there were many farms for sale at reasonable prices, so he delayed deciding until he could bring out his wife to help him choose. He arranged to move our family into a vacant, old stone house owned by Simon Huber. Because it was not in an inhabitable condition, we had to live with the Roths until that sturdy old house could be cleaned up and furnished. That took about a week to accomplish.

The old house was already more than one hundred years old. It was well built of precisely cut stone on the front and more random fieldstone on the back. Its walls were about two feet thick. It had four rooms downstairs and four rooms upstairs. A nice, wide staircase with a landing and turn in the middle connected the two levels. It had a large summer kitchen and a woodshed at the back entrance. There was a cistern and an indoor pump at a sink in the corner of the kitchen and a broken furnace in a cellar below.

The "Stone House," our first home in Ontario for the month of December 1948, purchased and refurbished by Pastor Gordon Bauman in the 1950s

We were happy for this house, though it needed a very thorough cleaning. It had been used as grain storage for the last few years. Rats had gotten inside and chewed big holes in the windowsills and under the doors. The wallpaper was also chewed up in places. Mom and Anita really scrubbed and cleaned. It was cold in there because the furnace was not working. Our folks set up a cook stove and heater, so it was not too bad. When used furniture was found, we were happy to move in.

Mr. and Mrs. Alex Hepburn lived on a nice 150-acre farm across the road from this stone house. They had one little boy, Doug, near my age. Mrs. Hepburn wanted her husband to sell the farm and move to town and become a carpenter instead. Alex liked to farm, and carpenter jobs were not that easy to find.

However, he was under pressure from his wife, so he offered to sell his farm to my folks with machinery and livestock. It was a deal. They moved out before the end of the month. As it turned out, Alex did not enjoy being a carpenter and living in town. He was sorry that he had sold the farm, so he bought another nice farm near Guelph and returned to farming. Alex was happy, and we were happy. I never heard about his wife's feelings though.

The Hepburn farm we bought and moved into on January 1, 1949

Finally on New Year's Day, 1949, we moved across the road into our own new home. We thought this house was very spacious. It was a grey, cube-shaped, cement-brick house built on a full basement that reached two feet above the ground. It had two floors with nine-foot ceilings topped with an attic that was fourteen feet from floor to peak and four feet from floor to eaves. The attic had two large dormer windows on two sides. There was a large indented front porch on the lower floor with a corresponding balcony on the upper floor.

Upon entering the ground floor from the back door, one passed into the washroom where work clothes were hung on hooks on the wall to the right, and the sink and washstand was on the left. A force pump stood beside the sink. It was used to pump water from an outside cistern up to a storage tank in the attic. A hot water tank stood along the opposite wall. Heat from the cookstove in the kitchen was transferred via a water pipe through the wall to the tank. In the wall between the pump and the hot water tank was a window in front of which Mom kept her Maytag washing machine. Straight ahead, a doorway opened to the kitchen.

The kitchen was a very large room with a cook stove on the left side of the entrance. Against the wall on the left was a buffet. A large oak drop leaf dining table surrounded by eight chairs stood in the center. Along the far wall were a couch and a few more chairs. On the right side of the room was the coal/wood-burning heater standing in the room between the table, the pantry door, and the hallway door. Turning a sharp right, one entered the pantry where all the dishes, pots, pans, cooking utensils, spices, and food were kept. There was a "dumb waiter" there to take perishables to the cool basement since there was no refrigerator, but it was not operational and was never made operational while we lived there. Connected to the pantry were the basement steps at the bottom of which were kept the canned goods, vegetables, and coal or firewood.

Off the kitchen to the right was a door to the hallway in which there was a flight of stairs to the right and two doors straight ahead. The left door opened into a parlor connected with double sliding doors to a dining room on the right to which the second door from the hall also opened. We rarely used these two large rooms. We made the parlor into a spare bedroom and the dining room into a sitting room, which we furnished with good furniture, but used only on special occasions. In the hall to the left was an outside entrance opening in from the indented porch at the front of the house.

On the second floor were four bedrooms and one bathroom which had running hot and cold water and a toilet. Something new for us. No more cold night trips to the distant outhouse! Each bedroom had a full-sized walk-in closet. Each doorway had a transom above it that could be tilted open with a control mechanism. At the very end of the hallway was an outside door opening onto the balcony that was directly above the indented porch. Halfway down the hall on the right was a door that opened to a stairway leading up to the huge attic. Although not big by modern standards, to us who were used to rather small, cramped living quarters, this house was like a mansion!

When we moved into this house, we boys were given the first bedroom to the left, and our parents took the first bedroom to the right. Anita was given the second bedroom to the right. Later, when Uncle Chris came, he was given the second bedroom to the left.

Our bedroom had a stovepipe hole in the floor above the kitchen. It was a very convenient hole, although there always was the danger of a little boy's foot slipping through with the possibility of severe distress following. The warm air came up that hole from the heater in the kitchen.

If we could manage to stay awake long enough, we could use the hole for eavesdropping on our parents' late night secret conversations, hoping to pick up those tidbits that were not meant for little ears. It was a good shortcut for dropping things downstairs when they were called for, saving many steps. We even found it handy for sweeping the dirt down when we had to clean our room. But this use had its pros and cons. For some reason, Mom was not amused when she was cooking the morning oatmeal on the kitchen range below. Her extraordinary objections came through loud and clear. We also gave up that use of the hole when the strong updraft of the rising hot air blew the dust sweepings back up into our faces.

The stovepipe hole also served as a fair intercom system, especially on those many mornings when Mom issued her tenth "final" warning about drastic measures that were about to be taken if we did not get up at once. I still feel pity for the many little boys and girls in our land who will never know the advantages of having a stovepipe hole in the floor of their bedrooms!

Hansen's home from January 1, 1949, to February 1956

There was a big barn on this farm. It was forty-five feet wide by ninety feet long and forty-five feet tall. The lower part was where the animals were kept. This downstairs was constructed of stone and mortar walls and a concrete floor. The pens were made of wood, and the stalls were made of concrete. The frame of the upper story was made with huge, long, wooden beams to which were fastened vertically hung unpainted siding boards on the outside.

The loft floor was made of heavy timbers with a sheath of two-inch thick planks. It was strong enough to hold a granary with several thousand bushels of grain, all the hay forty cows could eat in one winter, enough straw to bed them, and to store some of the farm machinery, including a tractor or a threshing machine.

There was a large bank of earth built up against the side of the barn leading to two huge doors. One could drive the horses or a tractor with a big load of hay up this bank into the barn. The haymows had ladders twenty feet straight up from the floor with cross beams at that level. There was a chicken house at one end under the straw mow.

Front view of Hansen's barn 1949

My parents bought this farm of 150 acres of land with twenty cows, a few calves, some pigs, four horses and a bit of old horse drawn machinery for a total of $16,000. They had to take out a loan to make the purchase.

Between the house and the barn was a small garage, big enough for one car and one tractor. There was a lane from the road that ran past the house and the garage to the barn. There were not many trees in the yard, but there was a cedar shelter belt that ran from the house down the north side of the lane, turned right for 120 feet, turned right again, and ran up to the house again, leaving a sheltered garden spot between the two hedges. Between the ends of the cedar shelter belt and the house was a nice big lawn.

This farm was located one mile northeast of the Bosworth School in Peel Township in Wellington County. We had five miles to Drayton, a small town west of us, where we sold most of our cream and purchased most of our groceries. Alma, our post office town was seven miles to the east of us. Mail was delivered daily to our box on the 14th of Peel. Our mailing address was R.R. 1, Alma, Ontario.

Drayton, Our Hometown

We did most of our business at Drayton. The Conestoga River meanders through this small town, creating the need for two bridges. At that time there were many thriving businesses serving the community. There was a creamery, a garage and farm implement dealer, a bank, a telephone office, two grocery stores, a variety store, a hardware store, a hotel, a restaurant, several churches, a primary and high school, a fair ground, and many other offices and small businesses.

The creamery was particularly important to us. The creamery staff sent out their truck on a route twice a week to collect our cans of cream. There they weighed the cream, graded it, and churned it into butter.

The creamery also had a frozen foods locker. This was before every home had a refrigerator or a deep freezer. We would rent a locker drawer or two and store our meat there when we butchered an animal. They would cut it up, wrap it, and freeze it for us and keep it in our drawer. If we wanted to keep anything else there, we could bring it. Almost every time we went to Drayton to do business or to buy groceries, we would make a stop at the creamery to pick up our check, buy butter or cheese, or bring something home from the locker.

We did most of our Christmas shopping in that small town. On a Saturday before Christmas, our folks would take us all to town, either Drayton or sometimes Arthur. They would give us each a dollar and turn us loose. We would use several hours to carefully spend that dollar. When we were done, we had Christmas presents for everybody. We might even have had enough left for a five-cent chocolate bar or a seven-cent soda for ourselves. This way we got to know the stores quite well and knew just where the bargains could be found.

Lamberts Garage was another place that played a key role in our lives. This was where we got our car or tractor fixed, bought our gas, ordered our farm fuel which they would deliver, bought our tractor and farm machinery, or just admired the latest machine that came in.

Carl E. Hansen

Bosworth, Our New School

As soon as we got settled into the old stone house, on a wintery December day, our dad brought Peter and me to the door of the school we would attend. He knocked. I was feeling very shy and afraid. I did not know what to expect in this strange place. Would the teacher be nice, kind, and helpful? Or would she be cross, demanding, and violent? Would the kids be friendly or mean like the bullies we had back home?

I did not have to think such thoughts long, for there was the teacher opening the door. She was noticeably young, slender, and sort of pretty, but she greeted us formally and properly.

Our dad introduced himself and told her our names. She introduced herself as "Miss Rosemary O'Reilly." He told her to "Make them behave!" and then turned and left.

Miss O'Reilly welcomed us in, found us seats, and proceeded to test our reading ability to see what we knew. I was placed in grade one with Samuel Huber. Peter was in grade two with Mabel and Clara Huber.

At recess and at noon hour, we soon got to know the kids. As usual, the big girls welcomed us the most. The big boys sort of ignored us at first. Our classmates became our friends quickly. When it came time to go home, there were quite a number of the kids, mostly Huber kids, that lived beyond us, so we had companions with whom to walk the mile home.

Happy Bosworth students from grades one through eight in 1949

In time, we got to know this school like an intimate part of our lives. The Bosworth School, S.S. No. 14, Peel, was an old dirty yellow brick building with dark green trim. It was built in the 1880's on the corner between Highway #13 and our sideroad, about one mile from where we lived. It had one big classroom that served eight grades.

Bosworth S.S. No. 14, Peel, Elementary School

One came into the school from the main gate. A flagpole was fastened to the front of the vestibule. There was a large, rusty cast-iron bell in the belfry above. One approached the school by going up two steps onto a twelve-foot square concrete patio in the right-hand corner between the school proper and the vestibule. From the patio, one turned left through a green side door into the small vestibule that had a rope hanging from the ceiling that was attached to the belfry on the roof overhead.

There were double doors to the right, leading into a large cloakroom that spanned the full width of the school. There was a window at each end of the cloakroom. To the right were coat hangers and a shelf for the girls lunch boxes and books, and to the left were the same for the boys. Also on the right was the girls' toilet, and on the left was the toilet for boys. The toilets were the open bottomed deep pits that had vent pipes going up through the roof, but still smelled revolting.

A central door led into the classroom, which had a twelve-foot ceiling and two windows on each side. A blackboard spanned the front of the room; a brown wooden wainscoting surrounded the room to the height of the windows.

There was a furnace in the center of the room towards the back. It was open at the top but was surrounded with a protective shield of heavy tin. It was situated in such a way that when one entered through the door, he faced the door of the furnace. A long stove pipe connected the furnace to the chimney at the front of the classroom.

Along the back wall were additional coat hooks and a shelf. There was a storage closet and a water dispenser to the right side and a library bookcase in the left corner. The plastered walls were painted a light green, and the inside woodwork was painted an ugly light brown. The floors were rough, worn, hardwood, tongue-and-grooved boards that looked an oil-soaked black.

There were five rows of desks screwed to runners that kept them joined together in an orderly line, about twenty-two desks altogether. Each desk consisted of a cast-iron frame with a folding hardwood seat, a slanted hardwood top with a groove for pencils, a hole for an inkwell, and a shelf underneath. A teacher's desk faced the pupil's desks at the center in front of the blackboard. A piano stood in the corner to the right.

Attached behind the school proper was a green dilapidated wooden woodshed. It served to store firewood and coal for the winter. It also served to store extra desks, broken desks, and other items that needed storage. Many a recalcitrant boy spent hours there splitting wood to atone for his misdemeanors.

The woodshed also served as a gymnasium for restless boys on a rainy recess. Sometimes it served as a "church" when it suited us to play "weddings," or as a jail when "cops and robbers" was the game of the hour.

Outside, its roof served as a convenient stairway to climb onto the school roof when the teacher went home for lunch on the rare occasion, or a good slide on normal days. Its worn shingles with the occasional nail sticking out was an inconvenience, but not a deterrent to daring boys eager to out-do each other in sliding off and jumping to the ground below. Many unsuspecting mothers were baffled as to why school clothes needed so much mending.

The schoolyard was about two acres in all, surrounded by a page wire fence, with a front gate facing the highway. There was a row of maple trees on three sides of the front half of the yard. There was a teeter-totter near the trees to the left, coming in through the main gate.

At the corner of the school was a well on top of which stood an old, green, cast-iron pump. To anyone desperate enough to use it, the pump produced rusty-colored, bitter-tasting water. We kids suspected a direct connection underground with the toilet pits nearby.

Beyond it was a tall swing set with two swings, also painted green. In the front yard, east of the school was a large mound made into a flower garden with about four concentric circles of whitewashed rocks outlining rows of perennial flowers mixed with grass and the voluntary weeds of the season.

Parker Mission, Our New Church

Our new church, called the "Parker Mission," met on Sundays in the Parker Primary Schoolhouse.

The "Parker Mission" was started in July of 1941, when several Mennonite families from the Elmira and Waterloo area moved into the community. Gordon Schrag oversaw opening a Sunday school that met every Sunday in the old Parker schoolhouse at the Parker corner. In 1946, three families from Virginia, the Clarence and Ira Huber and John Garber families, joined them. The Ontario Mennonite Board of Missions appointed John and Anna Mae Garber to give leadership on October 4, 1946.

A congregation was organized in a meeting in Garber's house on December 13, 1946, with twenty-nine charter members. It was a deliberate attempt to start a new church through colonization. They called it a "mission," but I never understood why. It only provided a church for economic migrants: people from heavily populated Mennonite centers who were attracted to cheaper farmland, mostly younger people who were struggling to raise a family and to gain financial independence as farmers.

John Fay Garber was the pastor. Later, he was ordained as "bishop." He and his wife, Anna Mae, had eight children: three boys and five girls. Their farm was between our farm and the Bosworth School. They taught their children by the home-school method before it was popular. Mr. and Mrs. Garber were both trained teachers, so they knew what they were doing. They figured they knew more about teaching than "that young Catholic girl" who just completed one year of Normal School. Some of the children were our ages, but we never really got to know them because they did not come to our school.

Of the two Huber families, Clarence was the oldest brother. He and his wife, Violet, had twelve children: four boys and eight girls. Their youngest two boys and four girls went to school with us. Their farm was on the 14th of Peel, less than a mile east of us. Clarence was a deacon in the church.

Ira was a younger brother to Clarence. He and his wife, Hanna, had ten or eleven children: five boys and the rest girls. Their farm was adjacent to ours on the east and across the road from Clarence's farm. Their oldest seven children went to school with us.

The Hubers and the Garbers were quite conservative Mennonites. They were non-conformists. Each of the three had their own standards of what constituted "worldliness." All three families wore plain suits or cape dresses of plain colors. Their women wore bonnets. The Huber men wore black felt hats with rounded tops, but Garber men could wear hats of other colors and shapes. Garbers could drink soft drinks; Hubers could not. Garbers could have a radio; Hubers could not. Garbers could drive any color of car; Hubers drove black cars. Ira needed to paint his bumpers black.

The rest of us families of the church were less conservative and had more flexibility, so we had an interesting church life.

My parents, coming from a different Mennonite community in Duchess, Alberta, felt removed from the intense feelings of loyalty to certain traditions prevalent in the East. This bitter fighting about what constitutes worldliness and holding to a rigid set of definitions and rules really disturbed my parents.

When they asked the pastor to take them in as members, they were not told that there were clear regulations about women's apparel. On the very day they were to be officially "received" into membership, the pastor, John Garber, cornered my mother in the entry way and asked her to promise to wear the "cape dress" and the "bonnet," so he could proceed with the program. Mom was shocked at the lack of sensitivity and the suddenness of the demand, so, being a woman of peace and submitting to authority, she weakly promised. What could she do? She felt like a hostage.

Later, when she had time to reflect on it, she was angry. He had no right to do that to her; it was indecent and disrespectful. She had always worn a very modest long dress of modest colors, and she covered her head with a kerchief of modest color. Besides, a kerchief was superior to the bonnet as a headdress in keeping one's head warm and comfortable. Her attempts at keeping her promise did not last for very long. There was simply no reason to be bound by such a promise extracted under duress, she reasoned.

Then there was Rufus Bender, an outspoken adult Sunday school teacher and song leader. He was the "pentecostal" among us. He liked to say "Amen," "Hallelujah," or "Praise the Lord." He had testimonies of visions, healings, and miracles. While the others worried about staying "not conformed to this world," Rufus was concerned with saving the world for Jesus.

The Parker schoolhouse was a very unsatisfactory place for church. The congregation started a building fund. Pastor Garber donated a plot of ground in a woodlot just up the hill from the Bosworth School as a place on which to build the church. Groundbreaking and building began in November 1950. By this time Rufus Bender had left the fellowship because the Lord called him away to an itinerant revivalist and healing ministry. Dave and Lavoy Roth moved their families back to Alberta because of arthritis and asthma (and homesickness?).

It was in that little Parker schoolhouse that Peter and I were baptized on September 24, 1950. Our parents took us to some "revival meetings" where a young man, Wayne North, was the preacher. Peter, less than ten years of age listened and responded to the invitation to accept Jesus Christ as his personal savior. This meant that arrangements for a baptism would follow.

Peter, concerned that he might be the only one to be baptized, exercised his "evangelical gift" and persuaded me to join him in that sacred ceremony. I, being ever the follower of my big brother and reasoning that sometime in the future I must be baptized anyway, and I would not want to be alone in that experience either, acquiesced and informed my mother that I wanted to be baptized also. She, being pleased with our early desire to follow the path of the righteous, informed our pastor, John Garber, who made the arrangements.

Bishop Oliver Snyder baptized us. His text was "Make every effort to live in peace with all men and to be holy; without holiness no one will see the Lord." Hebrews 12:14 KJV. A song was "Something For Thee."

For Peter, it meant a lot, but for me, it was not a happy experience. At eight years of age, I was still a child in understanding, and unready to make a life commitment. I had not yet experienced any love from Christ, only the fear of God. I had an overly sensitive conscience. I knew that I must accept Christ as my savior personally and be baptized to become a Christian. Inside, though, I felt unworthy and unprepared for this important step. I had lied to some people, and I did not have the courage to go to them and confess my sin and ask their forgiveness, so I came to my baptism day with a cloud of guilt and unworthiness hanging over my head. I could not tell anyone. I kept my feelings and thoughts to myself.

To make it worse for me, that particular Sunday the sun did not come up with its usual brightness. We noticed how dark it seemed as we drove to the old Parker schoolhouse. And as we entered the worship place, the sky got darker and darker. The lights were put on, and after the service, it was so dark that we used the car lights to go home. It rained a bit in the afternoon, but it stayed dark all day. It was a strange, strange day. The sky had a kind of reddish glow.

Mom figured it was one of the "signs of the times" that Jesus warned us to expect. The secular news anchors speculated it was simply caused by smoke from the burning forests in northern Ontario. I do not know, but I have never seen anything like it, before nor since. I was sure the judgment of God was manifest against me, the scared little bad boy in Ontario! I struggled for years with the feeling that somehow, I had entered the church through the back door, so to speak, but I would discuss my feelings with no one.

Life on an Ontario Farm

The first year on that farm was a learning experience for us all. Farming was done differently than in Alberta. Our uncle Chris Hansen worked for us and lived with us. Anita was there to help with the housework, the milking, and the gardening. Mr. Hepburn had been farming with horses.

Dad had become accustomed to using a tractor, so he bought a new Ford tractor with a plow. He and Chris used the Jeep for fieldwork as well. Dad sold some of the horses but kept three for a few years. They were used less and less, until Dad bought a second tractor several years later. Then all the horses were sold.

That first spring, 1949, Dad got infected with painful boils on his rectum. This unexpected, strange affliction resulted in his being hospitalized from June 5 to 25. The doctors operated. Mom would go to Kitchener on Sundays to visit him, and we would go along. We were not allowed to go into the hospital. On one visit we boys climbed up the outside fire escape and had a chance to see our dad. No one caught us.

Finally, he returned home, but did not heal properly, and suffered all summer. The church members, especially Clarence Huber and his two sons, George and John, helped finish seeding and put up our hay. There was no charge. We boys were impressed with their kindness and concern. Brotherly kindness! Good Christian people!

That fall, the crop was not so good because of the late seeding due to Dad's problems. The Jeep broke down that summer and was repaired, but Dad was not satisfied with it, so he traded it for an old used 1936 Oldsmobile sedan. We boys were upset about that because we were very proud to have a Jeep, which was uncommon in the area.

Hansen brothers, Carl, Peter with Charles, Paul &
George proud of their Jeep - Ontario 1949

In 1951, my parents bought the one-hundred-acre farm across the road to the west of us that had a stone house on it. Simon Huber, Clarence and Ira's father, had used it as a summer home. They spent their winters at their home in Virginia. Now they were getting too old and no longer came north for the summer, so they sold it to us for $4,000.

This farm had about fifteen acres of forest and about nine acres of swamp. There were about twenty acres of pasture as well, so we kept our cattle there much of the time. The rest was seeded to grain or hay. A creek, starting in Ira Huber's farm, went through our farm, crossed the road, and emptied into the swamp on the new farm. Occasionally, when the swamp filled to overflowing, the extra water spilled over into another stream that went through Beal's farm to the Conestoga River about a mile away.

Our First Telephone

For the first time in our lives, we were privileged to have a telephone in our house. This unique invention was mounted on the wall just outside the kitchen doorway, in the downstairs hallway. It was the model that had a long wooden box with two bells on the upper face, a mouthpiece in the middle, a slanted shelf near the bottom, a receiver or movable earpiece cradled on the left side and attached with a short chord, and a crank handle on the right side.

Our telephone was connected with the Drayton operator, so our number was "Drayton, 625 ring five." It did not matter whether you rang five longs or five shorts. Ours was a party line numbered 625. If you were making a local call, you could get us on the line by turning the crank five short "dings" or five long "ding-a-ling-a-lings." If you mixed the two longs and shorts, you would get one of the other twenty or so families on our party line.

If you were calling from long distance, you would ask the operator for "Drayton, 6-2-5, ring five." If none of the twenty neighbors were talking, the operator would ring five times and connect you to us. Otherwise, she would butt in and say, "Sorry, a long-distance call," and then proceed to ring the five longs or five shorts. The neighbors could all listen in to our conversation if their curiosity overpowered their code of ethics or sense of human decency. This was our first telephone. What a wonderful timesaving, step-saving, mile-saving, money-saving, life-saving invention!

Our neighbors did not all have telephones. Elton Cressman, just across the road north of us, and John Foster, a half-mile north of us did not have telephones. They often came to use our phone. That was always a good opportunity to catch up on the gossip. Many times, we had to take "urgent" (or not so urgent) messages to them from the telephone. This was a considerable inconvenience for us, but we saw it as an opportunity for a social event. Then, it was not so bad.

Our First Electricity

Rural electrification was underway in our community. In the fall of 1949, electricians worked at our place for many weeks. They went throughout the house cutting holes in the walls for switch boxes and in the ceilings for light boxes. Then, they strung wires in the ceilings and in the walls. We boys collected the little round slugs that popped out of the boxes. We used them for play money.

The line crew came with caterpillars and drilling augers and truckloads of posts and cable. They parked these huge, strange machines in our yard for the weekend. We boys came to observe. The crewman in charge looked at us with the utmost seriousness, and said, "Now do not forget to give them oats and hay in the morning!" We puzzled over his instructions after he left. We knew that machines did not eat oats and hay, but he was so serious. Was he really joking? We asked Dad, and he just laughed, so we decided it was okay to ignore the order.

On October 18, 1949, the momentous day came. The barn and house were all wired and connected to the power line, and the inspector approved the work. How exciting when the main switch was pulled, and bright electric lights flooded all the rooms of the house and barn. It was a wonderful day! This was the first time in our lives we had the wonders of electricity in our own home, and we were excited. Although the coincidence was not intentional, what a fantastic way to celebrate baby Charles's first birthday!

Having electricity brought about major changes to our lives and to the lives of everybody in the community. The first change, of course, was that we could put away the sooty coal oil lanterns, fragile glass lamps, and gas pressure lamps. The houses no longer smelled of burning oil, gas, or coal oil fumes. The ceilings no longer got darkened with the soot of smoking lamps. Yard lights made the dark nights less threatening.

Electricity also completely changed the way people worked. Old skills were no longer needed, and new skills needed to be learned. People were relieved of the old labor-intensive, hand powered way of doing work and enjoyed the conveniences of electrical appliances and electric-powered tools. Gradually, over time, they bought electric-powered water pumps, milking machines, cream separators, milk coolers, air pumps, feed grinders, grain augers, bale elevators, barn cleaners, etc. for the barn, and electric stoves, refrigerators, freezers, vacuum cleaners, mixers, eggbeaters, toasters, hot water heaters, washing machines, irons, clocks, razors, fans, and curling irons for the house. This involved a lot of spending and was a boon to the manufacturing and retail businesses.

The next year, Mom got a new Beatty electric stove, of which she was immensely proud. No more gathering firewood, building fires in the sweltering summer, or carrying out ashes just to cook a meal. How handy it was! However, it was a bit slow when doing a quick warm up, and Mom insisted the bread baked in her electric oven did not taste quite as good as that baked in the old wood-burning cook stove. When the old kitchen range was thrown out, they had to get a new electric water heater also, for the former one got its heat directly from the firebox of the range.

Then, a super slick salesman came along and enticed my parents to buy the latest in waterless stainless-steel cookware that was "guaranteed for a lifetime!" He agreed to put on a big demonstration dinner to which neighbors would be invited. This was too much for Mom to resist.

The big day came, and the neighbors came, and it was a great social success. Mom got to show off her new electric stove too. So, out went her old enamel or aluminum cookware, as she bought a nice big set of the super cookware to match her modern stove. She was incredibly happy with our prosperity. For the rest of her homemaker life, she still cooked with that same cookware. A sound "lifetime guarantee!" It was a great investment.

Mother proud of her new Beatty electric range and stainless-steel cookware

Interrupted by Medical Trauma

On October 31, 1949, Dad was re-admitted to the Kitchener-Waterloo Hospital, for the infection in his rectum would not heal. This time they kept him there until December 3rd. It was a long time for us little boys to have no dad with us on the farm. Mom would drive to Kitchener to visit him on Sundays. Finally, she brought him home, and we were happy. This time he was healed. Again, the Huber brothers came to our aid. They cut up a winter supply of firewood for us and stored it in our basement.

During this time the church people had a ground-breaking service for the proposed new building.

The next summer, on June 20, 1950, Dad was in the barn moving pigs from one pen to another when our four-hundred-pound Tamworth boar attacked him from behind, knocked him over, and trampled him before he could escape to the silo nearby. He managed to walk to the house, took off his soiled clothes, took a bath and went to bed. This was sometime between ten and eleven o'clock, a.m.

However, he felt awful pain in his abdomen. By the time we came home from school, Mom was getting prepared to take him to the hospital.

Dad had a perforated bowel. The doctor, Frank Harvey, operated, fixed the wound, cleaned him out, and sewed him shut. Dad recovered nicely, for which we thanked God. Clarence Huber and his sons came to our recue once again. They helped with the chores that night and came again the next day and took the boar away from our place. They castrated it and later sold it for us. It was too dangerous for us kids to take care of. Such good Christian neighbors!

We would go along to Kitchener with Mom when she would visit Dad. Although we were not allowed to go into the hospital, Mom would have him come to the window to greet us. That made us feel better. He came home on July 6th. It took several weeks before he was able to work again.

It was haying time, and again Dad was incapacitated. Once more, the Christian neighbors came and put up our hay for us. Clarence Huber even saw to it that they put up our hay before they finished their own. This deeply impressed us boys. This was Christianity in practice!

Making Hay

Putting up hay was not easy in those days. The timothy and clover crops were cut with a horse-drawn mower that cut a seven-foot-wide swath and left the hay laying in the field to dry for several days. Then it was gathered in piles with a dump rake until we later bought one of those more modern side-delivery rakes, which gathered the hay into nice even windrows, also driven by horses.

When the hay was cured properly, it would be loaded onto a hay wagon with a horse-drawn hay-loader. This was a device that, as the horses pulled it, its wheels turned by ground friction, turning a pickup that lifted the hay off the ground and deposited in on a chain driven conveyer that moved the hay up, dropping it onto the wagon.

Someone would be on the hay wagon with a pitchfork receiving the hay as it dropped and distributing it evenly over the wagon to build a good balanced load. Another person would also be on the wagon driving the horses. I, being at the ripe age of nine years, was big enough to do that job that year. My brother, Peter, had learned to drive tractor that spring while putting in the crop.

John Huber driving a team of horses towards the barn with a load of hay

After the hay wagon was loaded fully, the horses pulled it home, up the steep bank, and into the barn loft. This final pull was extremely difficult and took all the reserves of strength the horses had. They would approach the slope of the bank with utmost speed for momentum. About halfway up, they would dig in with all their mighty strength and lean into their harnesses for all their worth to maintain the remaining momentum into the barn until the wagon reached the level of the barn floor. Then, they would stop in the middle of the barn floor, their sides heaving, their breath coming in great gasps, and sweat running down.

Sometimes they would lose their momentum and fail to make it. In that case, the heavy load would pull the horses backwards down the steep incline. This was dangerous. If the driver allowed the horses to turn just a little, the wagon was in danger of upsetting and dumping its load and driver, and even breaking the wagon.

One time we had teamed up a new horse with an older experienced horse to do this job. When the horses reached the barn floor, the sound of their hoofs on the floorboards rang hollow, a very different sound than that of hoofs on the soil embankment. The new horse spooked at the change in sound and stopped pulling. The weight of the hay wagon pulled the team backwards and the horses ran away down the lane with the load of hay careening wildly behind.

Dad instinctively ran after the runaway team and managed to steer them into the cedar hedge alongside the lane where they had to stop. It could have been much worse.

One time we saw the horses coming rapidly up the slope, leaning into their harnesses with all their might, when a little kitten scampered right into their path. The horses could not stop now. A huge foot came right down on the poor kitten with a mighty force. There was nothing more left of the kitten than there is when you squish an insect.

The horses would rest while the hay was being unloaded. There was a special grapple fork used for unloading the hay. Using a system of ropes and pulleys, and powered by a horse or a small tractor, the hay could quickly be removed from the wagon and conveyed to the hay mow of the farmer's choice.

One of my jobs was to drive the horse pulling the rope. One had to stop the horse at the right time, or the rope would smash the grapple fork against the barn wall and maybe break something. I was fascinated by the technology, but I feared the responsibility.

July was haymaking time. In Ontario, July had some of the hottest, muggiest weather found anywhere. Sometimes, it was oppressive just to breath and stay alive. Haymaking was hard, dusty work. The sweat ran freely, and the chaff and dust would stick to the worker's skin until it could be wiped off in great big gobs.

We little boys were kept busy running to the well under the maple tree to pump cool drinking water into one-gallon syrup pails and taking them to the men who were sweating the hay into our barn. They would stop their work, grab our bucket, gulp down the water, and send us back for more. Without a refrigerator, there was no thought of adding ice cubes.

Winter Recreation

Winter on the farm in Ontario was rather dreary, busy, and predictable. For us growing boys this meant keeping a heavy schedule of doing morning chores and gobbling down a hasty breakfast before running off to spend the weekdays in school. In mid-afternoon, after walking home from school and eating a little snack, there were evening chores to be done, a late supper to be eaten, then going off to bed.

Saturdays allowed little reprieve. After breakfast there were pig pens and calf pens to clean, grain to grind, and sometimes firewood to be hauled or cut up on the tractor-powered buzz saw. It was seldom that we had free time, except on Sundays, to do the many winter things that boys would like to do.

Sitting beside the drive shed among other debris was an old faded black cutter sled that the Hepburns had left. One winter, we boys resurrected it and hooked it up to old Barny, one of our remaining work horses. It provided some excitement as we drove it around on a mild winter day.

Our uncle Chris bought us a long toboggan one Christmas. We were ecstatic. When the snow was right, we would take it down to the river on a Sunday afternoon where there were some steep riverine hills.

Somehow, we were given some old used skates, and we tried our best to learn to skate whenever we could find a piece of ice that was not too rough or covered with hard snow. Needless to say, with ill-fitting skates that caused plenty of blisters, with less than pristine ice conditions, and limited time opportunities, we never developed the finesse or reputation of a "Rocket Richard." But we could wobble on our feet and managed to learn to stay upright on the two blades, most of the time.

The "Cedar Hedge Farms"

Between our two cedar hedges was a fruit orchard with two rows of young apple trees and a wide row of raspberries and grapes. There was about a twenty-foot strip of unused land between the cedar hedge and the raspberries. Our parents said we could have that space to play in. It became the site of our "Cedar Hedge Farms." In the first years after we came to Ontario and before we could be trusted to do much farm work, we spent many happy summer days playing there.

We divided up the land, so each farmer had his own. Each farm had to have its own fence. We used old raspberry stems for fence posts. We built toy tractors, trucks, and plows out of pieces of wood, insecticide cans, jar lids, shoe polish cans, wax-can lids, and nails. We built little barns out of fruit crates and set them on foundations of bricks. We heaped up soil against one side of these foundations to made barn banks up which we could drive our toy tractors into the lofts. We stored "hay" in the lofts.

We dug wells and underground silos in which we stored wild cucumber "ensilage." We plowed fields and planted grain. The grain grew, and we harvested it and stored it in our barns. We were surprised and delighted when we found that mice had moved into our barns and made their nests close to the grain stores. We had real live livestock!

Barn fires were exciting happenings in the community, so of course we needed to have barn fires too. We persuaded our younger brother George, who was usually willing to please us, to sacrifice his barn. So, we filled it with hay and then created lightning and watched it burn to the ground. What excitement!

We mixed mud into little bricks and baked them in the sun until they were dry. Then we made a muddy liquid "mortar" and cemented the bricks together to build a house. It had a real fireplace in it complete with chimney. Then, we put down raspberry floor joists and rafters and covered them with cardboard flooring and roofing. Then, of course, we had to try out the fireplace to see if it would really work. It did work nicely, and the smoke curled out of the chimney. However, the fire spilled out of its place and caught the floor on fire. Soon we had a major "disaster" as the house went up in flames!

No community is real unless it has a currency, so we made money to make buying and selling possible. We also assigned a certain value to razor blades. They were our gold bullion. They were scarce in our home, so they kept their value until Bob Beal visited us and understood their value. The next time he came, he brought dozens of "contraband" razors that he picked up somewhere. So now we had a problem of "inflation."

No community is real unless it has a problem with crime, so we made some provision for that too. It became acceptable to tell lies and steal while you were on site among the Cedar Hedge Farms. Of course, conventional ethics continued to prevail while we were not there. So, you could steal things and hide them there and lie if questioned. If you could keep them hidden for ten days, then they became yours.

Of course, when the former owner found out who successfully stole his things, nothing could prevent him from attempting to steal them back, so we had quite a lively business in disappearing goods. Secret chambers were designed underground, or under the barns, or under our pit silos.

The "Old Swimming Hole"

Jack Johnson was an eighty-four-year-old man who had lived with his unmarried sister in their father's old stone house on their one-hundred-acre farm about half of a mile northeast of us. They were too old to help themselves much anymore. Their farm was long and narrow, with the buildings situated in from the road, connected by a long lane. The buildings were neglected for many years and quite dilapidated. Everything was of great sentimental value to these old people, and nothing should be changed.

But time and decay and the seasons were changing everything. This, they did not seem to recognize. They wanted things left just as they were. The farm was fenced and cross-fenced with split cedar rails, sometimes called "snake fences" because of the zigzag pattern in which the rails were placed. These rails were more than a hundred years old and were slowly disintegrating. Trees had grown up between them so that each fence resembled a shelterbelt, so the whole farm looked bushy and unkempt.

At the back of the farm was a creek running across it. On the far side of the creek was a small woodlot with some very nice timber.

Dad rented this farm for several years from 1951. We just used it for pasture. We were not allowed to plow the land or change anything. I remember the old man showing the place to Dad. He was boasting about how good the land was and how good this machine or that building was. We figured he must be about blind because everything we saw that he boasted about looked old, decayed, outdated, in disrepair, and completely useless and worthless to us.

Just to prove the point, as the old man was boasting, he took us through a gate. As he turned to close the gate, even against the old man's feeble touch, the main gatepost broke off at the ground level. He seemed surprised and remarked that he would have to "fix it sometime." To our eyes, the whole fence was sagging and would fall with one healthy pull. The old couple lived there for another year and then moved to a home for the aged.

We boys were interested in the creek. Our creek would dry up during the summer, but this one seemed to always have water flowing through it. It had a place where the water was deep enough to reach our navels. This became our favorite swimming hole. Unlike the river, this hole was safe enough that our parents allowed us to go and swim there unaccompanied.

Berry-picking and garden-weeding tasks got done a lot quicker, although maybe not as thorough, on a hot muggy summer morning if Mom promised that we could go swimming in Johnson's creek after we were finished. We would hurry through our work, grab our swimming trunks, and run off down the road before Mom had time to check our work. Many a time, she sadly went about picking over the patches again, gleaning what we had missed.

I was such a coward when it came to water. Peter and Paul learned to swim before I did. Mom thought it was because the nurse put me into cold water when I was a baby! We might as well blame somebody; it is easier than admitting that we have a coward in the family.

I would sit for a long time on the bank and watch my brothers having a good time before I would finally dip my feet into the stream. Eventually, I learned to submerge myself, and then we had the most delightful time fighting and playing in the water.

The water was shallow, and the creek bottom muddy, so the more we played, the muddier the water got. After a few hours of exhausting fun, we climbed out refreshed, but not necessarily clean. I learned to swim without a lesson or an instructor in Johnson's creek. Years later, I earned a lifeguard certificate.

One evening after a hard, hot day of work, our parents took us to the Conestoga river for a picnic supper and a cool, refreshing swim. It was fun swimming with Dad. Mom was not about to get in. She did not have the proper attire and was much too modest to come in otherwise. But Dad came in with his underwear briefs. We explored the deepest places in the river. They weren't more than up to our armpits, so Dad said it would be okay for us boys to come swimming by ourselves if we wanted to after this. We were delighted because the river, though small, was not muddy like the old swimming hole in Johnson's Creek.

After that, we came to the river to swim when we had free time. Like Johnson's creek, the river was only about one mile away. The water was quite deep under the bridge, but we did not swim there.

Sometimes we would catch our poor dog, Rex, and throw him off the bridge into the water. We thought it was fun to hear him yelp as he whizzed through space on his way down, then to see the big splash as he disappeared in the water twenty feet below. Finally, he would resurface, snort and yelp and swim to shore, and come whining and shaking his wet self on us.

Today you could be jailed for treating your pets that way. But we figured the stinky dog needed a bath anyway. We never thought about the pain of taking a "belly flop" from twenty feet!

Fishing with Bill Foster

Bill Foster was the eighteen-year-old brother of Jim Foster. He took an interest in us young boys. One day he offered to take us fishing. We went to "Foster's creek," as we dubbed the small stream that ran through their farm. It was the same as "Johnson's creek," only further downstream. There he showed us all the good places to catch fish and showed us how to put the worms on the hooks and how to cast them into the right places.

We caught some bass and some other species. If the fish were too small, he just threw them back in the water. He cut a short, forked branch and showed us how to put the big ones on it by sliding one of the sharpened prongs through the gills and out the mouth. The other prong was a handle for carrying.

Fishing seemed terribly cruel to me. Bill assured us that fish could not feel the way we do. I wondered how he knew; had he ever been a fish? Had he ever talked to one? How could anyone know what it feels like to be a fish and have a hook in your mouth and then be pulled up into the air by it, and thrown on the bank to drown in the thin air, and then have a piece of wood thrust through your gills and be hanged on it? How can we say it does not hurt them? How can we know what it feels like to be a worm and be impaled on a hook and cast into the water? Can we know that does not hurt?

I preferred to not fish and give them the benefit of the doubt. But we really admired Bill and appreciated his taking an interest in us. I, a mere nine-year-old, could not voice all my protests to him.

Bill was really our hero, like a big brother. Then, about two years later, he signed up to be trained as a Royal Canadian Mounted Police officer. We hated to see him go and missed him. After his training, he came home for a brief visit. That was the last time we talked. Sometime later we heard he was made a constable and was assigned to the intelligence branch.

Then, we heard that he was sick in the hospital where he had an appendectomy, and he would be home on medical leave just as soon as he was discharged from the hospital. We were very eager to see him again, as were his parents and brothers.

Then they got the shocking news that he had contracted an infection and had died in the hospital very suddenly. We were too shocked to believe it, but a few days later, there was a funeral at the funeral home in Drayton. His family members were not church people. The R.C.M.P. provided the pallbearers and the service. Bill looked so handsome in his scarlet and black uniform with its gold embroidered decorations lying there in his beautiful oak coffin. His pallbearers looked awesome to us. That moment, and for years after, I planned to join the R.C.M.P. when I grew up!

Some months later, Bill's folks received his brand new 1953 black and white hardtop Belle Air Chevrolet, a very sporty looking model car that he had just bought before he died. His loan was insured against death, so it came completely paid for.

Broken Bones

At school there was a teeter-totter on which we entertained ourselves during recesses. One day in September 1950, there were about four kids on each side. I was at the end, and my side was down. The four kids on the opposite side were up in the air, when, at a signal unknown to me, the other three on my side jumped off at once. Suddenly, the other side was much heavier than mine and came crashing down to earth, and I was catapulted into space in a large gravity-defying trajectory.

The flight was fine, but my re-entry into earth's gravitational pull had a shattering effect on my poor arm, as I reached out to protect my neck from the headfirst landing. My left wrist hurt terribly, so the teacher sent someone to the Garber home to phone my mother. (There was no phone in the school.) Mom came and took me to the doctor who x-rayed it and found fracture lines in it. He put a plaster cast on it and told me to come back in three weeks.

That was sort of nice, for now I was relieved of helping with the harvest for that year. By the end of the three weeks, I discovered that the cast made an excellent club with which to hit my "enemies" over the head. By the time I returned to the doctor, the cast was already broken. When the doctor heard what had happened, he took the cast off and said he would normally put on a second cast, but since he had concern for the safety of the other boys, he would send me home without.

On November 13th, Mervin Shantz and Menno Roth, church members, picked up the grade one and two kids to give them a ride on their way home from school in the back of Mervin's pick-up truck. He forgot to stop at our driveway, so Paul just jumped out of the moving vehicle. He had no concept of the effects of momentum on an object that falls from a moving vehicle to the stationary ground. He flipped over on the frozen ground and fractured the base of his skull.

Mervin stopped the truck, picked up the dazed boy, and brought him home. My parents called Dr. Sandwith out from Drayton to examine him. The doctor, in turn, called the ambulance from Drayton that took Paul to the Kitchener-Waterloo Hospital, where he stayed for six days. He rested at home for another week before returning to school. He suffered headaches for years afterwards.

Grandmother's Visit

In June of 1951, Grandmother Friesen came from Alberta with David to visit us for six weeks. That was a highlight for all of us. We took time off from farming for several excursions, including the farm show at the Agricultural College at Guelph.

A trip to visit Niagara Falls was unforgettable. We had somebody else milk our cows and feed our calves and pigs that day so we could get an early start. Early in the morning, Grandma, Mom and Dad, and us six boys all squished into our '36 Oldsmobile, along with enough picnic lunch and drink to last a whole day and set out in an easterly direction. It took about three hours to reach Niagara. We were really impressed with the Queen Elizabeth Way, our first time to see a four-lane road. I think we had only one flat tire on that trip. In those days that was a good record for us.

We enjoyed the day at Niagara very much. The Falls were awesome. We took a ride on the cable car that crosses the river over the whirlpool just below the falls.

We visited the museum where they talked about and showed photos and other memorabilia of the "dare devils" which we had never heard of before. They were those daring souls who went, illegally of course, over Niagara Falls in barrels or huge rubber balls or other containers, and those who walked on a tight cable stretched across the whirlpool below the falls. Some survived and some did not.

One was said to have driven a wheelbarrow across the chasm on a cable, and to have brought a stove along, and stopped to cook and eat his meal midway across! For me, I would have to see it to believe it.

We did see the "burning spring" and so believed a natural water spring can burn if natural gas bubbles up with the water. Somehow, in pre-history, natives discovered it would burn. Now it had become a tourist attraction.

Mom and Grandma were very impressed with all the beautiful flowers and botanical gardens. The floral clock impressed even me. We arrived home, sleepy, tired, and happy around eight o'clock that night. It was one of the very few vacation trips that we ever took during my growing years.

Grandma would be up early in the morning, picking raspberries or weeding in the garden before we lazy boys woke up. She was always such a happy, sweet, loving, helping, hard-working woman.

Building a Church

The sod had been turned in November of 1950 for the new Berea Mennonite Church. Construction had been going on intermittently through the winter. There had been many delays and disagreements.

Pastor John Garber wanted to make a tall, sturdy cathedral structure. The Hubers and others wanted a simpler building with a lower profile, humbler, and a lot cheaper. The bishop had it his way. The members would have to pay more for a building they did not really like. They would have to borrow the money and pay interest for many years. There was some grumbling. Unbeknown to everyone, the bishop would move away shortly after the building was dedicated, leaving the members to pay for the design they did not want.

The building site was along the highway, less than a quarter of a mile up the hill from the Bosworth School. We older students were keenly interested in learning how buildings were built, so we made regular checkups on the progress. After school, before we went home, we would go out of our way to see what had been done since the last time. Such site inspections were done clandestinely, our parents not knowing. We watched the brick walls rise slowly through the spring. The roof went on in the summer. By fall of 1951, the inside finishing was in progress.

On October 4th, we Hansen boys, Bob Beal, and John and Jim Larsen made our regular side trip after school to check on progress. When we arrived at the building site, we found that the workers had all gone home. They had been installing the paper fiber ceiling board. These were eighteen-inch squares that were nailed to the underside of a grid of 2" x 4"s twenty-two feet from the floor. Half of the ceiling was already installed. The scaffolding was in place, and no one was looking, so why not go up and see how it looks in the attic?

Therefore, we all climbed up the scaffolding, one after the other, Peter leading the way. Having reached the top, why not walk around in the attic? There was no one to stop us, so of course, we walked around.

All at once Paul's foot slipped off the 2" x 4" grid, and of course, the other foot slipped onto the same side of the 2" x 4," and he fell through the paper ceiling tile.

A feeling of utter horror ripped through my soul! He was standing beside me one moment, then all at once he was going down, then he was gone! There was a terrible sickening thud some twenty-two feet below.

Our hearts all stopped for a few seconds; then, we all scrambled for the scaffolding and got down in a hurry. Yet it seemed like a long time before we could see if our brother was still alive.

We found him sitting on a roll of building paper, stunned, and gasping for breath. We gathered around him to diagnose the extent of his injuries. We asked him if he could stand up? He could. No broken legs at least. Could he walk? He could. Then we better go home!

It hurt when he walked, so two of us helped him, one on each side with his arms around our shoulders. We took the short way across Beal's field to our road. When we reached our road near Beal's lane, Paul said he could not go any further. So, we sat down, and one of us ran home to get Mom to bring the car.

Mom rushed out with the car and took him to the doctor in Drayton. The doctor called an ambulance, and he was taken to the Kitchener-Waterloo Hospital. Mom came home from Drayton and got Dad. They decided for Mrs. Clarence Huber to come over and take care of us. Dad promised us all a very severe whipping, "one that you will never forget!" when they returned. Then they rushed off to the hospital.

We enjoyed having Violet Huber with us, but that was an awful evening. We kept wondering about Paul's condition, and we dreaded to imagine what was going to happen to us when our parents returned. We were very co-operative with Mrs. Huber in going to bed early that night. Surely our parents wouldn't wake us up to whip us if we were sound asleep!

And they did not. The next morning, we found out that Paul had a cracked vertebra this time. He had black bruises under his biceps where he hit the 2" x 4"s as he tried to break his fall. We never did hear more about the "whipping." Dad was merciful and forgiving. Although he could be tough, he really did understand and loved his boys.

Paul was hospitalized for six days and then convalesced at home for three weeks. The school children made a scrapbook and gifts for him. Many people stopped to see him. He got lots of attention. For years after, people would meet us and ask which boy it was that fell from the ceiling. Then they would look at him and marvel, "And not even crippled!" We had much for which to be thankful to God.

After the accident, the builders reported to us that the floorboard on which Paul landed was broken. We went and looked, and sure enough it was cracked enough to dip down a little. Years later, one could still see the tile in the ceiling from which he fell, for it had to be nailed into place again, and the nails were faintly visible to anyone who knew the story.

The Berea Church building was finally completed, and a dedication service was held on August 24, 1952, the same time our family came down with the measles. It was not a big building, but it was a very tall, red brick structure. It was sitting on a full basement that was half out of the ground. It had a twenty-two-foot ceiling and a very large attic because the roof had a steep high pitch. From outside ground level, one had to climb ten steps to reach the level of the vestibule. No consideration was given for the elderly or anyone depending on wheelchairs. Obviously, there were no elderly folks among the planners.

The Berea Mennonite Church building

School Days

School soon became the center of our lives. It afforded an opening to a larger world than our home, though the one-roomed schoolhouse was not really a big world at all. All the twenty students, give or take, were from rural farm families. With the large Huber and Hansen families, the majority of the students were Mennonites. The teacher was from a farm family and was Catholic, as was Joe Priester. The rest of the students were of various shades of Protestant.

Our daily routine was ordinary and predictable. We boys would get up in the morning, help our dad with the chores, gulp down our breakfast, and with one of us carrying our lunch bag, we would walk or run to school, depending on the urgency of the clock. As we neared the schoolyard, we often heard the bell ringing. Then we would put on that final burst of speed and slide into our seats just in time for roll call.

The teacher, Miss O'Reilly, would stand at attention facing the class, waiting for all to get in their places. Then she would ask us all to stand and sing, "God Save The King." We continued to sing this even a few weeks after King George VI died, before the word was changed to "Queen." Then she would read a Psalm from the Bible, after which we would recite the "Lord's Prayer." There was no "Pledge of Allegiance" nor saluting the flag.

Then she would ask the pupils to get out their books and make sure each grade had an assignment. She would then turn her attention to the first and second grades, helping them to learn their reading, writing, arithmetic, or spelling. Each grade was to work on their own, at their own pace. Our teacher was strict and demanded respect, and she got it. She, also, was very fair and considerate of our individual needs.

On recesses we would go outside, if the weather permitted it, and play games such as "prisoner's base," "pom-pom pull-away," "tag," or we would play on the teeter-totter or the swing. Sometimes we'd play baseball. In winter, snow allowing, we might play "Fox and Goose." Other times we would invent new games where we could set the rules. All these pastimes took some organization and a willingness to co-operate. When we were little, we were the learners, but when we, Hansen boys, numbered four or five out of twenty kids, Peter pretty well dominated the decision-making and organization of the school's recreational activities.

Like in every school, there was a definite social order in the Bosworth School. That first year we were small and had the status of learners. We grew very fast, and by the end of third grade, Peter began to be a force to be reckoned with.

There was a group of big boys in grades seven and eight, namely Jim Foster, Jim Walker, and Joe Priester who picked on David Boyle. They would torment him terribly. He was from a poor home and wore funny clothes, including an old WWII pilot's cap that tied with a strap under the chin. It had big round holes for the ears that had a rim around that stood out from his head an inch or so. His tormentors would catch him and push snow into those holes, forcing it into his ears. They would fight with him until the blood would run from his nose or mouth.

It did not seem fair or just to us. So, small as we were, Peter and I took sides with David Boyle, adopting as our policy to stick up for the underdog. I was still a peewee and did not make much difference, but David sure did appreciate Peter's weight on his side. He still lost his battles, but it was more costly to the other side.

The next year, Jim Foster and David Boyle graduated. Joe Priester was a gentleman. That left Jim Walker in grade eight as the only bully to be reckoned with. Peter was in grade four. One day there was some bullying going on, and Peter challenged Jim Walker. There was a fight and, in the end, Peter, the grade four self-appointed "minister of righteousness and justice," was chasing Jim around the schoolyard. After that, for the next four years, the Hansen boys policed (and at times bullied) the school! In September 1949, our brother Paul joined us in school.

Otherwise, we liked Jim Foster, a neighbor to the north of us. He was very athletic, good looking, fun-loving, and creative, but his fun-loving sometimes put him in the role of a bully. We looked up to him as a role model and hero. He went on to high school and later got a good job with television.

One day there was a knock on the door, and the teacher went out into the cloakroom and closed the door behind her. She stayed a little long, and as usual, our attention was distracted, and the kids made a lot of noise. Finally, the teacher returned and was very angry with us. She demanded that those who were making the noise identify themselves by raising their hands. I knew I was a participant in the noise making, but I did not raise my hand. Nobody raised his or her hand. The teacher scolded us severely.

Though I never felt sorrow or guilt for making the noise, I carried deep guilt for not raising my hand in an admission of wrongdoing, when asked. I felt I had told a lie by my non-compliance.

This happened shortly before I was baptized, and I decided to confess my deceit to my teacher before the baptismal day. But I was afraid and kept on procrastinating until the hour passed. That was one reason my baptism day was an unhappy event for me. I was loaded with guilt and was afraid of God, but I must have been even more afraid of my teacher!

In looking back, what did this say about my theology? If I were more afraid of my teacher, whom I could see, than I was of God, whom I could not see, then did I really believe that God was real? Or in whom did I believe the most?

It was many months later, that I finally got the courage to write a little note to my teacher saying, "I told you a lie. I'm sorry. Please forgive me." Ever the coward, I watched until she was busy, and then I sneaked it onto her desk just before heading for home. The next evening, she called me aside and addressed me in a kind manner, and I explained what I had done.

She was so understanding and thanked me for telling her. That was all. I was forgiven. A big load of guilt rolled off, and I felt great.

But I remembered that I had told Dad a lie once when I was six years old, and I could not confess that to him either, so I was still miserable in my conscience, a compulsive perfectionist that was far from perfect.

In our second year, the Wheeldon girls joined our school. Bertha Ann was in grade eight, and Vivian was in the grade below me. She was my secret girlfriend for a while, but I doubt she knew anything about that, since I never told anybody.

The fourth Hansen brother, George, started school in 1952. When he was about ready to start, we older brothers surrounded him out in the barn and made him solemnly promise (As Mennonites, we did not swear!) to never tell our parents at home what we do in school, and in turn, we would never squeal on him either. What happens in school stays in school! Our parents did not need to know. George was always a loyal sport, and he covered up for us very well. We always appreciated his participatory spirit.

The teacher encouraged creativity among the students. One day she asked the students in George's grade to make up and tell a short story in front of the class. George was in grade two. When his turn came, he stood up with a most confident exuberant expression on his face and began his "story": "Once there was a pony, and it died." Then he sat down. His story was complete. Job well done! The class and the teacher were a bit surprised. The teacher commented that his story was rather short.

So next time she asked the students to tell a story, George stood up and with that same exuberant expression on his face began his story. This time it went on and on, George making it up as he went along. After some minutes, the teacher, perceiving that this story might not have an ending, suggested that perhaps the story would come to its conclusion. But George, secure in his ability to entertain his captive audience, said "No, the story is not over yet!" And he went on and on and on. Finally, the teacher had to remind him that time was passing, and the other students wanted to tell their stories also. George was never shy about stealing the limelight, once given the opportunity!

From grade five on, Peter was definitely the leader of the student body. At noon hours and at recesses, we always looked to him to help decide what games we would play that day. Sometimes he would make new rules to make the games more interesting. There was always harmony and unity as all the younger children joined in the fun. Those were good times for most of the kids.

Of course, it helped that I was the second biggest kid, and Paul was equal to the third. In a small school of twenty kids, there were not many alternatives. Then when our youngest brother, Charles, joined grade one, there were five Hansen boys in that school out of a total of twenty. And we stood united. Who could challenge us then?

Walking to and from school was a major part of our social lives. We usually walked with neighbor children such as Bob Beal, John and Jim Larsen, and various combinations of the Huber clan. We would laugh and talk and sometimes play on the way. Sometimes we would stop to explore something that attracted our curiosity. Sometimes we would get home quite late and get scolded, or at least interrogated. When we were young, there were things to fear, like imaginary animals that might attack us, or some big bad men that might kidnap us, so we would stick together, and we would never accept a ride with strangers.

One of the real dangers, on our twice-daily journey on this road, was Garber's dog. It was a medium-sized mongrel that always came out and yapped at us as we tried to sneak by. We were terrified of this hostile beast. No matter how hard we tried to sneak past, when we were almost at the Garber's lane, this dangerous canine would suddenly spring out of somewhere, ferociously yapping and striking terror into our hearts afresh. We dared not run because then it would really come after us. We just marched past as quickly and as non-threateningly as possible. We even tried to make big detours around Garber's place through their fields, but the snow was deep, and still the savage mutt detected us and set up its threatening howl.

Then, one day, it actually did what it threatened to do twice a day for so many years. It bit one of my brothers. It did not bite hard, just nipped him, but that was traumatic enough. I got angry. Why did we have to put up with this unrelenting hostility twice a day, year after year? We had not done a thing to deserve this kind of hostility.

So, the next time we went by, and the dog came running down the lane in its usual manner, barking savagely at us, I turned up the lane and walked straight towards it and gave it a scornful savage kick in the face. It yelped, and turned, and ran home. That was the last time it ever barked at us, and so we co-existed in mutual respect, until some good saint ran over it with his car. No tears were wasted on our part.

Later that same year, the Davison family moved to our community. Carole and Ruth came to our school. School was never the same after that. Carole was in grade five with Peter and Mabel, and Ruth was in grade one with George. We soon became close friends. Mrs. Davison was a sincere Pentecostal, but Mr. Davison did not go to church. Carole said her dad was always miserable to live with when he used to go to church, but now that he quit going, he was nice to get along with.

Carole's worldview tended to favor her dad's. Where Carole was, there was bound to be fun. She was highly creative in adding a spark of excitement to an otherwise drab situation. She got along well with us and helped Peter give leadership to school life. Whenever one of them thought up something interesting to do, the other would add a suggestion that would add another dimension to the fun. If Peter and Carole were behind the same idea, the whole school was bound to have a good time.

Sometimes Carole's fun loving took a sadistic turn, like the time two new German immigrant children, Heinz and Fritz, came to school. Carole decided it would be a ball to persecute them. She rallied some other girls to join her. She undertook to blame the two tiny boys for all the horrors that Hitler imposed on the rest of humankind. They went around singing, "Hi! Ho! For silverware, Hitler lost his underwear. Hitler says, 'Me no care. Me go buy anoder pair.'"

They sang it repeatedly. When they started to get physically violent towards the two innocent little immigrant boys, Peter stepped in and told them that was enough. That was the end of it. Nobody went beyond the limits he imposed. The little boys were safe, a "protected species."

When Garbers moved away, the Elswick family moved onto their farm. Ann and Marian Elswick joined us in school. Ann became a good friend to Carole and us. Marian was in George's grade. They added a new dimension to the social life of the school.

Around that time, our teacher married Carman Phillips and began living on his farm about four miles west of the school. Sometimes she would go home for the noon hour. I doubt if it was legal, but she did. That left the children unsupervised over the lunch hour. We made the most of it.

What a wonderful opportunity to climb up on the school roof! We enjoyed it, until one day our teacher returned early. As she drove over the crown of the hill, she saw, on the peak of the schoolhouse roof, several of us boys silhouetted against the pale blue sky. She saw us before we could see her. She put a permanent stop to that!

It was amazing that none of us fell off the roof. In retrospect, it is also amazing no good citizen passing by on the highway took enough notice to report this spectacle to the authorities!

Another time we decided to play "church" in the cloakroom while she was gone. Carole was good at that sort of thing. She could preach or lead the singing. This time I was the "deacon." I had the "parishioners" all kneel for prayer. They were all reverently silent as I was leading out praying my way around the world in an authentic deacon-like loud voice, and I was just reaching a desperate crescendo of beseeching the Almighty to save the terrible sinners when the teacher walked in. I was so embarrassed that I could not go on. The meeting broke up then and there.

Sometimes in the winter when the weather and snow conditions were right, the teacher would give us permission to take the school's toboggan down to the river over the noon hour. She would allow us an extra fifteen minutes because of the distance. It was about half a mile away. There was a nice hill down to the river. We would have a wonderful time sliding down the hill and then walking up again. We would see how many kids could fit on the ten-foot toboggan, or we would see who could reach the bottom standing up alone. When we got back to school, we were tired, and sweaty, and happy.

Other times we found a piece of ice in the adjoining field. We would bring our skates and practice at noon hour. If there was fresh snow, we might play "fox and goose." When the weather was warmer, we got permission to go out to a nearby wood lot and play "cops and robbers," but we did not get back in time, so that was cut from our list of permissible activities. The teacher was also uneasy because somebody might get hurt, and she was not out there supervising.

Sometimes in autumn, we would spend our recesses and noon hours raking up the maple leaves and then playing in the huge pile. I'll never forget little Colin Campbell sitting in the leaves, legs outspread, moving his arms and hands in a rotary fashion in front of him like the cylinder of a threshing machine, literally "threshing" the leaves, and saliva running down his chin as his mouth made the necessary noise to accompany the imagined activity.

When the weather was bad outside, we would spend our recesses indoors. There were table games like "crokinole" or "monopoly." We would spend days, even a week on a continued game of monopoly. We would amend the rules to suit our whims like adding factories and making credit arrangements.

Other times we had group games like "clap-in-clap-out" where the one sex would go out to the cloakroom and assign numbers to themselves. The other sex would sit as singles in double seats. Then each would take a turn to choose a number that was taken to the cloakroom. The person having that number would come in and try to sit in one of the double seats. If he/she sat with the one who chose his/her number, he/she would sit there for the duration of the game. If he/she did not choose the right seat, the one there would clap his/her hands and the numbered person would have to return to the cloakroom. We older boys liked this game just fine.

When I was in fifth grade, I really "fell in love" with the buoyant Carole Davison. I was shy and reserved, so I never told her or anybody else about my feelings toward her, but I think she guessed, and I think she liked me too. That year we had a "shop" class in which we did woodwork. I enjoyed woodwork and discovered I had a gift in that area. I made a nice little corner cupboard out of scraps. Carole liked it, so I gave it to her. I would do anything to make her happy.

Life took on new meaning. I decided I would become a carpenter, build a house, marry Carole, and live happily ever after. I had always been a laid-back, careless, lazy, quiet type. Now, I got new energy and often ran to school early, hoping that she would come early too. She was fun person to be with. I decided I should take some initiative and cooperate with God to improve on my limited natural endowments. I started to comb my hair, wash myself more often, and look in the mirror now and then, make the most of my meager assets. I tried to pay at least some attention to cultivating manners, being polite, and being more considerate of others.

My efforts were not totally wasted, though I never got Carole. She was soon having a "courtship" with Paul Huber, but I did keep up my interest in self-improvement, which I hope, made a difference in the long run.

A couple of months into the 1953-54 school year, Mrs. Phillips took a maternity leave. A grandmotherly Mrs. Hicks took her place. This elderly lady had been a schoolteacher in her day, but her day had definitely passed some time ago. She was a large and heavy person. She walked with a bit of a forward stoop. She wore her long gray hair in a straggly bun at the back of her head. Her facial skin was loose and wrinkled. Her teeth were originals mostly, but sadly discolored by age.

She always wore the same brown dress. We wondered if she ever washed it. Maybe she had two alike? One of us sprayed ink on it when she had her back turned, to see if it would get washed off. Was it permanent ink? I can't recall the outcome of that research project.

Mrs. Hicks was an elderly saint, a real kind grandmother at heart, but she was no longer a teacher. She was a disaster in the classroom. Students did what students do when not under control. Discipline broke down completely. While she would be helping the young ones, the older ones would be talking, throwing paper wads, laughing, getting out of their seats, and sneaking around.

Once, little George, in grade two, was making noise. Mrs. Hicks swung around, clapped her hands, and pointed at George. Just as quick, George defiantly clapped his little hands and pointed at Mrs. Hicks. She did nothing about such open defiance.

Soon the paper wads, flying back and forth over the furnace, were mixed with rubber boots and other heavy projectiles. It became a question of security to risk going to school. It would become complete chaos.

Then Mrs. Hicks would stand in the front of the school and cry and plead with us to co-operate so the school could go on. Her tears evoked a thread of sympathy from our calloused hearts, and we would try to modify our behavior for an hour or two.

One time Peter, now in grade seven, was standing at the front of the room going over spelling mistakes or something. He was bored. He pulled out his pocketknife and threw it across the room where it struck the back wall with a startling clatter. Why he did this, except to provoke the teacher, I do not know. The teacher was provoked, and demanded the knife, which she kept in custody for a few days. Finally, Peter wanted it back, so he simply walked up to the teacher's desk and took it back.

We were all getting a little bored with school, so we would spell words wrong or give wrong answers on purpose, even on tests. A health test question was: "If you saw a person's clothing on fire, what should you do?" Peter's answer: "You should pour gasoline on him, so he would burn better." I cannot recall the grade he was awarded for that test.

Mrs. Hicks liked coffee. She had a special kettle in which she boiled her coffee on the stove. We decided to put pieces of rubber in the water, thinking that it would add a rubber flavor to her brew. Looking back, I doubt it had any effect on the flavor, but it gave us a certain sadistic joy to imagine it would.

The stove standing in the middle of the rear of the classroom was sometimes used as a wastepaper receptacle. If we had wastepaper, often we would get up and go over to the furnace and put it in.

A couple of times, one of us would put about an inch of water in a glass bottle, close the lid, wrap it in paper, and put it in the furnace on top of the red-hot coals. We would sit down and study while the paper burned away. After about ten minutes the water in the bottle would be boiling and building up steam pressure.

Finally, there would be a mighty explosion, as the bottle disintegrated, and the pent-up steam scattered all over the hot coals and pushed a mighty cloud of expanding gas and ash up the chimney and out through every crack and crevice of the stove pipe and out the air vents in the cleaning door at the bottom of the furnace. Then the whole room would reek of sulfide gas.

Later, when the teacher was out, we tried the same trick with twenty-two caliber bullets. At first the paper burnt and there was a long silence, and we thought nothing was going to happen.

Just when one of us was going to open the stove door to see what was wrong, the first bullet went off. Then the others went off, one after the other. They really made quite a pinging sound as they struck the iron of the furnace. Little Roy Huber's face turned completely white. I wondered what his thoughts were, as he feared this could possibly be the end.

One day it was good snowball weather. The big boys could pitch them pretty hard. On that particular day, a well packed snowball came shooting across the school entrance and struck the open green wooden door, just as the teacher stuck her head out of the doorway to ring the bell.

She was thankful it did not hit her (and more so we!). She called us all in and warned us not to throw snowballs around the school. It might injure someone. What if a little kid got hit by that icy missile?

So, of course, the next recess, Peter, Paul Huber, and I made a nice hard ball of snow, and all put our hands on it and threw it in through the open school window where it struck the tin skirting on the furnace with a resounding bang. Sure enough, the teacher was out there in six seconds, asking who threw that ball. Three different hands went up. So, we were all marched into the classroom.

Mrs. Hicks broke into tears, "I am so disappointed in you. You are the leaders among the students, and I thought I could depend on you to be good examples to the little ones." We were smitten and ashamed and apologized, and she let us go. Poor Mrs. Hicks: we respected her as a very upright, God-fearing human being and a kind grandmother, but not as a teacher.

Mrs. Phillips resumed her duties the following September, and order was restored to our school, and we all were relieved. Sometimes things happened that she did not know about, like the terrorizing of little kids.

Some of the older children would tell a little kid about the awful things we did to some fictitious kid last year: How we cut off their ears, or chopped off their heads and buried them, etc. Then they would say we are going to do the same thing to you.

One time I saw some boys doing this to a little one back behind the woodshed. One made the kid lay his head on the ground, while the other lifted the axe up full height and brought it down with full force sinking it into the ground just inches away from his head. In retrospect, one wonders what psychological scars such terrorist tactics must have inflicted? We did not know about PTSD in those days!

Sometimes after school let out, we would go on the highway and stick out our thumbs for a ride. Occasionally, a kind-hearted, dignified gentleman would stop his car, lean over, and open his door for us to get in. Then we would say to him, "If you'd keep driving, you'd get there faster!" The man would not understand at first and look at us in a puzzled way. When it dawned on him what we were up to, he would turn red, slam the door, and roar off down the road and out of sight as quickly as possible. We were not going that direction, and anyway we would not take rides with strangers.

*In the school year 1954-55, all five Hansen brothers made up one quarter
of the student body: L. to R. Peter, Carl, Paul, George, and Charles*

At the end of June 1955, Peter, Carole, and Mabel graduated from
eighth grade. The next fall was sad for me. I really missed them in school.
I had always depended on Peter for leadership at home and in school.
Now he was gone. The other kids missed him too. Suddenly the weight of
leadership fell on my shoulders, since I was the only one in eighth grade,
and the oldest in the school. Samuel had quit at the end of grade seven
after he turned fourteen years of age.

Somebody had to take initiative, and so I did. This was a new burden
for me, and I felt very inadequate to the task. But I did my best, and we were
getting along quite well when suddenly Dad sold our farm, and we were to
move back to Alberta in the middle of February. Our world was shattered.

The student body consisted of twenty students in eight grades in the fall of 1955

A Special Sister, Linda Marie

It was "Leap Year" and on February 29, 1952, the Children's Aid Society brought us a pretty, little fourteen-month-old girl for potential adoption. We were elated. We were so proud to finally have a sister in our family. Compared to us rough boys, she appeared so tiny and dainty. She had blond curly hair and pretty blue eyes and such a cute smile. She was a real live doll, and we were so proud of her.

Her origins were a mystery to us as the policy of the Children's Aid Society in those days was to give no background information. We knew that she had been kept in a foster home situation since her birth and that her name then was "Lynn." We quickly named her "Linda Marie." Many years later Linda tried to get information about her origins. In 1992, she finally received information about her birth parents and siblings, and the circumstances of her birth.

Linda Marie was a happy child after she got used to living with us. She liked to play outside and in the barn, rather than in the house. She liked to be out there with her dad and brothers.

One day when she was about two and one-half years of age, she witnessed the birth of a calf. She did not ask any questions nor make any comments. She just watched in awe and wonder. Then she went to the house and with great excitement told Mom, "A cow ate a calf!"

Linda liked to play with some kittens. One scorching summer day, we picked up a one-gallon syrup pail she had left outside on the barn bank. We noticed there was something inside it, so we opened it. There was a kitten, almost dead. It was obviously relieved to be released from its hot oxygen deprived prison tomb.

*Hansen brothers welcome a special sister - back Paul, Carl & Peter
holding Linda Marie, front Charles & George – 1952*

Charles & his new sister, Linda Marie

Assisting an Immigrant Family

In the early 1950's, Dutch immigrants were coming from the Netherlands to Canada, attracted by the inexpensive and available farmland. Many of them settled in our community. In general, they were very industrious and hardworking people.

These people would come and work for a Canadian farmer for a few months or a year, save most of their small wages until they had a few thousand dollars. Then they would buy a farm, sometimes for as little as $500 down payment. They would borrow as much as they could and buy as many cows as they could afford. They would work hard, spend as little as possible on themselves, build up their herds, and improve their farms until they would double or triple the previous production of the farm.

They almost always met their debt obligations so established good credit ratings. Then they would help their relatives immigrate too or help their children buy farms in the neighborhood. Drayton was fast becoming a Dutch community, and a Christian Reformed Church was built.

In the spring of 1952, our parents sponsored a Dutch immigrant family, the Anthony Van Manens. Sponsorship meant that we would provide a job for the father on our farm, and the family would live in our stone house. The family arrived with twelve children. The oldest son, Henry or "Hank," got a job working for Elton Cressman, our neighbor. There were several older girls that got jobs around. One, Kobie, aged 14, worked for us for a while. Tony, Kase, Jenny, and Henny went to school with us. Then there was little Franzie, the baby.

It was interesting to meet these people who knew no English and watch them adjust to the Canadian way of life. It made me understand what my own parents and grandparents must have gone through a generation earlier. Our mom was a big help to them at first with her Plattdeutsch, which is a Dutch dialect, and limited German. They were able to communicate quite well.

One day in the spring, our dad was driving our little Ford tractor around the yard when little Jenny Van Manen asked to drive it too. Dad took her on his lap and let her learn. She did not know anything about steering and steered straight for the clothesline. Before Dad could get control, they were hitting it, but it snapped just before they touched it. If it had not snapped it would have caught Jenny right on the throat. Dad just marveled, "It snapped before we hit it!" Another time the "Guardian Angels" were alert!

A part of the plan to sponsor this family was that we would finance it by growing sugar beets. The Dutch people knew how to grow beets, so Dad made a contract with the sugar company to plant ten acres. The Dutch family would work on the beets, and the income would cover the costs of the labor. There should be some profits for the grower, as well. It sounded like a good plan all around.

Like a lot of good plans, when tried for the first time, not everything worked out. In the first place, we had to buy expensive equipment to seed and cultivate the beets. The Dutchman turned out to be rather lazy and unenthusiastic about this type of work.

We contracted several other Dutchmen to help with the hoeing and thinning. It went so slowly, and they were getting behind for the season. Finally, our uncle, Chris, who was working on bridge construction, came home for a few days to help finish. We were amazed at how he could work. Chris worked alone, hoeing, and thinning two and one-half rows for every one row the Dutchmen did.

When the time came to harvest the beets, it was late October, and the Van Manen family had long since gone. The beets had to be lifted out of the ground, the tops chopped off, and piled. Then we had to load them on wagons by hand. This was dirty, cold, arduous work as there was light snow and frost already.

We boys had to stay home from school to help. I was just turning eleven years old. It was real torture loading the wet, muddy beets from the snow-covered piles onto the wagons. A cold, damp breeze penetrated our jackets, chilling our bones; the cold mud on the beets soaked our gloves, numbing our fingers so we could hardly feel what we were touching. Water dripped off our noses.

It was a joyful day when the last beet was unloaded at the train station at Drayton in November. When the final check was cashed and the accounts were settled, we found that there were no profits to compensate us for our hard, torturous labor. That was the last time we grew sugar beets!

After we got to know this family, we did not appreciate them all that much. The father, Anthony, was a hot-tempered man. He swore too much. I can still remember some of his most vulgar Dutch phrases. The family seemed rather dirty to us. They made demands on us that we had not anticipated, and they did not seem happy with our terms of agreement. Sometimes, the father acted like he hated the work on our farm. Dad could not depend on him to do a meticulous job. However, we kids did play with their children and had good times together.

Having a hired man was not altogether good for us growing boys either. When he came, we had fewer responsibilities. We were happy about that of course. He would do the milking every other Sunday.

One Sunday, Anthony was doing the chores, and some of the neighbor boys came to play with us. We played in the barn while the man was doing the work. First, we were rolling old tires around upstairs in the barn. Soon one of us rolled a tire down the hay chute directly in front of the cow the Dutchman was milking.

It was very unusual, of course, for a tire to appear so suddenly, clattering down the chute, and bouncing in the feed aisle with a cloud of dust in front of the placid cow, dreamily chewing her cud and giving down her milk. The cow was so startled, it about had a heart attack as it jumped and jerked around. Of course, justly provoked, Mr. Van Manen bounded up the stairs in an instant, and, with a very red face and shaking fist, swore with some of the most unprintable Dutch vocabulary one could imagine!

Then, Peter went out to the cornfield, and picked an armload of cobs, took them upstairs in the barn, and climbed up to an upper window. There he had a good view. Below were the well, the pump, and a cattle-watering trough. The Dutchman was coming to the trough to fetch water with two big buckets for the barn. Peter threw some cobs of corn down from a height of nearly thirty-five feet and hit the water in the trough, just inches away from the man. That, of course, not only startled him, but soaked him as well. You can imagine what that did to the man's sense of humor, especially when he looked up and could not see from where the cobs came, as Peter, of course, ducked back behind the wall, out of sight.

A part of our responsibilities was to operate the cream separator, which separates the cream from the skim milk. We were not doing it according to the wishes of our hired man, so he came over and swore at us again. Peter was shelling some corn and had a handful of kernels, which he threw at him. This provoked more Dutch profanity, as the enraged Dutchman chased us useless fellows out of the barn!

It was not surprising that shortly after, Anthony Van Manen quit working for us. He found a better paying job somewhere else where he did not have to put up with so many of the boss's spoiled brats. In a way, we were glad to see the whole family go, even if it meant that we boys would have to do much more of the work. We were getting bigger now and were able.

A Creative Playmate, Bob Beal

Bob Beal was another tough fellow who was two grades ahead of me. He was sort of a "Huckleberry Finn" type character. He lived alone with his father on the farm across the road west of the school. His mother had left his father, leaving his home life deficient. His father had a reputation for using too much alcohol. Since Bob was alone and had very lax supervision at home, he usually was available as a friend any time you needed one.

He enjoyed coming to play at our place, and he came often, but we never went to play at his place. Our parents, like most parents, did not really approve of us keeping his company, "a bad influence ..." But they never forbade him to come to our place.

Bob could tell lies and spin stories, so we could never be sure if they were true or not. He had creative ideas or suggestions of things to do; some of them were fun, and some of them, if we would have followed through with them, would have landed us in jail for sure.

I remember getting into a fight with Bob one time, outside in the school yard, when I was in grade three. I could not beat him, and he could not beat me either. We were really angry and going at it. The teacher came and caught us fighting and forced us to stop. I cried because I was so angry. The teacher scolded both of us and hustled us into the school. She blamed him more, maybe because of his reputation, and partly because he was two years older than me. However, overall, we were friends.

Bob would often come over to our place after school, or on a weekend, to play a game of "cops and robbers" in our barn. There was an empty chicken room that we used for the jail. Two kids would be the cops; the rest were robbers.

The cops would chase the robbers up the ladders, across the beams, over the haymows, down another ladder, down the hay chute, between the cows, across the cleaning aisle, through the milk area, up the staircase, and throughout the barn until one was caught. The surprised cows would jerk in their stalls, the pigs would all say, "Ouph, Ouph," and run to the far side of their pens, then stand and look, and the cats would flee away in terror. If touched by the "cop," a "robber" could not resist arrest. He would be tied up as securely as possible with baler twine in the jail. Then the cops would go after the others.

The objective was to have all the robbers tied up in the jail at the same time. This was not as simple as it sounds. We became escape artists. Robbers would sneak into the jail and rescue their accomplices. Jailbirds would untie themselves, sometimes chewing the sisal twine with their teeth. They became experts in hiding razor blades in the cuffs of their pants, or the sweatbands of their caps, or in their shirt collars. The cops, in turn, had to search for hidden razors and invent new ways to tie a prisoner so that he could not escape, even if he had a razor blade on him.

Finally, the cops had to engage the services of little brother, Charlie, to serve as a prison guard, since he was too small for the rough and tumble of police or thief life.

Sometimes Bob was a bad influence on us. For example, one day Bob got this brilliant idea that we should put some live frogs in the beds of these new Dutch neighbors living in our stone house. Peter and I thought this was a splendid idea, and so did Jim and John Larsen, who were foster children staying with Elton Cressman's, our neighbor.

So, on our way home from school, we stopped at the creek, near our place, and caught some frogs and put the poor wretches in our pockets. Then we walked towards the stone house. Now we had a slight problem: to reach the Dutchman's bedroom, we had to crawl across a fence, sneak through weeds up to the side of the house, climb up the perpendicular stone wall to the second story window, crawl in, put our jumpy wet load under the blankets, then retreat the way we came, as noiselessly as possible without being caught! We were to do all this at four o'clock in the afternoon, when there were about eight little Dutch children watching us. Indeed, a prodigious challenge!

First, we climbed over the fence and walked past the window to survey the situation. Sure enough, the children saw us coming and gathered to watch. We had to pretend to be about other business, so we walked on past the house to a machine shed, which we entered. There we had an emergency strategy conference.

By this time, the children had notified their mother. She, suspiciously, came out with a broom to inquire what we were up to. Language was a problem with her, so we could ignore her words, but we could not ignore her broom and the hefty arms that wielded it. She was getting increasingly menacing every second as she interrogated us in this unknown tongue. We never knew what experiences these foreigners may have had in resisting Hitler's S.S. men, so we did not want to underestimate what they might do to us if they perceived us as a threat.

We decided to make a beeline for home. We bailed out of the shed the way we came, back past the open bedroom window. Bob, or was it John, had the presence of mind to not forget the original purpose of our coming, and threw the now dead frogs into the window as we rushed by. Unfortunately, a flying dead frog knocked a small vase off the windowsill to the floor inside where it broke.

In the meantime, we were running for our lives. The biggest boys ran the fastest, and I was coming along with Paul behind. This middle-aged Dutch matron, mother of twelve, was no joke, weighing not an ounce under two hundred pounds, and yet, could she run! We stragglers could feel her breath on the back of our stretched necks and hear her gasping between her Dutch cuss words as we mustered another ounce of strength for our flying feet!

The boys ahead made it to a big maple tree and scrambled up into its protecting branches. We were right behind, not a bit slower than if an angry mother bear was pursuing us! We made it just in the nick of time and heaved a big sigh of relief.

But, before we could begin to laugh, the color really drained from our faces when we heard the determined beat of the woman's feet going up our lane. Of course, the old lady would tell our mother! No maple tree ever grew big enough to save us now!

Occasionally, our mother did surprise us. While what we did was bad, she took a reasonable mediator role and cooled the old lady's wrath. She made us apologize to the woman. Then, she got out her glue bottle and glued together the priceless treasure. So now the keepsake has even more sentimental value than it did at that time, for the cracks will forever engrave our memory on their hearts! I think our mother secretly attributed this incident as part of the price that had to be paid for having Bob Beal as a playmate for her boys.

Another time Bob, Jim, John, and we made elaborate plans to scare the Dutch neighbors. We would get some cap guns resembling authentic pistols, then we would put on some masks and unfamiliar coats, and on the first night after pay day, we would hold them up and take all their money. Then, because it was just a joke, we would leave the money on their doorstep! Brilliant! Bob did not really agree that we should leave the money there. If we get it, why not just keep it?

His ethics were a shade different than ours. When we were by ourselves, we did not feel right about such a joke. In the first place, without money, how were we to get the required guns? What if they should resist and fight us? With our toy guns, we would be quite helpless. When we would be exposed, it would become a police case. Who would believe we were just joking? We decided that we could not go along with that plan, but it was fun contemplating the scenario anyway!

Shortly thereafter, John and Jim returned to their home in Preston. Their parents were going to try to live together as a family again. They were good boys, and we missed them a lot.

Russian Immigrants

Sometime after the Van Manen's had left, four families of Russian immigrants came to our community. They were refugees who had undergone untold suffering during the war and more suffering afterwards in post-war Europe. Now, they finally had sponsors to receive them in Canada. They all came to our church at first. Most of them did not know any English.

There was the Orlov family with several teenage boys, who were already wise in the ways of the world, and who taught us boys a twisted version of all the facts of life that our parents were embarrassed to teach us. The Orlovs worked for Mervin Shantz.

There was the Tertishenoi family with their one little son, Alex, who came to our school. Then there was Alex and Elvina Sawluk, an older couple, who later rented our stone house for twenty-five dollars per month. The husband of the fourth family was named Peter Hnatkov. Peter was later killed in a tragic car accident, leaving a widow and three small sons to mourn him, all in a foreign land. His was one of the saddest funerals I ever attended.

After they learned English, Alex and Elvina Sawluk became good neighbors. They entertained us with their stories for hours. Alex had been a Russian soldier during the war. He had been captured and practically starved to death in a German concentration camp. Elvina had been married before. Her husband was taken away by the KMVD (Russia's secret police) and died in Stalin's prison somewhere. She had had several children, but, in those unspeakable suffering times, had lost all of them. Somehow, she escaped from Russia into Germany. In a refugee camp after the war, she met Alex, and they married. Alex was ten years younger than her, but he wanted her so badly that he lied about his age. After he became a Christian, he had to confess his deceit.

Alex was a carpenter and worked away from home every day. He kept about one hundred rabbits and some chickens for meat. Since he was quite busy, he gave us boys a job of picking fresh green clover or dandelion or sow thistle each day. We got paid ten cents a gunny bag for it. We made quite a business out of it. We also learned how to keep rabbits. We bought four does and a buck from him. We soon had forty rabbits of our own.

The Sawluks bought milk from us every day. We looked forward to the hour when Alex would come into the barn to get his milk. Often, there would be an interesting story, or at least a comment on a current issue. If he had eaten garlic that day, we could always tell before he got near to us.

We felt sorry for Alex Tertishenoi because he was an only son and because he had an over-protective mother. He would come to school and get hurt. When he went home, he embellished the extent of his sufferings. Then his mother would get all worked up, like a mother hen. She would ruminate on it all night and report to her Russian neighbors. In the morning, she would rush over to the school and try, in her anguished broken English, to demand justice for her poor little persecuted cherub.

One Sunday, she cornered Paul in church, and, in front of everybody, scolded him harshly. Paul did not understand what was going on. Then, she and another Russian lady found Mom and accused Paul of locking her son up in the latrine and hurting him. Mom asked questions and finally discovered that Paul was innocent. Other children had teased him and locked him in the latrine. This behavior was not out of the ordinary, since the top of the latrine was opened, and boys, being boys, often crawled over the top. When the mother found out her son had misinformed her, she turned on him and accused him of lying. We felt sorry for Alex. He would have been much better off if he had four brothers, or if his mother would just keep quiet.

Influenced by Preachers of the Gospel

John F. Garber was our pastor and later, bishop. He was a diligent student of the Bible and preached messages that were Biblically based. He was gifted as a teacher. In fact, during the winter months, he would go to Kitchener to teach at the Ontario Mennonite Bible School and Institute. His sermons were deep and oriented towards an adult audience. Most of what he said passed over my head. From the little I remember, he relied heavily on the Pauline Epistles, especially I or II Corinthians, for his preaching material.

I did not like him as a person all that much. He seemed so stern and strict, and his preaching seemed directed to scold and discipline us. Like my view of God, he had very high standards, and we never felt quite good enough to be acceptable in his sight.

I was probably wrong; maybe it was that I was so far from the "bishop" qualities in him? Since he always preached from St. Paul's writings, I began to dislike St. Paul too. It took many years before I was able to really enjoy reading St. Paul's writings with complete objectivity and to find powerful challenging truths for my life in them.

Sometimes we would have "revival meetings," a series of preaching services every night for a week or so. The preacher was usually an invited guest from elsewhere. The object of these meetings was to challenge, encourage, stimulate, and nourish the faithful; to warn, rebuke, discipline, chastise the wayward and backsliders; and to present the good news in such a way to move the sinner through knowledge of Jesus Christ, to faith in him, to repentance, to assurance of salvation, and to a commitment to holy living in obedient discipleship.

Three of the more notable of these preachers were Roy Koch, Peter Wiebe, and Raymond Kraemer. All three of these men made a positive impression on me. For once, it was exciting to go to church. Kraemer was such a clown. He could tell the funniest stories, complete with actions, in such a way that people were crying with laughter, and then he would skillfully drive home the point. We enjoyed applying the descriptions in the stories to the real people in our church whom we knew fitted them very well.

Sometimes I had to apply the truths to myself. When I did so, I became uncomfortable and felt very unclean, guilty, and afraid of God. But I never "went forward" when the invitation was given. I would just sit, feel miserable, and wish that somebody would go forward, so that the preacher would not feel like he was a failure or be so disappointed in all of us.

In Ontario, apples would fall off early due to worm activity or some other default. These fallen apples were usually okay to eat, and we would often pick up a nice one to chew on, avoiding the worm holes, as we walked along.

I remember walking along the road passing an apple tree growing wild in the hedgerow on Johnson's farm. I looked to see if the trunk was rooted in the soil inside the fence or outside the fence. If it was outside the fence, I would eat the apples without guilt. If it was rooted inside, I would not eat an apple from there; although, I knew that the owner was in a nursing home and would never come to collect his apples. To do so would be "stealing." That is how much of a slave I was to my conscience, and how oppressed I was by the "Accuser."

Another time, when I was about nine or ten years old, while vacuuming the upstairs floor of our house, I was humming and singing along with the whine of the vacuum cleaner. I was also saying nonsense things to myself, and my tongue slipped and instead of saying, "got" I said "God." Then to my utter horror, I realized that I had used "the Lord's name in vain," which in my understanding was the "unpardonable sin." "For the Lord will not hold him guiltless who uses his name in vain." (Exodus 20:7 KJV) Now there was no pardon for me!

I was overwhelmed with horror; I would go to hell for sure! I pleaded to God to forgive me, but there was no answer. I reasoned that perhaps God would see that I am just a little boy, and if I tried hard all my life to make it up by living like a good Christian, even though I had committed the unpardonable sin, maybe He would just bend the rules a wee bit and let me slip into Heaven after all? I resolved that that was the best I could do. What a burden, and what an impossible quest. I tried hard to be good, but the more I tried, the more I failed.

Obviously, my view of God was rigid to the extreme. To imagine that He would fry a little boy over the glowing coals of hell forever and ever because his tongue slipped is inconceivable to me now in light of what I know as an earthly father of love for one's children. "How much more will your Heavenly Father give good things to those who ask him?"

I do not know how I arrived at such a view of God, but that was what I believed, and I was completely miserable. I was shy and timid and never talked to anyone about my inner turmoil and guilt. I suspect it was my stubborn pride that kept me bound up in fear of what my parent or pastor or counselor would think if I revealed to him how bad I was.

In the summer of 1950, a group of leaders of the Ontario Mennonite Churches invited the "Brunk Brothers" to hold an evangelistic and revival "crusade" in the Waterloo area. This would be a region-wide event.

George and Lawrence Brunk came from Denbigh, Virginia, with a convoy of tractor-trailers carrying a huge tent, 5000 chairs, and a lot of equipment, including their own generator, and several late-model Oldsmobiles pulling campers and carrying their families. They set up this huge tent on a farm and arranged their living quarters in an orderly fashion at the back. It was quite an impressive setup.

George and Lawrence were giants of men in every way. Physically, at about six foot four, they stood out in the crowd of fellow leaders. Intellectually, they were deeply knowledgeable about the Bible and all things theological. Mentally, they had great imaginations and were gifted in the art of public speaking with profound ability in using communication skills. Spiritually, they exuded an air of authority and holiness that made us little boys believe they must have a special hot line to the Almighty. George Brunk did the preaching, and Lawrence led the singing. They could reverse roles just as well, but they preferred to do it this way.

That year, the meetings were held for four weeks. Every night, the tent was near to full. Hundreds of people were convicted of their waywardness and turned to Christ. It was a blessing to many people and churches. Lives were changed, God was honored, and people were encouraged. We got to go sometimes, but not every night. Sometimes we drove the thirty miles. More often, some of us would go with some of the Hubers.

The next year Howard Hammer came to the area with a similar setup and held meetings. Somehow, we did not go very often, so the memory of it does not stick in my mind. Howard later went to Brazil as a missionary. But there he got involved in a scandalous affair with a sixteen-year-old girl and took his own life. What a tragic ending to a life that was used of God in a mighty way. "How are the mighty fallen!" It is a sober lesson to all of us, to be on guard. The enemy of men's souls seeks to destroy God's work. "He who thinks he stands should take heed lest he fall."

In the summer of 1952, the Brunk Revivals group came back. This time they came without the brother, Lawrence. There had been, like in the case of Paul and Barnabas, a disagreement, and a parting of ways. Lawrence gave his life for another ministry, and someone else took his place as song leader.

This time the tent capacity was eight thousand. The meetings were so popular that they were extended for six weeks. Again, it had a profound impact on the lives of thousands. My brothers and I listened in awe of George Brunk's oratorical skills. He became one of our heroes for many years following.

Again, I listened and felt guilty. I thought I should respond to his long invitations and go forward, but I did not. We picked up the measles there and missed the last two weeks in solitary confinement at home instead.

By now, it had become a tradition to have these evangelistic "crusades." In the summer of 1953, Myron Augsburger came with his big tent. J. Mark Stauffer was his song leader. Myron outshone all that had come before. He was only twenty-two years old at the time, was better educated, and could talk faster, tell more stories, and repeat more jokes than George could. He also gave more carefully thought out and daring explanations for the more controversial topics of the day. Myron became our superhero. We all wanted to become preachers like him.

Dissention in the Community of Faith

Meanwhile, back at the Berea Mennonite Church, there were problems. It seemed to us that the rift between the Garbers and the Hubers was growing. The bishop, John F. Garber was changing his views on several basic issues. As he studied and taught Bible at the Institute, and as he worked with the leadership of the Ontario Mennonite Conference, he was influenced to change his views on eschatology from supporting premillennialism to espousing amillennialism. He also moved away from rigidly holding members to a prescribed dress code.

The Huber families could not go along with this. They felt betrayed by their co-founder of our church. However, there was more to the discontent than that. Arguments over the church building left bitter feelings. People held resentments over the highhanded way the bishop ruled the church. As the discontent and murmuring increased, the pastor struck back, using his sermons to scold his rebellious sheep. Although I was still a kid, I learned from him about how not to lead a church.

One Sunday the atmosphere of disagreement was getting so thick that you could almost cut it. After church our mom said that she was hungry for a good Gospel message, and that there was a woman preacher at the Pentecostal Church in Drayton that afternoon. She would go and hear her. Later that afternoon she came home and said she was really fed and blessed.

Her openness to other denominations and even women preachers back in the 1950s really impressed me. Mom and Dad did not like the fighting in the church and would have no part in it. They often discussed the issues with us boys. They could see the strong points and weak points of both sides. They loved both sides as brothers and sisters in the family of God. They just longed for both sides to live together in peace, with love and toleration all around.

In 1953, a new family moved into the neighborhood that gave a boost to our little church fellowship. Dan and Lillian Jantzi moved onto a farm on the 12th of Peel. They came with a family of five children. Dan was an electrician who farmed on the side, or was it a farmer who did electrical work on the side so he could afford to farm? I was never sure. Lillian was a good homemaker and mother. They found the farm to be a good place to raise their kids.

They both were very sociable and hospitable. They contributed much to the spiritual and social life of our little congregation. They often invited us to their home for Sunday lunch and we had them over to our place now and then as well. Since their eldest daughter, Damaris, was a few years older than us boys, we did not have a lot in common at that stage in life. Darrell, however, was just a year older than Peter, and Dalton was about George's age, so we were happy to welcome them as new friends.

During those times, the Conference encouraged the pastors to teach their congregations to start supporting their pastors financially. Up to that time, pastors were completely self-supporting. It was suggested that they begin by having one "love offering" each month for their pastor. John Garber introduced this at Berea.

This innovation was not popular at first. It could not have been introduced at a worse time, considering how the feelings were running high against the leader who had to introduce this new practice. I remember one Sunday, the "love offering" amounted to four dollars, and we learned that that was contributed by one saint. A normal offering those days ran at about sixty dollars per Sunday.

In 1954, our bishop, John F. Garber notified the congregation that "the Lord had called" him to pastor a church in Ohio. He would be going soon, so we should find a man to take his place.

After searching, a young man from the Bible Institute was found. He was trained but lacked experience. Would we accept him? To the majority of the congregation, he was a breath of fresh air, so Gordon Bauman became our pastor.

But he wore a necktie before he was ordained. That was unsatisfactory for the Huber families, so they both left our church for a more conservative church near New Hamburg. With the loss of these three large families, our church was reduced in size.

Gordon Bauman came with a wife and three small children and would need a house. They were recently students so were not rich in resources. They wanted to buy our stone house. What could we say; we did not need it, and they did! We agreed to sell the house and two acres of land for $1500. They did an extensive remodeling and had an excellent house.

The "love offerings" at the church for the new pastor, without the contributions of the two big families that went away, usually amounted to between sixty and one-hundred and twenty dollars per month that first year. We could overlook his inexperience and other minor flaws. We were happy to have him for a pastor and for a neighbor.

Fun in the Bush

Ever since grade three when we read "Robin Hood," we boys developed a romantic relationship with the "forests" around us. These were actually just little farm woodlots, which were often called "the bush." "Foster's bush" was just kitty corner across the road from us. It was really only a small cedar swamp.

We used to imagine dangerous robbers hiding out in that bush and sneaking over to our place at night. We developed a fear of going upstairs in the barn at night or down the cellar steps in the house. There just might be one of those dangerous guys lurking in the shadows to "get" us. In the daylight, however, we enjoyed playing in the bush.

When we got bigger, we enjoyed playing in our own bush, a fifteen-acre woodlot about a half-mile from our house. We would go out there in the summer Sunday afternoons. Under Peter's creative leadership, we built a "cabin" of old fence rails and roofed it by nailing on old paper fertilizer sacks. It made a nice clubhouse and headquarters.

When we played "Cops and Robbers," this cabin made a good jail. All five of us would be involved. Trusty little Charlie could be the guard. The rest of us would be either "cops" or "robbers." We found out it was more fun if we had more people, so sometimes we would invite the Huber boys or Bob Beal. When we persuaded the Davison girls and the Elswick girls to come, that made it even more exciting.

The girls had problems getting permission from their parents to go to a bush to play with "those Hansen boys," so they could not come very often. Carole had her ways of getting to where she wanted to go. Her parents were more lenient, and her mother liked and trusted us boys. The Elswicks, however, were stricter, so they could only come clandestinely, which made it more interesting any way.

Other times, we used the cabin for a laboratory. We executed extensive experiments studying the burning qualities of gasoline and diesel fuel. We took a small barrel, cut a door in the side, and made it into a stove. Outside in front of the cabin, we would make a fire in this stove, put some gasoline or diesel fuel in a small floor-wax can, punch a small nail hole in the lid, push the lid on tight as it could go, then put the can on the stove.

After a while, the gasoline would start to boil nicely. The lid would bulge outwardly due to the pressure, and a nice jet of steam would shoot out the nail hole. We found that the jet of steam would not burn, unless one held a nail, screwdriver, stick, or any pointed thing, to just touch the stream of steam. Then it would burn like a blowtorch.

We also discovered that if you made the hole big enough to leave a flat headed nail in it, the gas would come up around the nail head and burn like a stove burner. That is, until the pressure got too great and blew the nail into orbit.

We discovered that boiling diesel fuel burns as well as boiling gasoline, though it burns much slower when cold.

One thing we never discovered was why the lid of the wax-can never blew off spraying boiling gasoline all over our foolish faces! I am sure the guardian angel must have got his hand badly burned holding that lid on that boiling bomb!

A Halloween Like no Other

It was the eve of "All Saints Day" commonly known as "Halloween." In those times, in our rural Ontario, we never heard of such a tame thing as "trick or treating." We only knew it meant "tricks." Our parents never let us go out on Halloween night. To sneak around at night, pulling pranks on unsuspecting people, simply was out of character with the kind of people we were, or at least ought to be. We knew better than to ask for permission to go out. We did not even think to ask.

It was the evening of October the 31st, 1954. We were quietly doing our barn chores at seven p.m.

Suddenly, out of the dark appeared our friend, Carole Davison. Could we not join her, her sister, Ruth, and Ann Elswick and her brother for a little stroll in the countryside this fine hallowed evening?

"No way!"

"Why not?"

"Dad would never let us!"

"Let me ask him for you!"

And Carole was off to conquer our invincible Dad. She was such a sweetie when she wanted to be, and Dad just melted. Just maybe he was not as hard as we had assumed? Dad tried to wiggle out of saying, "No!" by finally saying, "Go ask their mother!"

Well, Mom was surprised and felt let down by Dad's weakness, and she did not want to be the "ugly old witch" in front of our friends, so she had to say, "Okay, if their Dad agrees!" Well, we had it made, thanks to the mighty Carole. This was beyond our fondest dreams. We were actually going out on Halloween night!

We hurried and finished our chores. Then, before we left, Dad strictly ordered us to behave ourselves and specifically warned us, "Do not go near Archibald's place!"

Billy and Becky Archibald were siblings who lived together on their parent's farm. They were in their eighties, and as eccentric worriers, had a reputation for getting extremely upset by Halloween pranksters. It was an established custom for every serious prankster to converge on the premises of the Archibald farm sometime during the evening of the 31st, to participate in the annual harassment. Dad did not want us to be involved.

It was a warm, dark, clear fall night. We set out east on the 14th of Peel, the road that went past the Huber farms. We went on a spree of destruction, ripping off or pulling out mailboxes. We unrolled a roll of page wire across an alfalfa field, unrolled a snow fence roll across the road, put straw bales on the road, and that about sums it up as far as the pranks we did. A bright full moon came out, and we just enjoyed walking along in its light on this special night.

After two miles, we reached the first crossroad. We needed to turn either right or left. If we turned right, we would reach Archibald's place one mile away. Carole was just dying to go. But we remembered Dad's stern warning, so we turned to the left. That led us to the next crossroad and junction with the 16th, one mile down. We turned left again and went two miles west on the 16th.

As we were about to turn left again for the final mile home, we heard several gunshots ringing out on the quiet, clear night air from the direction of the Archibald's. We heard no more, so we went on home, arriving at the reasonable hour of ten o'clock. It was a memorable evening.

The next day at school, everybody was excited about the awful shooting at Archibald's place. As it turned out, in the tortured thinking of the elderly couple, they devised a plan to stop the harassment once and for all. They hired a man with a double-barreled shotgun from Guelph. He came and opened fire into the darkness that was just crawling with pranksters.

One of those struck was Carl Lambert, a thirty-five-year-old father of six. He was a prominent community man and owner of "Carl's Garage" in Drayton. They say he had been coming faithfully for the fun every year since he was a child. He had forgotten that he had grown up. Now he had to pay dearly for his entertainment, for the blast took out one of his eyes and destroyed the hearing in one of his ears. He was hospitalized for months but was fortunate to be alive.

The police came and found at least thirty-five pranksters had been there at the time of the shooting. One or two others received a few of the pellets as well. A big court case followed that took most of a year to settle. Mr. Archibald had to pay damages to Mr. Lambert and pay a fine, and the hired gunman went to jail. We were very, very thankful that we had respected and obeyed our father that night!

Years later, of that night, Carole recalls in a letter to me:

> *The Halloween night we all went out, I was on my way to your house and decided to scare Pastor Bauman's children. It had just darkened a little, so I sneaked in their driveway hoping to peek in their window. Just as I got to the back of his car, I heard the door open, so I ducked down behind his car.*
>
> *Well, wouldn't you know it, he was getting something out of his trunk! I thought, if I am going to scare anyone, it must be now, so I snarled and jumped at him. His reaction was so quick, his foot flew in my direction just missing me by centimeters. It never occurred to me I might get hurt, I scared him so bad it was pathetic. He then was so worried that he had hurt me. He told my mother that I almost scared the life out of him.*

My mother was approached more than once about my shenanigans. She was embarrassed but probably gave up. She had cabins built and sold them at the end of our lane way. One day she sold one. Well, I proceeded to tease (Cokey) Colin Campbell, that I knew his older brother Ken had stolen our cabin because it was missing. Two days later my mother nailed me. What are you doing? Mrs. Campbell had phoned her and said, "Mrs. Davison, honestly Ken did not steal your cabin!" My mother had no idea what she was talking about. She immediately knew who the culprit was, and I had to apologize for my nonsense.

Farming

When we bought the second farm, Dad saw the need for a bigger tractor, so in the spring of 1952, he traded the little Ford tractor for a new Fordson Major Diesel.

It was an ugly-looking thing. It had been a demonstrator and had been painted a grayish white in contrast to all the blue Fordsons. It was very clumsy and old fashioned, the last of the old models, before the new modern low-profile blue line of Fordsons came out with their three-point hitches and hydraulic devices galore.

This model could not go more than eight miles per hour and took half an acre to turn in. It came with grossly undersized tires. But it had a good Perkins Diesel motor and had a lot of power. We were very proud of our Fordson Major Diesel. That was the year we had the Van Manen family living in our stone house, and the year we grew sugar beets.

One day, the new tractor was standing in our lane beside our house. Six-year-old George was sitting on it pretending he was farming. All of us older ones were in the house. Suddenly, we heard the diesel start up and go. We had left it sitting in gear with the ignition switch on. George had pressed the start button, setting it in full forward motion. He had never driven before and had no idea how to stop it or how to keep it on the road. It turned out into the field, and he just kept it going in a big circle until Dad ran out and rescued him or it. What if it would have run into the open green septic pond nearby?

It was a wet spring in 1953, and we were still trying to get the crop seeded in June. One day the Fordson got stuck in a muddy spot, which had happened quite often that year. This time Dad called Peter to help him.

He had a new, easy plan to dislodge the tractor from its muddy prison. He would tie one end of a chain around the rear wheel, and the other end to the lower end of a crowbar that he had embedded deeply in the soil. Then he would hold the top of the crowbar at an angle away from the tractor while Peter would put the tractor in gear, and it would pull itself out of the mud, so easy.

Well, it was a nice idea. However, even with the advantage of the leverage of the long crowbar, not even Dad was a match for the Fordson. When the wheel turned, pulling on the chain, the bottom of the crowbar held, but Dad could not hold the top. It tilted forward, and the chain slid up the bar, catching Dad's little finger against the flange at the top end of the crowbar and cutting it off.

Mom had to take him to the doctor to get it cleaned, sewed, and bandaged. The doctor sent him to the hospital. It did not heal as infection set in. At one point he developed blood poisoning, and they feared there might be lockjaw. He was there for three weeks. They finally let him out on July 7th, the day our parents had to go to court in Guelph to get Linda's adoption papers finalized.

Again, Dad was an invalid during haying time. This year we hired someone with a baler to come in and bale our hay. The church people again rushed to help us put it up in the barn. We older boys were very much involved in the farm work by then. We did a lot of the tractor driving, and we learned how to stack hay bales.

By that time, we had made the transition to tractor power and had disposed of our horses. Uncle Chris had a Farmall H tractor with a new power mower that simplified cutting the hay. We had a good side-delivery rake. That fall we bought a small new International pull-type combine harvester with a grain box on it. The grain box with unloading auger was new technology in the area.

Up to that time, most farmers used the old threshing machines. They would bring in their sheaves of grain when they were dry and store them in their barns. Then during the winter, when the threshing machine was available, each farmer would thresh grain in his own barn. That was a very dusty job. It was also very unhealthy, as farmers frequently got pneumonia from the dust.

The Hubers used older Allis Chalmers combines, but they had grain baggers on them. While the tractor pulled the combine around the field, someone else rode on a platform regulating the flow of grain into gunny bags, tying them when full, and unloading them at designated places. After harvesting was done for the day, the farmer would have to come with a wagon, lift all those heavy bags off the ground onto the wagon, haul them home, and unload them inside his barn.

We were so proud of our new machine. It simply filled its box; then a wagon would be brought, and the machine augured the grain into the wagon. The only work was in unloading the wagon with a grain shovel, which was easier than breaking your back on heavy bags. The disadvantage of combines, though, was that after threshing, the straw was still in the field and the chaff was lost, which was the best part of the straw for feeding and for bedding the cattle.

It was also this year that we did remodeling in our barn. We tore out the old horse stables and put in nice new steel Beatty cow stanchions in their place. We also built a proper concrete and steel bullpen.

Up to that time, we had no bull. We had been using artificial insemination and had built up the quality of our herd significantly. But there was a problem getting some of the cows to conceive on time, so Dad got a bull. We were milking about twenty cows, separating the milk, selling the cream, and feeding the skim milk to pigs and calves.

In December of 1953, Mom took little Linda to Alberta by train. It was her first time to go home in five years. While there, she attended her sister Neta's wedding. Neta married John (Jack) Broadfoot and moved with him to his home farm near Watrous, Saskatchewan. It was our first time to be without a mother for several weeks.

In 1954, we worked together with Chris in haying and harvesting. This was the year he rented the Vale place. Together we put up over seven thousand bales of hay. We did it without hiring any outside help. That might not sound like much by today's standards, but, in those days, we had no bale loaders or elevators, and we were still children, Peter being not fourteen years of age. We boys really learned to work that year, and we were proud of our achievements.

When it came to harvesting, Dad sold the combine and bought a new Mount Forest threshing machine. It was a good machine, but it meant that we had to go back to using a binder again to cut our grain, and then to stooking it like we used to. Dad knew it was more work to do it that way, but he was a dairy farmer, and wanted good straw with all the chaff in it to feed and bed the animals. Baled straw from a combine just was not up to his standard, and there was no other way to go. Besides, although he did not mention the additional advantage, his boys provided cheap labor!

So that year we harvested and threshed all our own grain by ourselves. Dad had his own threshing crew. It took a long time to finish because of the wet weather. Harvest started in August, but we had rain and then snow in September and October. The grain just would not dry out. It began to grow in the wet stooks. The stooks turned a dark brown and then gray black as mold set in. In November, we finally had dry weather. When we threshed the black moldy grain, clouds of black mold dust filled the barn and our lungs until we were sick. We never thought of using masks.

Thousands of mice had been procreating under the stooks all those months, and a significant amount of grain was lost to them. The yield that year was dismal indeed, and the quality was even worse. Yet, we were thankful that we did not have a combine under those circumstances. The grain would have rotted completely.

It became customary to miss school in the fall, due to helping with the harvest. But there was not any competition in school, and nobody seemed to mind when we were not there.

By this time, the 1936 Oldsmobile needed repair, so Dad traded it for a maroon 1948 Oldsmobile. Shortly after, we found that it needed a new engine. He had been the victim of what became the proverbial "used car salesman." It had been "doctored up" so that it ran good on the demonstration drive, but by the time it reached home twenty miles away, it was rather "sick." (No guarantees on used cars in those days!) After spending more money to make it "well," it turned out to be a good car.

Dad never liked the baler as a way to put up straw or hay. It bothered him every time the plunger went in, to see a handful of chaff fall to the ground at the back. He hated to buy the twine for the baler. He hated to lift the bales. He grumbled about tearing the slices of straw apart for bedding.

The piles of useless, used baler twine that accumulated around the farm, got into the manure, and clogged up the manure spreader annoyed him.

So, when it came to haying time in 1955, Dad decided to buy a forage harvester and blower and to put up his hay the latest modern way. No more baler twine to buy and no more used baler twine to stumble over in the barn! No more heavy lifting of bales! It was so much easier to put up the hay with a forage harvester.

With this machine, we picked up the hay in the field, chopped it up, and blew it into the special forage wagon. With the wagon, we took it to the barn, and there we unloaded it with a fork into a blower, which blew it into the barn loft. It was so easy, only touched by hand once. If we could have bought the latest self-unloading wagon, then we would not have had to touch the hay at all. It was a terrific way to make hay!

But then wintertime came, and we found that the barn was not set up for feeding chopped hay. It was much more work to move the chopped hay from the mow to the mangers.

Also, since the hay was just blown into the loft, as it piled up, it put pressure on the walls that they were not designed to withstand. One wall was pushed out from the foundation and a cross beam broke. We were worried that the barn would collapse. Obviously, some more work needed to be done in modifying the facilities to handle this new way of making hay.

Spared for a Purpose

Our neighbor, Pastor Gordon Bauman, wanted to clean out and remodel his well and install a modern electric pump and pressure system for his house. We went to assist him in installing thirty-six-inch diameter concrete culverts for curbing. To do this, we used a tripod standing over the uncovered hole. At the top of this tripod, was a pulley with a rope through it. One end of the rope was fastened to a culvert, and the other end to the tractor. Dad drove the tractor, and other men were helping to direct the culvert as it was lifted by the rope, swung it over the hole, then slowly let it down the hole, as the tractor slowly reversed. As it reached the bottom, someone would guide it into place.

They had the first culvert firmly in place and were swinging the second out over the hole. I was standing at the very edge of the well looking down watching the action below. Suddenly, I noticed the tripod was coming my way. Reflexively I stepped backwards to avoid being struck by it, only to back into the barbed wire fence behind me. One pole of the tripod struck me, grazing and scratching my face. It settled on top of me, as I settled on top of the wire fence.

I was not hurt badly, but I was shaken up a bit, as I pondered my fate had I been knocked forward into the well instead of backward. I became very conscious of God's protecting care and began to think about the possibility that He had a purpose for sparing my life.

Each culvert weighed about 700 lbs. This one made a very rapid descent and landed exactly on top of the bottom one, and neither of them broke. It remains exactly as it landed to this day. They completed that well and later installed the same kind of culverts in our barn well.

One day that winter, as we did on many a Saturday, we went out to the bush with a tractor and bobsled to bring home a load of firewood. We piled the logs and tree limbs on the sled, chained them fast, climbed on the load, and then set out for home. Dad was driving the tractor. The sled was moving along at a good pace; I was sitting towards the edge, resting and half-asleep dreaming as we went along.

Suddenly, one hefty limb came loose, and the front end fell to the ground. It dug in, and since it was chained and the sled was moving, it flipped over end for end. The heavy end came down hard just grazing the back of my sleepy head. I was unhurt, but it made me think. Again, I was spared what could have been certain death or serious injury. Was there a "guardian angel" on duty on the sled that day?

My life could really be summed up as a story of narrow escapes. I had to think of all the times that I could remember coming close to death yet was always spared and unhurt. I thought of seeing the underside of the horse's foot, walking on the thin ice of the pond with my brothers, falling into the well, my narrow escape at Bauman's well, and now this. Did God really love me in a distinct way? Did He have a purpose for me on this earth? If so, what could it be? I felt as though I was the most average and ordinary of all people; why would God have an interest in me?

Working with Dad

When we boys were still quite small, whenever a salesperson or neighbor or anyone stopped by to talk with our dad, out of curiosity, we boys would come out and listen. When the visitor would see us, he would often remark something like, "Wow. What a fine bunch of boys. Enough for a baseball team!" Dad, would correct him, "Enough for a threshing crew!"

This was characteristic of our dad. Productive work was always more important than play or frivolous entertainment or sports. Somehow this value was instilled in all his sons and none of us excelled in sports, nor did we care very much about those who did.

One of the special benefits of being a boy raised on a farm is the privilege of working with and learning from one's dad. We boys always felt we were important to our dad. He acted like he needed our help on the farm, whether he really did or not. From early on, he taught us, not only how to work, but that work is important, good, and necessary.

Even when we were small, he would let us "help" him, even if we got in the way and he would have to do our job over after we left. If he was carrying water in two big five-gallon buckets, we could carry water too in little tin cans. "Help" was never rejected. Later when we boys were older, our little brother or sister would come with a can, a fork, or shovel to "help;" we would lose patience with them, but Dad always encouraged them with, "That's a good boy now. You are a big helper!"

He would teach us to do something, and then he would trust us to do it. By the time we were nine years old, we could drive tractor by ourselves doing fieldwork. Occasionally, we knocked off a gatepost, or tangled a machine up in a fence, or got stuck in a ditch, but we were never scolded. We would explain what had happened, and our explanation was accepted. Then he would help us get going again. We learned to work and like it. We tried to do our best, and he knew it, and we knew he appreciated it.

When we worked together with our dad in hand labor, like fixing things, or stooking, or doing chores, Dad would always have time to talk. He never seemed to be in a hurry. After working for a few hours, he would often say, "Let's rest a bit." Then we would sit down and visit some more. We thought he was doing the resting for our benefit, but sometimes we were not tired yet and would have been just as happy to continue. Years later, when I reached the age of fifty, I understood he probably really was tired.

Dad never went beyond seventh grade in school, but he put what education he had to effective use. He was a reader and built up a respectable understanding of historical and current world issues, as well as church affairs. We spent many an hour in the barn, discussing or arguing about historical or political issues, while we should have been doing chores. Sometimes, we got so involved in our discussions that the milker stayed on a cow for twenty minutes when it should have been finished in four. Chores that should have taken an hour and a half took three.

Those were precious times for us boys. We absorbed everything we could from our dad. We were fully aware of the financial situation of our family. We knew the costs of everything and the incomes of each product, and how much we owed to the banks and the Farm Credit Corp., how much the annual or semi-annual payments were on the machinery, and how much interest we were paying, etc. We knew the reasons for everything we did on the farm. There were no secrets kept from us even though we were only twelve or thirteen years old.

Dad enjoyed arguing, and he taught us to argue. Whichever position we would take on an issue, Dad was sure to challenge and test us by arguing for the opposite side. He was trying to teach us that there is always more than one way to look to an issue, and to be open-minded, fair, and reasonable in approaching them.

Dad taught us, by example, to treat one's neighbors as one would wish to be treated. One day the Elswicks called and wondered if they could borrow our manure spreader. Now, many people had been borrowing our new manure spreader, and it was getting worn and needed repairs. Dad said, "Sorry, it is broken down." Later, he noticed them out in their field spreading manure by hand from a stone-boat. Consequently, he fixed his spreader, then phoned them and told them to come and use it.

Dad taught us to value a good name above riches. As we were preparing to move back from Ontario to Alberta, one of our neighbors insisted that our bull had impregnated one of his heifers before she was mature enough, causing her to be a substandard cow. The neighbor demanded compensation.

This irritated Dad since he did not agree that it was our fault and since we had been on good neighborly terms for many years. We boys urged Dad to just ignore the man. In a few days we would be moving away, so what? But, on the day we were leaving, Dad stopped by and paid the man what he demanded. Dad reasoned, "I do not want to leave a bad name behind."

Chris Hansen

Our uncle Chris was an interesting character who was somewhat shorter and smaller than my dad, but stocky and strong. He tended to work very quickly and enthusiastically. He talked with a strong Danish accent. He was very sociable and had many friends. He was well informed and highly opinionated, but his opinions reflected a rational grasp of facts and basic common sense. When he talked, his words come out forcefully and emphatically in rapid staccato fashion. He had a good sense of humor and enjoyed using exaggeration in his speech to that effect.

When Chris moved to Ontario, following us in early 1949, he helped Dad get settled into farming. Then, he went looking for work. It was not hard for him to get a job, having the experience of three years in construction under the Nazis in Germany. Soon he found a job with a construction company, building bridges and other things around Fergus. He worked there most of the time during the first few years, but some of the time he was home helping us on the farm.

Then, he rented the Lloyd Mark farm just a mile west of our place, next to the Conestoga River. That was not a very satisfactory deal, so the next year he bought fifty acres about seven miles away on the 16th. To add to that, he rented another run-down farm, the "Vale place." His fifty acres were good, but the Vale place was no good, so he rented the one-hundred-acre "George French farm" just across the road from his.

During those years, we worked together in sharing machinery and in helping each other, especially during haying and harvesting time.

Later, Chris bought the one-hundred-acre farm from Mr. and Mrs. French. They were elderly and had only one young daughter, Doris, who later became a schoolteacher. We used to tease Chris about her, but she was so much younger than him. Anyway, Chris was a confirmed bachelor, so there was not much danger. Chris lived with the Frenches for several years. Finally, they moved to Arthur, and Chris lived alone and farmed for about sixteen years.

In retirement, Chris sold his farm and bought a house in Drayton where he lived for a few years. As he got older, his longtime friends, Leif and Margaret Larsen, took on the role of "family" and assisted him with his business.

Finally, he spent his last years living in a nursing home in Arthur, Ontario, where he died in 2005, aged ninety-two. His remains were cremated, and his ashes were scattered on his former farm. Chris was the only uncle on the Hansen side that I ever knew. When his estate was settled, each of us nephews received about $1,000.

Retreat from Ontario

Although Ontario was a good place to live, and we had a good farm and were getting ahead financially, Dad and Mom were not settled in their minds to stay. They were often homesick for Alberta and the home and family they left there. Mom did not like our big, cold, drafty house. She did not like the damp, cool climate that made her arthritic joints ache. She was not happy about the church situation at Berea, and she longed to be closer to her family.

Dad did not like keeping the cows in the damp, sweaty, stinky barn. He longed for the clear, dry, open skies of the prairies where he could keep the animals outside and feed them on the clean snow and where he never had to fork their manure. Therefore, for several years, they had advertised our farm for sale, but there were no takers.

In the fall of 1955, Peter had finished school and was helping at home. He was an industrious worker at age fifteen and had a great ambition to work together with Dad and the rest of us to make our farm shine. Things were beginning to fall into place for us, and our parents had about given up their quest to sell and return to Alberta. They had almost decided to settle down for good.

Then, one day in November, John Santing brought his Dutch father-in-law to look at the place. They looked it over carefully and talked awhile in their language. They wondered how much we were asking for the place, and whether we would sell it with the machinery and livestock included.

Dad was caught off guard and responded by quoting the price we had hoped to get a couple years prior. He forgot about the fact that we had bought quite a bit of new machinery since that time and the fact that land prices had begun escalating. The Dutchman, Mr. Radstake, said he would take it. Therefore, our 248 acres of land, forty-five head of dairy cattle, forty to fifty pigs, and a complete line of fairly new machinery were sold for $28,000, a real "steal!"

We boys were shattered, our dreams were shattered, and our world was shattered. Ontario was our home. Our friends were there. Our memories were rooted there. We did not want to move. We even threatened to commit suicide, rather than leave! Our parents were unmoved. Kids had no say. Not even fifteen-year-olds. The decision had been made. The agreement of sale signed. The money transferred. There was no turning back!

Hansen family in 1955 before leaving Ontario

The Radstakes were good people with whom to leave the farm. They were also a family of five sons and two daughters. Only, their youngest son was fourteen years of age, the same as our oldest. They were all big Dutchmen, all over six feet tall, strong, and diligent workers. They took over the chores at the end of December. Two of the boys lived with us for a few months until we moved out. We were amazed at how much the two could eat, more than all of us put together! Yet they did more work as well.

Dad went by train to Alberta to find a place for us to live. He came back with the report that he had bought a quarter section of irrigated land, just one mile south of the Clancy School on the highway, and he had found a temporary place for us to live until that farm could be vacated.

When Dad got back, we decided to sell all the contents of our house: furniture, dishes, and canned food. The exception to this was Mom's Maytag washing machine, sewing machine, stainless steel cookware set, a few dishes, and our clothes. We negotiated with the Radstakes and finally agreed to leave it all for $1,000: another "steal."

Then, Dad bought a nice used light blue 1953 Super 88 Oldsmobile. This was a beautiful car. It had a big V8 engine, automatic transmission, and radio. We had never known such luxury.

We packed the things we were shipping back to Alberta and sent them by train. Then, there was a round of farewell appointments with our dear friends.

Finally, on February 20, 1956, we had our last meal in Ontario at Clarence Huber's place. They had been such good neighbors. Now, we were leaving them as we drove away from all that was familiar and dear to us boys into a future that was unknown. We were sad, angry, and bitter. We tried to be open minded about the possibilities of a bright future in Alberta, yet stepping out into the unknown can be intimidating.

Our trip to Alberta was a historic undertaking for us. We had never had such a nice car. We had never taken a real family vacation trip of this magnitude, and we had never traveled in the United States before. For the first time in our lives, we got to sleep in motels. Our car was packed with eight people, and the trunk was full of our luggage. We were not little children anymore as Peter weighed two hundred and fifteen pounds, and I weighed at least one hundred and fifty.

We took the northern route through Michigan, rather than trying to go through Chicago. The bridge at the Mackinaw straits, which connects upper Michigan with lower Michigan, was under construction, so we had to use the ferry. We were impressed by the size of the new bridge. It was to be about five miles long. The pillars that hold the suspended roadbed were four hundred feet tall, and the roadbed was about two hundred feet above the water.

Finally, we reached the wide-open spaces of the prairies. The atmosphere was noticeably different. The air seemed lighter and clearer and the sky bluer. No more hazy, cloudy, dark, and dreary days. Five days and four nights after we left Ontario, we arrived at our grandparents' house near Duchess, Alberta.

It was already dark on that Friday evening, and no one noticed our car drive into the yard. We sent Peter to the door to ask if they could give a poor guy a bite to eat. Our fifteen-year-old aunt, Esther, came to the door in answer to his knock. She had not seen Peter since he was eight years old. She turned and said to her mother, "Mom, there is a bum out here who wants something to eat!" Grandmother came to see, and said, "Ah Peter!" She knew him immediately.

S I X

RE-PLANTING IN ALBERTA

We spent that night and the next two days crowded in the Friesen house. The next day, our parents went about arranging temporary lodging at Herman Grossfield's second house. On Sunday, we attended the Duchess Mennonite Church. It was surprising how people changed in seven years, especially to a seven-year-old boy who was now fourteen.

Our parents soon got used furniture together, and on Monday we squeezed our family of eight into the little Grossfield house, where we lived for about six weeks. That gave time for Mr. Skrobot to get his things moved off the place we bought from him.

A Raw Land Deal

Mr. Skrobot was about sixty-five years of age. He was thin with gray hair and had deep dark sunken eyes. He spoke broken English with a very heavy Polish accent, which we found extremely hard to understand. Having recently lost his wife to cancer, he was still grieving and lonely and trying to adjust.

He was selling his home place in an attempt to cut back. He had another farm a mile and a half east where he was moving his possessions and his livestock. He bought a house in Brooks where he could live in comfort. He would drive out every day, in his red Ford pickup, to care for his animals.

Dad had purchased this farm of 169 acres for $16,000. It was located halfway between or about six miles from either Brooks or Duchess on the east side of the then #36 highway. We boys were not overly impressed with this farm. It was much smaller than the one we sold in Ontario, and the buildings were all poorly built wooden shacks in various stages of decay and disrepair. The house was fairly large with two full stories. It had six bedrooms, a kitchen, living room, dining room, and bathroom.

The bathroom was just that, a room with a tub. It had no sink nor toilet. Water had to be carried in from the only working faucet in the house, the one at the kitchen sink, where we also washed our hands and face and hair, and where we shaved. We had to go outside to a rickety old "out house" and sit with the smells and the flies and the mosquitoes in summer, or with the hoar frost and ice in the winter, to pay our respects to the call of nature.

There was a furnace in the cellar, a small excavation under the house. One had to go outside, open the horizontal trap door, and descend some dilapidated indistinct steps sloping into the cellar hole.

The house was not as big as the one we had left behind, and it was not as nice, nor as well equipped. It did have a telephone and electricity. It was a wooden frame house covered with faded yellow and ugly red shingle siding. The wood was old, cracked, and leaky. When the wind blew outside, it was also windy inside. When it was cold outside, it was also cold inside.

The yard and outbuildings were also in the same advanced stage of decay and disrepair. There was an old, faded, red wooden barn, measuring about forty feet by eighty feet with a hayloft. It did not even have a cement floor. Old horse stalls had been converted into grain storage bins. There were a few stanchions on one side for milking cows and a chop bin.

There was also a pump house built over a drilled water well. The water had such a strong soda content that it fizzed a bit and gave you diarrhea if you drank too much at first, but we got used to it and enjoyed drinking it. In those days we still did not have a refrigerator, so we felt fortunate to have a well that produced cool water in the hot season. Most other people in the area drank warm water out of cracked cisterns, which tasted like chlorine or like duck wash mixed with alkali salts. There was an unsightly attempt by someone to build a coal shed out of railroad ties and sawmill slabs.

The main entrance to the farmstead from the road led to a wide area where a lot of the farm machinery and fuel tanks were kept. Out to the side of the main entrance was a car garage in which we parked our Oldsmobile.

Upon entry into the yard, the first prominent feature one would see was two dilapidated old grey sheds. Probably built by the pioneers in the earliest days of the Model T Ford, these sagging relics of a bygone era welcomed all visitors and passersby to form their first impressions of this farm!

This driving area was a horrendous mess. Because of seepage from the canal, the thick gray clay subsoil was always soft and spongy. If heavy vehicles came in or drove in the same tracks too often, the ground would open, and the wheels would go down. There seemed to be no bottom to it. Consequently, this yard was a rough, treacherous, quagmire the few months that it was not frozen solid.

East of the house, there was a large corral and feeding area for the range cattle and straw sheds for their shelter. To the south of the buildings was a large irrigation canal running through the farm, dividing off twenty acres on the southwest corner. Across this canal was the pig barn. It was in an even worse state of decay than the rest.

The yard was surrounded on three sides with four rows of old dying poplar and willow trees. At one time, this had been a nice shelterbelt, but now it was an eyesore and a nuisance. Every time there was a wind, more dead branches scattered over the yard and lawn.

The poplar trees produced a crop of cotton every June that, with a slight breeze, covered the homestead with a thick blanket of this white fluff. It seemed to get into everything. It clung to the window and door screens and found its way into the house. It stuck to one's hair, got into one's eyes, tickled one's nose, and got into one's food. The trees released this plague for about five weeks. The fallen cotton collected in irrigation ditches, lodged in the grass and shrubs, and covered the ground around the buildings, making an ugly sight until it was finally, with the assistance of a good rain, absorbed back into the soil.

Living beside the busy highway was another annoyance. We had to get used to the noise of the whizzing cars and the shaking of the house every time a heavy truck rumbled by at all hours of day and night.

During the dry times, a prevailing westerly wind brought a cloud of dust into our yard each time a vehicle passed. The fine, gray-brown dust would hang in the air and settle on every blade of grass, or leaf, or flower in our yard. It would seep into the house through the cracks and settle as a thick film on every piece of furniture. Mom's clean white laundry, hung out to dry, was gathered an hour or two later colored a definite shade of gray.

Dad got started farming right away by going out and buying enough pigs to fill the pig barn. We bought wheat and barley, which we ground to feed pigs. They grew quite well, and we kept at least fifteen of the best females for breeding purposes. These became the foundation stock for our future pig business.

He bought a used John Deere G. tractor and a complete line of John Deere farm machinery from a farmer through the help of Jim Martin, the John Deere dealer.

That spring, we seeded fifty acres of wheat and a large field of barley and another of peas for a cash crop. We thought we would make good money. We boys had to learn how to irrigate. I was assigned to irrigate the wheat field. This was a new experience for me. I noticed that out of a thirty-acre field, there was a small area, maybe eight acres, where the wheat was quite dark green and healthy looking. Of the rest, there were large sections where the grain did not sprout, and these areas were surrounded with wide bands where the wheat sprouted but remained stunted. I did not understand but thought that it must be too dry, so I watered it very well.

When we came to cut the ripe grain that fall, most of the field was little else but a rich assortment of weeds. There were large areas where even the weeds did not grow. There was only a white crust of alkali salts. I also found that, on those areas, even though the ground looked dry on the surface, one could easily get stuck in the sticky gray clay just beneath the dry crust. Seepage from the irrigation canal had waterlogged at least fifty acres of our farm, bringing up undesirable alkaline salts from the subsoil, and rendering the soil useless for agriculture.

This was a great disappointment to us all. Not only did we get a farm with poor buildings, but even the land was useless. Our crop averaged less than twenty bushels of wheat per acre. We had left a productive farm in Ontario for this!

When Dad had come in January to "spy out the land," there was ten inches of snow covering the ground, and Mr. Skrobot had showed him the horse barn full of wheat and bragged about how good the farm was. Dad believed him and bought the farm in good faith. Later, we learned that the wheat, that Dad saw, had been trucked in from the other farm for winter storage. It had not been produced on this farm. We were deceived and cheated. We had been dealt a raw deal!

Struggle to Belong

In Ontario, we older boys had been popular leaders among our peers in our small social world. We had only friends in school, church, and community. Now, the social world was much bigger, and the pecking order was firmly established. Suddenly, we were reduced to being outsiders, invaders, nobodies, unknown, and feeling unwanted.

Peter and I had the hardest time making the adjustment. We were the oldest; he was fifteen years of age and I just fourteen. We had come from an environment where we were secure and confident. We knew we were loved, respected, or at least accepted. We had friends, and we knew just how we stood in relationship to them. Socially, we felt we were "insiders."

Now, suddenly, all of that was gone. We had to break in, as "outsiders," into very tightly knit social circles, if we were to regain what we lost. Our self-confidence was shattered. We felt rejection. Were we as good as others, or were we really inferior? Why did people not open up to accept us? Were we really that repulsive or undesirable? If people would only be kind and give us a chance to prove that we were okay to have as friends.

This was an extremely painful time for us as growing adolescent boys. It took us a full three years before we made the adjustment and felt comfortable, as though we really belonged in that community.

In the first few weeks, several flirty fourteen- or fifteen-year-old girls did pay attention to us, and we were foolish enough to hope that they would replace our lost friends back home and give us an entrée into the social circle. However, we soon learned that we were being set up to being used. When we could not produce a car and lots of money for running them around, they soon found others to occupy their time.

My loneliness hit an all-time low one day in school when I said, "Hi!" to one of the above mentioned as I met her in the hallway at school. She lifted her haughty snoot and said, in what I felt to be a most disdainful voice, "Oh, go home!" I felt so bad, lonely, rejected, and homesick. I just thought to myself, "Girl, you have no idea how much it would please me to do just that!"

The older, more mature young people were gracious and kind to us from the start. We had our age-mate aunt Esther and uncles Edward and David who always befriended us. That made it bearable. For the rest, I found myself making friends with the other underdogs, the social rejects. They were friendly, humble, and accepted me. Maybe they weren't my kind of people, but at least they weren't snobbish, haughty, and cruel. We helped each other and were friends. It made my situation bearable.

In looking back, some good came out of it. It helped us Hansen brothers to be more sensitive to the needs of the stranger among us. Whenever a stranger showed up in our church or community, if it was not a Friesen, then it was usually one of the Hansen boys who went over to welcome him, talk to him, and even invite him home for dinner. Many a stranger, some of them less than desirable characters, shared hospitality in our home. Some of them became our friends; others taught us things we would never have learned otherwise. There is always a blessing that comes back, when being a blessing.

Irrigation and Mosquitoes

About as soon as the frost left the ground and the season of cotton was about finished, the season of mosquitoes settled in and tormented us. In the EID, the abundant availability of water filled many sloughs and marshes with stagnant water. These made excellent breeding grounds for the mosquitoes.

Consequently, by late June, there were trillions of mosquitoes hungrily searching for any bare patch of skin in which to sink their long proboscises and gorge themselves on the life-giving crimson flow beneath. Even horses and cows were not immune to their smothering attacks. Farmers, who cared for their animals, often burned a smudge fire at night so their animals could find release from the mosquitoes in its smoke.

The mosquito population seemed to reach saturation point when it was time to irrigate the tall alfalfa, just before haying time. Unless the day was extremely hot with a dry wind blowing, the mosquitoes would bother the irrigator all day long. In the cool calm evenings, they would be overwhelming.

I used to put on a long-sleeved jacket to keep covered, even if the temperature was ninety-five degrees, because they drill right through shirts and even worn denim trousers. I would pull up the collar to reach the back of my cap, put on gloves, and then go out to do battle, while I tried to set the canvas dikes for the evening.

Wherever I went, a gray column of high-pitched, whining, bloodthirsty insects swirled above my head. While I worked furiously, I would wipe blood-ballooned mosquitoes off my face every few seconds, killing them by the dozens. At that stage, they showed no signs of fear of death. Like kamikaze fliers, they would just keep coming as fast as I could wipe them off.

The more I swatted, the slower I got the work done, and the more I perspired and gasped for air. The more I gasped for air, the greater the danger of one or more of the determined tormentors getting sucked down my windpipe and into my chest, which then caused me to cough and choke and gasp for air even more desperately, which, in turn, increased the likelihood that more mosquitoes would get sucked in.

When I finally got the water set for the night, I would stagger out of the field, looking and feeling like I had just survived a major battle: gasping for breath, sweat running down my face, mixing with the mud from my soiled gloves, my stolen blood, and the corpses from a thousand flattened foes, not to mention my face and neck, feeling swollen and hot like a burning pin cushion.

These mosquitoes were a large healthy strain. There were many mosquito jokes. It was said by those old-timers, who should know, that a certain enterprising man once tried to train some of these big mosquitoes to drill wells. However, one night they got loose and flew away with his horses! What a disappointing end to such a promising economic venture!

The Highway

The "highway" alongside which we lived was something to be experienced in itself. At one time it was called "Highway #1," the main "Trans-Canada Highway" that stretched from Halifax to Vancouver Island. By the time we moved to Alberta, it was called the "#36" as a new asphalted "Trans-Canada Highway" had been built, running east and west and by-passing Duchess. In the late nineteen fifties, a new highway #36 was built, running north and south and bypassing Brooks and Duchess altogether.

But at the time we moved there, in the mid nineteen fifties, this old #36 carried all the north-south traffic through Duchess and Brooks and the regions beyond. Although it was a busy main artery, it was a poorly maintained gravel road that was either muddy or dusty and always rough. In times of rain, it became a greasy, muddy quagmire from which cars often skidded out of control into its deep side ditches or got stuck in its many boggy places. Vehicles traveling on this road got coated with a thick layer of sticky, brownish-gray clay muck. In dryer times, every passing vehicle was followed by a huge lingering cloud of dust.

One enterprising neighbor had a large bog hole in front of his property in which vehicles often got stuck. He kept his tractor close by and charged the victims ten dollars, in those days a bit exploitative, for a tow through the mud hole. Rumors had it that at night he would haul water into the bog hole to keep it wet and profitable! What rumors! What neighbors!

When the sun eventually dried out this "highway," it became hard and rough, like a washboard, with sunbaked crooked ruts that made cars rattle and shake and swerve back and forth as they sped along.

Weeks after, a maintainer would come along and grade the surface a bit and fill the ruts with loose particles. As speeding oncoming cars hurtled past each other (and they never seemed to go slow), they left each other a shower of rocks, pebbles and a thick cloud of suffocating and vision-obscuring dust. Even the newest cars on this road soon had pitted, cracked, or smashed windshields and stone chipped paint. Insurance on windshields cost about the same as new glass, so most people took their chances. As a result, many local cars looked like they had spent a Sunday in a crash up derby.

To make it worse, this highway was crossed with an irrigation canal at least once every mile. This meant that there was a narrow wooden bridge at each crossing. At that time, these bridges were old and in such a state of decay that it made each one a potential bump or speed trap, with the potential to send a speeding car hurtling into an abbreviated orbit.

To meet a speeding car in a thick cloud of dust on one of these narrow, broken bridges, was a hair-raising experience, to say the least. One never could know if a second speeding car might be overtaking the front car somewhere in that swirling cloud of dust. One always took a deep breath, that well might be his last, before plunging blindly into the approaching cloud.

Some drivers on this road were madmen. It seemed like this road brought out the worst in a person. It was so horrible that they drove, not for pleasure, but to get the inevitable suffering over as quickly as possible. The occasional cautious driver, who stayed within the bounds of reasonable safety, was seen as a road hazard that needed to be passed by as soon as possible. No one wanted to stay behind to eat the other's dust, so normally sane, but now "demonized" drivers would pass at eighty or ninety miles per hour, even in a cloud of dust where the visibility was zero. On that road, many a vehicle was demolished, and many a soul took the shortcut to eternity!

Dad tried to keep his lovely Oldsmobile off this road as much as possible. One should try to have something nice when needed. We teenaged boys were given the keys to the shaky old "corn binder," our battered International pickup truck, when we needed a vehicle. On one rare occasion, when I was sixteen, Dad sent me alone to Duchess on an errand with the Oldsmobile.

So far, we had never assessed its maximum capacity for speed. On the way home from Duchess, I decided there was no time like the present to conduct this much-needed assessment.

Soon the Oldsmobile was hurtling over the loose gravel at one hundred miles per hour, and still gaining. I realized that I was no longer driving the car. I was just aiming it. If anything would happen, it would be over very quickly.

A microscopic grain of wisdom showed itself, or I lost my courage, and lifted my foot. I never did find out just how fast that "Super 88" could go. But I'll never forget how that rutted gravel road felt at one hundred! And I certainly never told Dad!

A New Consolidated School at Duchess

The Clancy School had been closed while we were in Ontario. We were picked up by bus and taken to the new consolidated school at Duchess each morning and brought back at night. This was a new experience. The school was so big with over 160 kids in twelve grades. All the grade seven and grade eight children shared one classroom and were taught by one teacher, Mrs. Krause. There were fifteen students including me in grade eight.

In Ontario, I had been the top student in my class of one, without working to stay ahead! I did not know what competition was, and I had developed very lazy work habits. Suddenly, well past the middle of the school year, I was plopped into a new school, which had a different curriculum, with a teacher who made us work, among students who were used to doing homework and who knew how to compete. I enjoyed the teacher, but the boys were rough and immature in my way of thinking. The girls were, of course, gorgeous, but hard for a shy boy to get to know.

In Ontario, our teacher expected us to work alone during the class period, while she helped the lower grades. We never had "homework." Here, the teacher talked to us through the whole period, gave us an assignment at the end of the period, then went on to the next lesson of the next subject.

How I wished she would keep quiet for once and let me work. I worked in class during the spare periods, but I never took work home. I did not know or notice that we were expected to do at least two hours of homework each night. I wondered how the other students had their assignments done the next day when I did not.

When the final exams were corrected in late June, I rated alarmingly low in the hierarchy of class percentage marks. In fact, I stood second from the bottom of the class, and the boy below me failed. I had scraped into grade nine "by the skin of my teeth."

In the fall of 1956, I entered ninth grade. Mr. Jonathan Siemens was our teacher that year. There were fifteen students in a classroom that we occupied all by ourselves. That was a welcome new experience for me. I started at the bottom of the list of achievers. I liked the teacher and the lessons, and I began to make friends. I had a long way to climb.

Sometime in October, I was riding home on the school bus, sitting beside my classmate and friend, Fred Hiebert. He, seeing that I carried no books with me, asked me if I did not have any homework. I said, "No, I never do homework." Then I looked at him and noticed that he was carrying a load of books. I looked at the other students and saw that they all were carrying books home. Then I asked Fred if he had homework and if he always took work from school to do at home. He did.

Suddenly, the light dawned on me that it was expected of us that we would complete our assignments at home if we did not finish them at school. Then I understood why the others seemed to have their assignments completed when I did not. After this realization, I determined to take my unfinished assignments home as well.

I would come home from school and do the farm chores like feeding the pigs and caring for the cows and calves, then eat supper at around eight o'clock. When that was done, there were dishes to do if it was my turn. After all was done, it would be nine o'clock in the evening when I would begin to do homework. Sometimes I worked up to eleven or twelve o'clock. The family would be sleeping.

My parents did not understand my doing homework. I was treading ground they had never trod. At first Dad scolded me, saying that schoolwork should be done at school. The only reason I could be bringing it home was because I was not working at school. Gradually my parents got used to it.

It paid off. In the November report, I ranked in the middle of my class. By the mid-year report period, I had risen to fourth place. I tied with Ronnie Klaut for third place in the Easter report. Ella Torkelson and Edith Burkholder were unbeatable. At the end of the year, we sat for the Provincial Examinations, and I passed with good grades.

That year in school, I joined the senior football team. I was a lineman. I was a healthy 165 pounds and stood five feet ten and three quarters inches. I was strong, but no athlete. I was good on the defensive line, because I could get in the way of the opponent, and stay in the way, but I was too slow and clumsy for anything else. We had a good team that year and beat all the other schools in the EID. Although we represented one of the smaller schools, we were the champions of 1956, and we were mighty proud of it.

Some of my special friends were Barry Rust, who wanted to be a politician, Fred Hiebert, and James Roth. Barry and Fred were both clowns. There were two closets in the classroom, one at the front, and one at the back. One day, they each hid in one of those closets. The bell rang and the teacher noted the two boys missing and started the class. Twenty minutes later, one of them could not stifle a sneeze. The teacher walked over and opened the door and out he came. Then he walked over to the other door and discovered the other missing person. The class roared with laughter.

The highlight that year was our class's weekly trip to take shop at the school in Rosemary, twelve miles away. The Rosemary School had facilities for woodworking and home economics classes. Our teacher was Mr. Parker. He had a twisted personality, was likeable, yet in some ways, was very gruff and repugnant. He was around retirement age. He was dirty, rumpled, and unkempt. He spoke rough to us, yet he was soft hearted. If you were respectful, which we seldom were, he would take a liking to you and do almost anything to help you.

However, he lost control of the class. Towards the end of the year, there was no respect left. Boys would skip class and run up town, go behind the class and smoke, or do whatever they liked. They began to play tricks on him, like lift a pile of boards in the supply stacks and squirt glue between them and set them down again or paint other people's projects.

One day he was giving us a lesson explaining some deep technical truth. Fred was bored. He looked out the window and saw some local girls going by, so he suddenly interrupted the boring monologue of the teacher, as if he did not exist, by saying, in a loud voice, "Bob, do you think there are any pretty girls in Rosemary?" The rest of the class just roared with laughter. The teacher lost them entirely.

That was the year I got my first pair of glasses, the kind with reddish brown plastic stems and tops, with gold-colored metal nosepiece and supports under the lenses. I thought, at the time, they were cool, but my children, years later, thought they were "nerdy." Anyway, I am sure of one thing, even if they did not make me look good, they did help me to see well.

At the end of school in June 1957, I took the final government administered examinations and bid all my new friends "Goodbye!" Even though I enjoyed it, I was through with school. I was fifteen and one-half years old. I had enough education. I was going to become a farmer!

Freda: A Bonus Blessing

In a way, Freda was as one born out of season, maybe that is why she is so special to us all. However, during the time of our mother's pregnancy and at her birth, to us boys, she was an unwanted intruder. Our mother was looking for a girl ever since Peter's birth. That I was not a daughter was her first disappointment. And after four disappointments, there still was no baby girl.

Then during the seven years in Ontario, there were no new births at all. Mom was not to be thwarted. She wanted a girl, and planned for a girl, and applied for a girl. Then we got our girl. We were delighted to have Linda to make our family complete. We were satisfied.

Then our whole world turned upside down when we sold our farm in Ontario. The jolt must have shaken something loose in our parents, for with the move to Alberta came an unexpected pregnancy. Perhaps the transition provided Dad with too much free time! We teenage boys were angry about that, too. We were embarrassed. Six kids were enough. Our family was complete. Large families were no longer in vogue. We did not want more kids. When would this stop anyway? Did we have to be like the Friesens or the Hubers or the Torkelsons and have a dozen kids?

When the birth finally came on November 4, 1956, we brothers were still upset. When our aunt Esther congratulated Peter at church that Sunday and asked some question about the birth, he growled loudly back at her, "I do not know, and I do not care!" Bystanders were shocked.

But when baby Freda was brought home, we had to admit she was irresistibly cute. We boys chose her name, "Freda Joy." She brought much joy to our home. It was interesting to have a baby around again. We enjoyed playing with her and teaching her to walk and talk. We would swing her around upside down and toss her into the air and catch her just before she crash-landed. She would scream with laughter. Freda was an indispensable addition to our family, an additional unsolicited bonus blessing!

Though she was small, Freda had a way of making an impact on our lives. I would sit at the dining table in the evenings doing my homework while Mom would go about putting the smaller children to bed. Freda's bedroom door was just behind my back. Mom would get her ready for bed, which meant taking her to the potty, washing face, hands, and feet, giving her a drink, taking her to the bedroom and tucking her in, telling or reading her a bedtime story, kissing her goodnight, and turning off the light. Then Mom would go about getting the older children into their places of rest.

When that was done, and Mom was about ready to settle her tired and aching bones into an easy chair, a small voice could be heard coming from the half-closed door behind my back,

"Mom, I want a drink!"

It brought the response, "You've had your drink. Now, go to sleep!"

That argument was never heard. Soon the little voice increased in volume with each repetition. And each response of protest that Mom made fell on deaf ears and only stimulated a louder demand.

Then Mom tried the silent treatment. Ignore the demand and maybe the need will go away. When shouting did not get the desired results, the young lady resorted to her last, most effective weapon: tears. The casual observer would have thought that such agony of thirst would have left no moisture for such tears. Soon there came from behind me a whimpering and then a rising storm of intense wailing. Soon Mom rushed in with the desired drink.

"Now, lay down and go to sleep!"

The satisfied "cherub" lay down quietly and closed her tear-filled eyes.

As soon as Mom's weight sunk into the deepest part of her chair, a small voice behind me would start up the next part of the nightly script,

"Mom, I wanna go potty!"

Again, there would be an exchange of a series of admonitions and demands, each round a little louder and more insistent, always leading through tears on the part of the underdog to ultimate victory.

After the second trip to the potty, and Mom just got through the first paragraph of her book, the little voice behind me would start up again with another round of demands.

This would go on for most of an hour, until finally, there would be the cruel but needed application of the firm hand of discipline, accompanied by howls of great pain and humiliation that quickly subsided into quiet sniffles and then the deep satisfying breathing of contented sleep.

Little Freda demonstrated a bent for scientific investigation. For example, she and her cousin Tom Grove undertook to verify if there were indeed little chicks in each of the hatching eggs. She also showed deep compassion and humanitarian concern for the unfortunate. One day her pet cat got sick. It was shivering, so she put it in the stove oven to warm it up. A cat really does have nine lives, for it was discovered just in time. But chickens do not have nine lives, for when she poured water down the gullets of sick chickens, they died.

Slowing Down

As Grandpa and Grandma Jacob and Justina Friesen got older, fewer activities revolved around them, and more of the action revolved around their growing children. By the mid 1950's, the older children had all abandoned the nest and spread out in every direction to seek their careers. Some found their mates and started nests of their own. The youngest were to finish their high school years within the decade. When our parents moved our family back from Ontario, it was possible to have the first Friesen Family Reunion at Duchess in 1956. A head count at that time indicated that the family had grown to forty-two in number.

In the late 1950's, Jacob Friesen gave up farming altogether. He had always been a part-time farmer, finding temporary employment away from home as a carpenter, laborer, handyman, or whatever. Now he would go into that kind of employment full-time. He never stuck to one job very long. He was always restless, finding something that did not suit him about the job, the working conditions, the boss, or the wages. There was always a good reason to move on.

When they reached age sixty-five, Jacob and Justina both retired on the government old-age pension. They were used to living on little, and now they were happy and able to retire on little.

SEVEN

REACHING FOR MANHOOD

Ambitious Peter Takes on the Adult World

From my birth I shared the same bedroom and the same bed with my brother, Peter. I was always in his shadow until he left school the last fall we were in Ontario. Then, I was forced to step into the real world on my own. While Peter stayed home from school that year, he started to take grade nine by correspondence, with the possibility that I would, in turn, stay out to help Dad the next year, and Peter would return to high school in grade ten.

However, then we moved to Alberta, and that changed everything. Peter dropped correspondence studies, and, since there was not enough work on the little farm to occupy two men, he accepted opportunities to work for neighbors on a day-to-day basis. I continued through grade nine. That year, Dad rented the Dumka farm. It had a quarter section of hard-to-irrigate land and two quarters of pastureland with about forty Hereford cows on it.

In Ontario, Dad had made a promise that when each boy finished grade eight, he would be given a heifer calf. Peter had received his calf a few months before we moved. The heifer was left behind.

Now since we did not have a dairy farm anymore, the agreement was changed to a pregnant gilt instead. Peter got to choose one out of Dad's herd. He chose the only black one. It gave birth to ten piglets, which he weaned and sold for ten dollars apiece. It later gave birth to ten more piglets, and again he sold them for ten dollars apiece. He was into big money. He became a confirmed capitalist.

In the spring of 1957, Peter got his first real job working out for Hero Takeda, a rancher, farmer, and feedlot operator near Rosemary. He was Japanese Canadian and had a Japanese cook and housekeeper. Peter boarded with them and was paid $125 per month and $175 for irrigating months.

During those first few months, Dad drove him to work every Sunday afternoon and got him back Saturday nights. It was nice to have him home. Then Peter bought his first car, a used 1950 Chevrolet, a gray two-door sedan with a long-slanted back. He was immensely proud of that car and spent a lot of money to fix it up with fender skirts and shiny black paint. He and his new friend, Doug Schindelier, fixed up the inside with red door panels, interior lights, etc.

Although he was only sixteen years old, Peter was already establishing a reputation as an industrious worker. He learned how other people lived, worked, and did things. He learned something about the Japanese culture.

The cook was a thirty-five-year-old woman who smoked. One day, Peter got into her cigarettes and dug out the tobacco from the end of one of them and implanted a nice little firecracker and covered the fuse with tobacco and put it back in its place.

Sometime later, the woman was in the outhouse doing what people usually do there. She decided it was a peaceful time to enjoy a cigarette. When it blew up in her face, she was so shocked, she jumped right off the seat and out the door! That evening she was still upset with Peter.

Hero was a hard-nosed and hard-hearted businessperson. He worked hard and expected complete loyalty and total devotion to his cause from his employees. Peter learned much from him about farm and feedlot management and about demanding work. After he worked there for five months, he felt exhausted and depressed by how Hero treated him.

Then one day, Hero provoked him to a confrontation and fired him. Peter was deeply humiliated by his "failure," but took consolation when an associate told him that his staying with Hero for a full five months was a record for Hero's employees.

Peter helped us brand the calves that summer and worked with us for a few days.

John Martin recognized Peter as a good man and offered him a job in his hay business. His wages were $150 per month, without room and board. This time, since he boarded at home and drove to work every day, we enjoyed having him home in the evenings and on weekends.

John Martin was a hay dealer. His customers were feedlot operators, ranchers, local dairy farmers, and some farmers in Saskatchewan who were often dried out and came to the irrigated EID area to buy the much-needed hay. John had two three-ton trucks and a crew of three to deliver the hay. In most cases, the hay that was to go to Saskatchewan was loaded onto railroad boxcars and shipped out.

The work was hard, and the hours were long and the wages exploitative. There were not many men that would stay with that job. But Jimmy Kingston, Cork Plett, and Peter Hansen were a tough team that worked well together.

Peter worked for John Martin for two years. During this time, he reached the full power of his manhood and could hold his own against the best, as far as work was concerned.

His Chevrolet had major problems, so he traded it for a pretty lemon yellow 1956 Pontiac. Now he was stepping around in style. He invested his wages in young cattle, which he kept with Dad's herd.

Jimmy Kingston left his employment with John Martin after many legendary years of service and got a job with the EID. Peter and Cork continued until in the spring of 1959, when Don Anderberg offered Peter a job driving his truck hauling mostly grain. The hours were only eight hours a day instead of ten or more, and five days a week instead of six, and the wages were $210 per month instead of $175.

Therefore, Peter left Martin's establishment and went to haul hay and grain for Mr. Anderberg. Peter enjoyed his new job. There was much less hassle, the hours were more agreeable, and he was more relaxed. He learned much about the grain and feed business, which stood him in good stead when he started his own business, later.

My Brief Farming Career

I had decided I was going to follow in the footsteps of my ancestors and take up farming as my profession. Having completed ninth grade, I thought I knew all I needed to know to be a good farmer, so I quit school. I planned to work with Dad for a few years, and then he would help me get started. Besides the farm we owned, we were renting the Dumka farm. Now, we also rented the other Skrobot farm. It was a hilly, hard-to-irrigate farm with about 120 acres of fairly good soil.

By this time, we had sold our John Deere tractor and bought an old WD9 International Diesel. We had an old Case hay baler that never worked properly. We wasted so much time trying to fix it that our hay crop was lost in the re-growth. In the end, the hay was black and worthless. The old baler cost us more in lost crops than it would have cost us to purchase a new baler- an expensive lesson we learned the hard way.

That summer I worked hard on the farm. While driving the tractor around and around the fields day after day, and while watching the water slowly flooding the parched fields, I had much time to think. I thought about my future. I planned how I would get my own farm and how I would fix it up and make it into the model farm of which every farmer dreams.

Then, I would think beyond that achievement and ask the fatal question that always provokes despair and disillusionment: "What then?" When all my farming goals are achieved, when all the buildings are built, trees planted, fences made, and everything painted up nice, then what next?

Well, there will be maintenance. Paint will peel off, wood will decay, barns and houses will become outdated, even trees will need to be pruned, or they will die and need to be replaced. But maintenance isn't overly exciting, and what will happen when the next generation takes over and remodels, rebuilds, or bulldozes and starts over again? What will remain of all my efforts? What of real lasting value will I leave behind?

I saw that all my goals were too shortsighted, too transient, and only of passing value. I only walk this way once. I only have one life to invest. What is the best way to invest it? What can I do during my short stay on this earth that will have permanent value? What can I do that will have made this world a better place for my having been here?

Slowly, the answer became clear to me that the only permanent things are the eternal realities such as God and human beings who are made in his image. The most lasting and worthwhile investment of my limited life's time and energies would be to invest it in other people. Ultimately, my life will be worthwhile only in as much as it touches and influences other human beings in a positive way that helps them realize their potential as immortal beings in relationship to an eternal God.

I pondered the question: Is my goal to be a successful farmer big enough to have any ultimate meaning? Is working hard to contribute to the stockpiles of surplus butter, surplus wheat, or surplus meat really all that God made me, protected me, and saved me for?

Even while seeding the fields in the spring, back in Ontario, I used to pray to God to bless our crops and our farming enterprise, but usually, he was not extra good to us and ignored my selfish prayers. He did not treat us any better than our neighbors who swore and worked on Sundays and did not go to church. In fact, some of our crops were downright failures.

I found it hard to accept. If God is able, and if he really loves us, then why doesn't he hear my prayers and bless our crops? Surely, we would soon be rich if everything produced according to its potential. It would be so nice for us, and certainly it would not cost him any effort on his part. Did he not love us? Did he have something against us? Maybe he has not forgiven or overlooked our sins?

Now in Alberta, the pattern continued. I prayed, but God did not bless our efforts. After finishing eighth grade, Dad gave me a bred gilt. It bore me three piglets. Two of them died. Obviously, God was not smiling on my ambition to be a successful hog farmer! I had even promised to pay him a tithe of ten percent, but he did not seem interested. Peter's sow produced and raised ten piglets twice each year. Was he a better Christian than I? I kept the one piglet and raised it for a brood sow. But it would not get pregnant. Its "modern mother" would not get pregnant again either.

Therefore, I eventually sold them both and invested the money in purchasing a two-month-old Landrace female piglet, shipped by train from Fergus, Ontario, for the steep price of $150. Local pigs of that size were selling for about twelve dollars at that time. This was the time when "Landrace" was the latest fad among Canadian hog producers.

The piglet was a lovely little animal if a pig can be called "lovely." It was long and lean with the characteristic drooping ears. I was proud of it. I anticipated my success. I would be one of the first Landrace producers in our community. I would sell each of her many offspring for maybe fifty to one-hundred dollars at weaning.

Dad bought a Landrace boar, so when the pig grew up, we had her bred by the boar. But she would not conceive. Did someone clue her in on the latest trend in family planning?

Finally, six months late, she conceived, and on a cold November night she bore thirteen long, lean beautiful Landrace piglets. But the night was cold. I was not home at the time to attend to her, and no one else attended her either. All but three of the piglets died on the spot due to the cold. Two of those died before they were old enough to sell. By this time, the country was saturated with Landrace pigs, and they were not worth any more than any other pigs on the market.

The mother again refused to conceive for about a year. Eventually she did, and we raised and marketed five pigs from her. In that way, since Dad provided the feed, I was able to recoup the excessive money I had paid for their mother. Then she would not get pregnant again for a long time, so I shipped her off to the market as well. That was the end of my envisioned "Hansen Landrace Hog Farm" business.

I invested the pig money in four sheep at the same time my brother, Paul, bought three sheep with the idea that we would start a sheep ranching business. Paul soon tired of sheep and sold his share to me. Then I bought seven old sheep for a cheap price of a couple dollars each.

About a week after I bought them from Paul, I noticed the sheep were not hungry in the morning when I went to feed them. I found out they had discovered a hole in the chop bin and had helped themselves. It seemed they had collaborated to commit mass suicide. Now they were sick and began to bloat. They started to die, one by one, until seven of my fourteen were dead. This provoked another theological question: If they had to die, why did God not let them die while Paul still owned a share in them? Why me?

But Paul was not immune to the suicidal intentions of his livestock either. For about the same time, when it was his turn, our dad had given him a pregnant gilt to raise. It was almost ready to deliver when it got out of its pen and was roaming around the yard.

Behind our house was a barrel planted in the ground to catch the drainage water from our kitchen sink. The barrel was uncovered and was, of course, full of sewage water, and the pig, being a pig, thought that would be just a fine concoction to assuage its thirst. I do not know if suicide to escape the potential horrors of motherhood was on its mind, but it put, not only its mouth in the filthy broth, but, being a pig, also put its front feet into its drink. Not finding a solid footing, the whole body lost its balance and went headfirst into the barrel.

It could not back out. Mom saw it from the kitchen window, struggling in vain to reverse itself from its suicidal decision. She ran out to rescue it, but it being a full-grown sow stuck headfirst in a barrel, was too heavy and it took too long to call the farms' "rescue squad." The men came running, but it was too late. The victim was pronounced "dead on arrival."

Paul, of course was devastated. But Dad, being a father and man of mercy and believer in second chances, gave him another pig to replace his grievous loss. In the end, Paul was able to prosper.

As for me, thankfully, the rest of my sheep bore lambs when lambing time came around the next April. I liked raising sheep. After another two years, I had about sixty head of them.

First Timid Ventures out of the Nest

During the winter of 1957-1958, I did not have much work to do on the farm. It was Christmas time, and my uncle Edward was driving to Tofield, Alberta, to visit his sister, Annie, who had married Lyle Roth and was living there. "Would I like to go along?" Would I ever! I had a deep longing to travel and see all the places that people talked about, so I went along.

It was a weekend. Lyle was working on a bread truck route and lived in Ryley at the time. Annie had two little boys, Art and Curtis.

I was not overly impressed with Tofield. It was cold, and the farmers kept their cows inside dark, sweaty little barns that were depressing to me. I met "Mennonites" there who were obviously Mennonites, but their behavior did not strike me as very "Christian." Up to then, I was not aware that you could be the former without being the later.

A middle-aged Mennonite man was with the young people at a hockey rink. He was using foul language and telling and laughing at filthy jokes. I was not impressed with his role model. My first exposure to Tofield and the church community there was negative.

If at that time you would have told me that I would live there some day and love it, I would not have believed you for a minute. I had made a negative judgement of a whole community based upon a limited exposure to a small segment of the much bigger and more wholesome body of God's people.

On very short notice, I heard that there was going to be a five-weeks long winter Bible school in the Mountain View Mennonite Church near Kalispell, Montana. I heard there was a vehicle going down from Alberta, and there was room for one more. I made sure that on January 11, 1958, I was filling that space.

The vehicle was a VW bus, one of those famous machines that can seat twelve people and store their luggage on top of the motor which was at the back. The driver had to shift gears every time there was the slightest change in altitude, and the motor gave out its famous whine every time he changed the gears.

Ed Yoder from Smith was the driver of this bus. From Duchess, he picked up Joanne and Doreen Ramer, besides me. We went down to Sterling in Southern Alberta to pick up Katie Wipf and then crossed the border at Cardston and crossed the mountains into the Flathead Valley. There we found the home of Dan Brenneman, a preacher near Kalispell, and his wife, Mary, where we were warmly welcomed.

I was billeted in the home of Dan and Mary Brenneman, along with four preachers: Clarence Ramer, Milo Stutzman, Harold Boettger, and Stanley Shantz. I shared a bed with Ed Yoder, the eighteen-year-old son of Willis Yoder, also a preacher. I really felt close to God in that holy atmosphere! These were real men of God. I was impressed by their piety, genuine joy, and fervent faith as they visited, joked, and shared. I wanted to have what they had. I wanted to know God the way they did.

The Flathead Valley was a different world. While the climate on the prairies was so cold, clear, and dry, this valley was like a different planet. The clouds hung over the mountains to the south and east most of the time. The winter weather was mild, and the air was humid. There was a lot of snow, but also a lot of rain and drizzle, and the snow melted soon. People burned wood or sawdust in their stoves. Many of the people worked in the forests or in wood-related businesses. The mountains were beautiful and protected the people from high winds. To me, it felt like a winter paradise, and I loved it.

Winter Bible School was held in the church building where Clarence Ramer, Stanley Shantz, and Milo Stutzman were the main teachers. There were about twenty-five young people and some community folks attending during the day. At night, other young people who worked or went to public schools during the daytime came from the community.

We were given two meals a day there. Our breakfasts were served at the host's home. During breaks, there was time to socialize, and I made new friends. I felt so free. People accepted me for who I was. I sensed no cliques, snubbing, nor snobbery like I lived with at Duchess. I found the lessons interesting and learned a lot, but I learned even more from the people with whom I lived and associated.

This was a very life-changing experience for me. I was away from all my family and relatives in a new setting for the first time in my life. Now I was under nobody's shadow, and I felt free for the first time. Now I could relate to strangers and make friends based on who they found me to be, not based on what they thought of my big brother or my parents or my grandparents. Now, it was up to me to be the real me and to fail or succeed socially on my own!

Another barrier I broke there was the dating barrier. Up to that time, I had never dated a girl. I was shy and timid and deeply hurt by the social climate at Duchess. I lacked self-confidence and had no idea how I should act on a date. By this time Ed Yoder and I were becoming good friends. He was two years older than I, and was, I presumed, wiser in the ways of courtship. He suggested that we create a little excitement for ourselves by asking some girls out, so we made plans. He got the vehicle reserved, and we decided which ones we would investigate first.

There was a certain fourteen-year-old girl that was very friendly to me that I thought was very pretty and easy to get to know. However, she hung around me too much and embarrassed me with the immature things she said. Then, there was a nineteen-year-old girl who was intelligent, sensible, modest, and pretty as well, but she was three years older than me. The time came to ask someone. I did not have a large reserve of nerve, but I managed to kill two birds at once when, in front of the immature one, I asked the more mature one, if she would go out with me for the evening. I scored when she said, "Yes!"

Ed and I had a fun time taking the girls home that evening. For a week or so the immature one was cool towards me, but then she started to warm up again. This time, I asked a bishop's daughter out right in front of her again. This girl was about my age, was intelligent, and good looking. She knew how to carry herself with confidence and courtesy and knew how to put a shy fellow at ease and show him an interesting time. I thought this one was about as good as I could do, so we had several dates. It was exciting, and I was up in cloud nine for sure. She agreed to write to me when it was time for me to return to Alberta.

I was different, and everything seemed to be different when I returned home. I was not as shy anymore. I had more self-confidence. I was okay and began to feel sorry for the "snobs." I began to see them as prisoners locked into their own little world while missing the much bigger and varied world out there.

I got home in time to do the income tax returns for my parents. They said, since I was the only family member who had completed grade nine and had the most education, I was the most qualified to do it. They gave me a shoebox full of receipts and bills and the bank records, and I went to work.

I discovered that our gross income exceeded our deductible expenses by $400, without deducting any depreciation for machines or buildings. This meant that Dad and I had worked for nothing, and our net worth decreased by the amount our assets depreciated, plus what the family consumed, minus $400. Farming was not going well for us in Alberta at all.

About this time, I had a keen sense of destiny experience. Mom and Dad were discussing something about our church leadership. Our pastor was getting older, and Dad said to Mom, "I wonder who will take his place when the time comes."

The thought came to me, "Perhaps it will be me." I did not say a word to anyone about this. But then and there, I just knew that I was "called." Unworthy, inadequate, and weak as I was, I was destined for church leadership. I was completely amazed by the thought, but I kept it inside and pondered how this could be so.

The Ecstasy and Agony of Courtship

Soon we were busy preparing the land for seeding. I received a total of three letters from the wonderful girl just over the Rockies. The first two were just the fuel I needed to keep me going. But the third was the standard "Dear John" letter. I was a wonderful guy, but at the ripe age of fifteen, she was too young, and her parents did not approve, so we better be "just friends." I did not agree with the arguments in the letter and did not like it much, but what else was there to do except accept the depressing fact that "life is nasty, brutal, and short!"

At the end of June, our congregation hosted the annual meeting of our Alberta-Saskatchewan Conference. Such conferences were known in the area by some as the "Mennonite mating season." These conferences were organized with the whole family in mind, with activities for all.

The young people from all the congregations in Alberta, Saskatchewan, and Montana would come, and of course, eagerly scrutinize the latest crop of potential mates. Youth activities were organized, and after the programs there was the remainder of the night for dating, if one was lucky enough to land a date. It was awfully long and lonely for those who lacked the courage or good fortune to get a date.

It was a time when local girls wouldn't even look at local boys. In fact, many local couples "broke up" just before conference time. They had to keep themselves available for the "prince charmings" that came riding in their steel chargers from exotic and romantic places like Tofield, Guernsey, Carstairs, or Kalispell.

This time it was Peter's good fortune to land a date with one of the princesses from Guernsey, Saskatchewan. His careful grooming and his yellow Pontiac paid off. It was his first date, and he was elated and madly "in love."

I was not so lucky, as one girl I asked said she was "booked." I wondered what she meant by that. Did she entertain "clients" like a professional, that she could be "booked" in advance? I was too timid to ask.

Peter's catch led to letter writing and then a trip or two to Guernsey in the fall. On his second trip, he took along his friends Ed Friesen and Doug Schindelier. Of course, they had to find dates there too, or the trip would have been a disaster. Ed came back very much "in love."

Soon after, Peter got his first "Dear John" letter. All the photos he had taken and all the lovely gifts he had lavished upon her were returned to him. How could young love wither on the vine and die so soon? Some "George" had replaced him. He was devastated.

It is true that courtship is a kind of "war." One's conquest is another's defeat. Joyful triumphant celebration for one means ignominious defeat and irreparable loss for another. It is a cruel, ruthless competition devoid of any brotherly sentiments. How can this competition be synchronized with the Christian's "Golden Rule"?

Peter had gotten Edward started on a relationship with a girl in Guernsey, Saskatchewan. Just that quickly, Peter lost his welcome there. Now, Ed had no one to keep him company on the next long, lonely journey he had to make to see his love, so I, as a subordinate nephew, was recruited for this task.

Of course, there were several incentives to persuade me to ride along. I was always eager to travel and to visit unfamiliar territory, and I had never visited Saskatchewan, nor Guernsey in particular. I also wanted to visit my two aunts, Helen Biehn and Neta Broadfoot, and their families. Then, Ed also promised that his girlfriend had a beautiful younger sister that would undoubtedly be of considerable interest to me. I was willing to explore the possibilities.

The opportunity came in the spring of 1960 when Ed got a long weekend off from Martin's Garage where he worked as a mechanic. We drove together the four hundred plus miles to Guernsey and stayed at Uncle and Aunt Mervin and Helen Biehn's place. We had a nice visit there.

Finally, the time came for me to meet the sister that Ed had been bragging up to me. Yes, she was everything he promised and much more beside. She was only fifteen years old at the time: young, innocent, and very pretty. She acted very mature and had a good sense of humor. We were both rather shy, but with Uncle Ed's help, we soon became friends.

When the time came for me to return home, we agreed to keep in touch. Thus began a relationship that lasted for two and one-half years. It was a good relationship that consisted of a lot of letter-writing and about two visits a year to Guernsey. The two sisters also visited us at Duchess on two occasions. We thought that Ed and the sister would certainly marry in the near future, but then suddenly, they broke off the relationship. He would not be going to Guernsey any time soon. I, being a poor student, had neither car nor funds, so there was a long lapse in my visits.

Meanwhile, Peter's romantic endeavors were going in another direction. He was hurt deeply by his first "Dear John" letter, but not so hurt as to keep him from trying again somewhere else. He went to Tofield and dated a young lady there who became interesting to him. They started corresponding, and he went for a second visit. He thought he was making progress when he got another "Dear John" letter.

It did not take so long to get over that one. He soon was dating one in Kalispell, the same "immature" one who two years later had become very mature. She knew just how to make a man feel good. However, a few weeks after his second successful visit to see her, he received another "Dear John" letter.

He was really hurt and angry this time.

"She no sooner says 'Goodbye' to me at the front door, than she welcomes 'George' at the back door!"

Repeated exposure to painful experiences can build up a certain immunity or resilience. There were "more fish in the sea!" Peter began to play the same game, dating many different girls, both local and far away.

One time he ran into an embarrassing problem. He pursued a relationship with another girl at Tofield but was also dating one locally. Then he got the announcement that his Tofield girlfriend was coming with a youth group to visit over the weekend. The local girl would be expecting to monopolize his time that weekend. After agonizing for a few days, he was forced to make a choice. It was his turn to write a "Dear Sarah" letter.

Paul, a Pillar of Sanity in a Less Sane World

Of all the brothers, Paul and Charles were the most gifted with the ability to keep their thoughts to themselves, or was it that the rest of us were too busy expressing ourselves that we had no time to listen? Anyway, Paul was quiet around home. He was a diligent worker, even though he suffered from backaches and headaches related to his many accidents.

Paul was always kind of reckless and fearless as a small boy. In Ontario, if I would jump from a high beam onto a hay pile, Paul was sure to jump from a higher one. He would just go up and throw himself down. I would not compete with him on that score. Sometimes you would think he did not like himself very much.

Back in 1957, Paul was just learning to drive. Dad had brought home a 1952 International pickup truck, which we promptly dubbed "the corn binder." It was a well-cared for used truck. It was a dull, light brown in color with black fenders. It was in better shape than our light green 1938 Ford, at least.

On one sunny winter Sunday afternoon, Paul decided to go to the Dumka farm to check on the cows. He took along his brother, George, and William Ramer. Apparently, Paul was a bit over-confident in showing off his driving skills to these two younger boys. While speeding down the narrow, icy Dumka road, he decided to do a U-turn without the benefit of slowing down first. Well, any experienced driver knows that it is impossible, even on the driest, widest, smoothest roads, to do a U-turn if you are proceeding forward at a high speed. But Paul was not experienced.

Of course, the truck went into a series of wild skids and ended settling nicely in a deep, snow-filled ditch, balanced neatly on its roof, facing the opposite direction, all four wheels in the air. So, they did negotiate the U-turn, sort of!

In the turmoil inside the cab, no one was hurt; only William's glasses were broken. The truck's roof was pushed in, and the right door was bent out of shape and would not close properly. The boys were lucky they were able to walk home to get help.

Dad never did fix that truck. For several years, we drove it just like it was, with caved in roof and damaged right door that did not always stay shut. It was somewhat embarrassing. It looked as if we had just come out of a crash up derby or out of a war, or perhaps escaped from a riot or a civil disturbance of violent proportions.

Whenever there was a youth activity, or we boys wanted the car for anything, Dad always gave us the "corn binder." I suppose not fixing it was his way of punishing us and protecting himself from worry over his nice car getting to look the same way! Anyway, we did not mind too much. Hot rods were in style. We were not rich enough to have a hot rod, but the old, beat up "corn binder" always turned a few heads, especially after the exhaust pipe fell off.

Before Paul bought his own car, he used to hot-rod around in this lovely "corn binder." One evening, he was running up and down the streets of Duchess with his friend Delmar Bast. Delmar was a bit overweight, let's say, "well-cushioned." Paul was making a fast power turn on the corner of Main Street when the broken door flew open, and poor Delmar slid right off the seat and landed on the street. Lucky for him, he was not hurt! There were no seatbelts in those days!

Paul had many friends in school, especially among the fairer sex. He was the most handsome of us brothers, and apparently the girls agreed with that evaluation. Sometime later, Paul bought a nice Pontiac, which made him even more attractive to the ladies. He did have some girlfriends, but he was not wild about them.

Paul was not a scholar, and he did not have the patience to waste his life behind a desk. As was the custom in our family, he stayed home after completing grade nine to help Dad for one year. After that, he also decided to return to high school. He and I both missed a lot of school days during harvest that year, but at least he was continuing.

Sometime later, he got restless and decided to quit school again. This time he found himself a position in Martin's Garage as an apprentice mechanic. He stayed there for four years, spending two months per year in technical school until he gained his license in automotive mechanics. He did very well in the technical school and became a very good mechanic.

One day while working in the garage, Paul was bending over a split rim truck tire, putting air into it. The pressure was mounting. Suddenly, the rim came apart and the tire exploded under him. Paul was seen suspended in space, above the John Deere tractors in the garage before he landed again. They had not taken the precaution of putting the tire in a mandated locked cage before filling it. He could have been killed, but he was blessed to have only a broken thumb, sand blasted into his eyes, and a few bad bruises. He was rushed to the Brooks hospital where he recuperated in a few days. Doctors were worried about his eyes, but they healed nicely.

Gregarious, Gorgeous George

For some reason, although Peter was closest to me, I always held a special bond with George. Maybe it was because he was far enough down the line that he was no threat to me, or maybe it was because we thought alike in so many ways. Whatever the reason, we always liked each other and got along well together. We often took sides together against Peter and Paul when we were smaller, back in the Ontario years.

I liked to work with George. He was always willing to do more than his share, and he was so cheerful. One time we read an article about the white highlands of Kenya, and we decided that we would farm together in Kenya when we got big. (Little did I realize that I would give six years of my life to managing a farm/development project at Ogwedhi in Kenya.)

George had a reputation for being strong for his age, and he took delight in trying to live up to it. Even back in Ontario, when he was in grade two, Henry Loppers, a grade five boy picked a fight with George. True to form, George never turned down a challenge. Soon the Loppers boy came into the school crying. The teacher asked him what he was crying about. He blurted out, "I had a fight with George, and he beat me!" The teacher said, "Shame on you picking on a little boy like him!" The whole class broke into laughter. George had a lot of fights. I never saw him get angry, and I never saw him lose either.

The big boys gave George a chance to play on the Duchess High School Senior football team when he was still in grade six. Maybe they were desperate for players, but George did really well on the line. He was still small and looked rather harmless, but he was quick, hard, and strong. He got through where the opponents never expected him. I heard one opponent talking to his teammate, "That big fat tub of lard is no problem, but this little guy, you better watch out for him!"

One day when I was sixteen, a group of us boys were outside the church house testing our strength by lifting the front of a Volkswagen beetle off the ground. Some of the older guys could do it, but I could not. Then twelve-year-old George did it! I was so ashamed. If George did it, then I had to do it! I tried again and lifted it!

George spent time with his friend William Ramer, often going to his home on Sunday afternoons. He learned things about dairy farming that he never learned at home. He played with barbells there too. Could that have had some bearing on the fact that he had to go to the hospital for a hernia operation when he was twelve years old?

George took seriously the biblical injunction "Remember your Creator in the days of your youth. ..." (Ecclesiastes 12:1 KJV) When Myron Augsburger held evangelistic services at the Duchess Church in the summer of 1957, George responded to the preaching and accepted Christ as his Savior and surrendered to him as Lord of his life. He was only twelve years old. It made such a change in George's life, that it was a challenge to me to take my own spiritual condition more seriously. He gave himself to reading the Bible and taking Bible correspondence courses and took an interest in spiritual matters and church activities. He changed his rebellious attitudes and behavior.

Growing with God

My spiritual life was still quite stagnant for the first year after coming from Ontario. The Duchess Mennonite Church at that time was steadfast in holding to the rules and practices of the more conservative parts of the denomination. None of the men wore neckties except two young men, Edward Friesen and his friend, Werner Barg. Peter and I decided to give them our moral support in their rebellion against tradition, so we bought flashy neckties too. Soon others followed.

I was quite proud of the stand I had taken. I was not a real rebel at heart. I liked the church, and I liked Clarence Ramer's preaching. He was a student of the Scriptures, was well informed of current issues, was a solid biblical expositor, had admirable oratorical skills, was friendly and approachable, was deeply respected in the community, and lived a life that demonstrated a close walk with the Lord. I knew that my stand did not please my pastor or the church elders, but I thought it was time for them to change, so I would do my part to push the issue. My attitude was naive, presumptuous, and egocentric.

In the fall of 1957, this began to change. I had dropped out of school, and on the farm, I had lots of time to think about my life. It was very hard for me to confess my sins and feel forgiven, and it was hard for me to make a new start without doing that. It was also hard for me to really feel that God's love was adequate to include me. On the other hand, I had a very sensitive and legalistic conscience. I wanted to live an upright life and to please God.

Now I was getting older and realized that I must make decisions about my inner life. I was still carrying condemnation for a lie I had told my dad when I was six. That was the time when I was to go bring a certain cow home to be milked. I found her in the company of our bull. I was afraid of the big mean monster, so I went home without the cow and told Dad that I could not find her. He went himself and brought the cow home.

I could just as well have told my dad that I was afraid of the bull. He would have understood that a fifty-pound boy of six was no match for a one-ton angry bull, but I did not want to admit feeling fear either. After all, a boy of six should be strong and brave and fearless! I could not appear as a coward. So, I chose the expediency of deceit, and I was paying a heavy price in self-condemnation and inner misery. There were a few other deviations from the standard of absolute truth that also bothered me.

Now we heard the horrible news that Mike McCula, my friend Andy's father, was killed in a baler accident. He got tangled up in the feeding mechanism and bled to death out in his field all by himself. I could not sleep. I thought about what had happened to him. Where was he now? Was he ready to leave this earth and face eternity? What would happen to me if I had a similar accident? Old age is not guaranteed. Am I ready to go in any given instant? Of course, I did not feel ready, and I wondered how much longer I would struggle with this guilt before I surrendered my pride and did what I knew I must do.

There was no easy way to get rid of this burden of guilt, except to admit that I was a liar, confess my deceit, accept forgiveness for it, and make a new start. But that was hard. I was a coward and too proud to admit to anyone but myself that I had done such a shameful thing. Somehow, I had the idea that once you were a church member, you should live a perfect life. If you did not, it was a great shame on you, and everybody else in the church would view you as a despicable hypocrite, which of course, in trying to cover up, I truly was.

It was after my experience at the Bible school in Kalispell that I embarked on a campaign to clean up the environment in my inner life. It was time to obey the inner voice of the Spirit of God if I was ever going to come out of this mess. I told my dad what I had done, and he forgave me. I exposed myself in those other cases as well. I lost all interest in the current pop music. I had to burn some books that were a hindrance and embarrassment to me.

Then I felt I should go before the whole body of the church believers and confess to them my hypocrisy and my pride and ask them to forgive me and pray for me, as I wanted to renew my covenant to walk with God with all my heart. As an act of contrition for my rebellion and as a symbol of my new determination, I stopped wearing the necktie. I needed to submit to the community of faith. There is no place for rugged individualism and egotistical self-determination in the family of God's people. Did not the biblical prophet, Samuel, rebuke King Saul with the warning, "Rebellion is like the sin of divination." (I Samuel 15:23 NIV)?

It was on a Sunday in the spring, when the congregation was preparing for communion, that I went to the front and clarified my stand before all. They forgave me, and afterwards, many came to me and affirmed me in my new direction. I was making a new start. The guilt was gone. I had nothing to hide anymore. I was so relieved and happy.

Now I enjoyed Bible study, sermons, singing, church services, revival meetings, even prayer meetings. I was interested in any activity that could draw me closer to God. I learned the joy of private prayer, of waiting upon God, basking in his loving presence. I experienced a deeper inner peace than I had ever known before. I looked to the future with awe and anticipation, eagerly awaiting the unfolding of the mysteries that God had in store for me as I yielded step by step to his leadership.

For the first time in my life, I had no fear of death, knowing that I belonged to God, and that he was in charge of my life whether here or on the other side of the "river" of death. No matter what happened to me, I would always be with God, and that is the best of all possible places to be. In fact, if I were to die, that would save me a lot of agony and suffering, and I would simply be getting a shortcut to Heaven, and who would turn down that kind of bargain?

Soon after that, I experienced an obedience check. There was a girl in our church about my age that I respected very highly, and we had many interests in common. She was a committed Christian. I wanted to get to know her better, so I asked her for a date. We drove to a little Evangelical Free Church in a neighboring town to hear a returned missionary give a talk about his work. He was a fantastic speaker, and the girl and I enjoyed being there together. The vibes were good. Should I cultivate a relationship with her?

This question was on my mind, when I was loading grain the next week at the Dumka farm. I finished loading, and there, all by myself, I prayed and asked God for an answer. He did not speak out loud, but he just put a very clear "awareness" inside my being that she was not the one for me. I should not pursue the matter further. I was hoping and thinking along different lines, but I did not argue with his answer. I dropped the matter there.

The influence of the preachers and the Bible lessons really impacted my life. I thought about my life even more than I had before. I finally decided to surrender my life completely to God and allow him to lead me from now on. Up to then my prayers had always been something like, "Lord, this is what I want to do, now bless my efforts so that my plans succeed!" Now I prayed, "Lord, I wanted to be a farmer. But what do you want me to be? Now I am looking to you. I want to follow your plans. I do not need to know what they are. Just lead me!"

All at once, just as real as if he had spoken, I knew in my heart that God was telling me to "Go back and finish high school!" I realized I was just a sixteen-year-old kid. There was so much I still needed to know. I did not know, and I could not know the future, but it was enough to know him who holds the future. Now was the time of preparation for whatever the future might hold. There was no question in my mind. The rest of his plan remained shrouded in mystery. I was incredibly happy, excited, and satisfied. I would obey, and I would do my best!

That September 1958, in obedience to what I knew to be the will of God, I was back in high school. Those next three years were good years in which I learned to pray and to listen to God speak to me in my inner being. There were places on the farm that became "sacred" to me, where I spent time alone with God and sensed his presence and love for me and received his guidance for issues I had to resolve. I sensed that God was calling me to be either a minister of the gospel, a pastor, a teacher, or maybe a missionary. I was thrilled and excited about the prospect and eager for the revealing of his plan.

I believed, with my denomination, that the call of God to an individual would always come with a three-fold confirmation. There is the inner call that one would sense in his spirit. There was the outer call of the need, in line with the will of God revealed in the Scriptures. Then there must be the call, or confirmation of the call, through the church, the people of God. When these three were in line, one could be certain beyond any doubt that he was indeed called of God. For me, I had the first two, but I must await the third, the confirmation of the call by my church.

I was active in the church, as best a teenager can be. One of the highlights was to be involved in a young people's Bible study and prayer group for the last two years of high school. We would meet every week with some older, more matured youth. We prayed for non-Christian people and watched them being drawn to Christ and become Christians. We prayed for weak Christians and watched them grow. We traveled to other churches and gave programs, and people were encouraged and blessed.

Our church grew until the little building was about to burst. But true to form, when we started to disturb the "enemy's territory," we stirred up opposition, and cracks began to appear in our group. Some youth left and began ridiculing what we were doing. Others in the group got "holier," more legalistic, more radical, and more judgmental of the rest of us. We were heading for conflict when I left for university.

A Return to Academia

Back in Duchess High School in grade ten, my former classmates were a year ahead of me, except for those few who failed to make the grade. I missed about twenty-four days of school during harvest. That put me back to a class standing of number ten out of twenty students on the November progress report.

I enjoyed getting back into school and tried to make the most of it. I joined the football team again that fall. We did not win all the games this time. Again, I enjoyed going to "shop" in Rosemary where Mr. Kadey, my mother's former teacher, was my shop teacher. I made a bookcase among other things. That year I bought a guitar for ten dollars, and Fred Hiebert tried to teach me to play. I wanted to play, and I liked music very much, but I just was not gifted in that line. After a year of trying, I finally gave it up.

That year I was appointed to serve as an usher in the church. I also was asked to make speeches in several Sunday evening programs. We had some conservative, old-fashioned preachers come to our church that made a profound impact on me. One of them was Eli Yutzi from Loman, Minnesota. The elderly evangelist James Bucher followed him.

Both men were real firebrands for God as they understood Him. They had a big impact upon our people for better and for worse. Some repented of real sins and sought to get into a right relationship with God.

Others got all fired up about non-conformity to this world in dress, which really meant that they became serious and expressed their desire to be obedient to God by returning to the old-style attire that some Mennonites had been keeping for two hundred years. In the end, this emphasis, instead of bringing a blessing to our church, brought division.

The fall of 1960 found me entering the twelfth grade in high school. I managed to get a chauffeur's license and was hired to drive our school bus. It was an excellent arrangement for me since it was the same bus and the same route I had to ride anyway. This way I got paid one hundred dollars a month for going to school and enjoyed the privilege and prestige of being considered responsible above my age-mates as a side benefit.

It was also a benefit to the County, for at least one bus could stay at school all day and thus save almost fifty percent of normal mileage costs.

I felt blessed. From my monthly paycheck, I tithed ten percent or ten dollars to the Lord, spent five dollars as pocket money, and invested eighty-five dollars in cattle.

I bought a big cow from my dad that was too mean to milk anymore. When she gave birth to a bull calf, I bought a second bull calf from Ramer's, and she raised them both. I bought two weaned heifers from Sander's that I wanted to raise to become milk cows. Therefore, my bus driving earned me five head of cattle. The two bull calves became nice big steers. One of the heifers got sick and after a lengthy illness, passed away. The other heifer became a cow and produced a calf. One of my fat steers was found dead one day in a ditch.

When I later sold all my animals so I could go to University, I recouped my investment, but I never made any profits. Obviously, the Almighty was not blessing my farming efforts to encourage me to reconsider farming. Yet in his kindness, he provided enough so that I could continue my education.

That fall, I was elected president of the student's union at high school. In church, I was chosen to be assistant superintendent of the Sunday school. I was also vice president of our church youth group that year.

Whether I did a decent job or not, I do not know, but these appointments gave me some opportunities to gain experience in exercising leadership skills.

We had some good times in high school. Almost everybody was my friend, though my real close friends were very few. My aunt and uncle, Esther and David, were in the same class with me. They added a lot of fun to the class. Deanna Galiz and Marlene Rogalsky joined the class in grade eleven. They were both friendly, attractive, intelligent girls who added to the social life of the school. Fulton Beck, Olive Roth, and Deanna were my chief competitors for second or third place in the class rank of academic achievement. We always gave deference to my "Uncle Jake" as we called David Friesen and let him be number one.

One time, we planned a class outing, an evening hayride and skating party. We borrowed a Farmall "M" from Dan Burkholder, the International Harvester dealer, and somebody provided a wagon with straw on it. The evening of the party, we all gathered at school and loaded the wagon with about fifteen of the class members. Some of the boys drove the tractor. The rest snuggled into the straw or ran along beside. Others fought, throwing straw at each other or pushing each other off the wagon, like young people will do.

We finally reached an isolated farm pond and parked the tractor on the top of a very steep hill, overlooking the pond. We climbed down the hill and spent a wonderful evening skating on the smooth ice. The winter weather was mild, and the stars were shining in the clear night sky. We had a fire on the edge of the pond for those who needed to rest or warm up a bit. It was a romantic and pleasant time. About ten o'clock we roasted wieners and had hot drinks.

Then it was time to return home. One of the boys had gone ahead up the hill and started the tractor. The rest of us climbed to the top of the hill, but we had not yet climbed aboard the wagon. For reasons unknown to the rest of us, the boy who started the tractor dismounted, leaving the tractor in neutral with the engine running and with the brakes unlocked. He came over and joined the group of us who were joking around.

Behind his back several of us saw the tractor slowly inch forward towards the slope of the hill, gaining speed by the second. Four or five of us rushed over to the tractor at the same instant. Some got in the way of each other as they tried to reach the brake pedal from standing on the ground in front of the rear wheel. However, the tractor was creeping forward at an ever-increasing speed as the slope increased. Their position of having to pull the unwieldy brake pedal towards themselves, while backing up to keep from being run over by the advancing machine was untenable.

I, seeing it was impossible, rushed to the rear of the tractor in an attempt to mount up into the seat, the proper place from which it would have been easy to control the tractor. But I was too late. I stepped onto the drawbar and grabbed hold of the steering wheel, but there was no time left to mount into the seat. It became obvious to me that I would not be able to stop the tractor on its mad race downhill. It now was equally impossible for me to dismount without being run over by the wagon trailing behind this runaway monster.

All I could do now was keep my feet on the drawbar, hang on to the steering wheel with all my might, and prevent the wheels from making a sharp sideways turn, which would have sent the tractor and wagon and me rolling sideways down the incline. I must only ensure that it went straight forward.

I did not have much time for contemplation as we three, the mindless mass of metal, myself precariously balancing on the bouncing drawbar and desperately clutching the wobbling steering wheel, and the empty wagon banging and leaping after us, all hurtling down the hill at ever increasing speed in the darkness. I had no idea what lay ahead in the path. There could be boulders or logs or a fence or even a cliff in our path. There was no way of knowing and nothing more to do but hang on!

It was a great comfort when the tractor suddenly leveled out as we reached the ice and sped forward across the dark frozen pond. I hoped that the ice would hold as I steered the tractor in a large circle over it. It did. I mounted the seat, put it in gear and drove it around to a place where the incline was less steep and then returned to the top. "All is well that ends well!"

As we went home that night I felt like a hero. That was a new and strange feeling. But I also realized that I could just as easily have been a mangled mess of meat strewn on that rocky, frozen hillside, my hot blood mingling with the ice and snow and then freezing with the mud that it created a few minutes later. God's angels were watching over me!

I took the grade twelve matriculation examinations in May of 1961. Out of fifteen who sat for the exams, four of us matriculated. I was the second highest, next to my uncle, David, in percentage points. Graduation exercises were conducted in the fall. I was awarded the fifty-dollar Duchess Home and School Association Scholarship. I had enrolled in the pre-medical program at the University of Alberta in Edmonton. David Friesen enrolled in the Ontario Mennonite Bible Institute. Esther Friesen enrolled in a nurse aid program in Brooks Hospital and then followed David to Ontario a year later. They both graduated from the Bible Institute after completing three years of studies.

EIGHT

SEARCHING FOR DIRECTION

Peter's Fascination with Business

The spring of 1961 was one of the driest and hottest on record in Alberta and Saskatchewan. The government of Canada declared it a "disaster area." The farmers in the dry areas had no hay to feed their cattle, so the government agreed to help them with subsidies to purchase hay from the irrigated areas and have it transported to them.

As usually happens in the world of commerce, one person's disaster is another's opportunity. Suddenly there was a big demand for hay. Prices soared as farmers from the dry lands converged on the irrigated areas searching for hay at any price.

Many of John Martin's old customers approached him for help. He had gone out of the hay business two years ago. He had sold his trucks, and his crew was disbanded. How could he help them?

John, sensing a chance to make a dollar, approached Peter with a proposal. If Peter would be willing to go into the trucking business for himself, John would help him with a loan for a down payment on a truck and would give him a contract to load hay from the field into railroad boxcars for four dollars per ton. John would be the buyer and seller, and Peter would get all his trucking business.

It sounded like the chance in a lifetime for a young man who was eager to become his own boss and own his own business. Peter explained the proposition to his employer, Don Anderberg, and found a sympathetic ear. Don told Peter that if he was going to quit driving for him, he might as well sell him the truck he was driving.

So, Peter bought the dark blue Ford truck from Anderberg and got Anderberg's grain hauling business as well as the hay contracts. Peter was excited and ready to go. He offered me a chance to go into partnership with him as I was graduating from high school. I turned the opportunity down as I was determined to start university in the autumn, but I was available for a summer job. We agreed at one dollar per hour. No fringe benefits.

In June of 1961, I matriculated from the Duchess High School. The day after the final exam, I started my summer job.

The Ford was a recent model, a three-ton capacity vehicle. Peter bought a pop-up bale loader, a contraption to be hooked onto the side of the deck of the truck and towed along beside in the field like a trailer. Whenever it came to a bale lying on the ground, it would pick it up. Its two wheels drove an elevator chain that would lift the bale vertically from the ground to about four feet above the truck bed where the person building the load would put it into place. He ordered a blacksmith to make two bale hooks exactly according to his specifications. We were ready for business.

We took turns driving and building the loads. The truck had to be driven very carefully around the fields gathering the bales because there were irrigation ditches that were incompletely filled and other rough places. The person on the back building the load was working hard and as the load got higher, any sudden twist or jolt could send the man and his load to the ground in a hurry. We built our loads eight layers high, with 210 bales, or approximately eight tons each. Then we would stop and tie the load with a small winch and chains. After that, we would speed to the railroad station as fast as the truck would move.

At the station, we would be assigned a boxcar into which we would unload each bale by hand. The boxcars were usually old-style freight cars. They were forty feet long, nine feet high, and enclosed with walls and a roof made of steel and painted a dark rusty red. We were to fill them completely, with no room to spare.

It was a dry, hot year, so day after day, the sun beat down on us in the field and on the oven-like boxcars as we loaded. Some days the temperature was 105 degrees Fahrenheit in the shade. Inside the steel boxcars it climbed up to almost oven-like temperatures over 140 degrees. If there was no wind, the sweat poured off our bodies, mixing with the chaff and the dust forming thick gobs of wet dirt in the crevices of our face and sunburned neck and arms.

We usually started the work with the first streak of dawn, which in Alberta at that time of year, meant 4:30 a.m. We would go out and load one load, stop for an early breakfast, then work until eight or nine at night. If the field was not too far from the station, we could bring in five loads in one day. Some weeks we averaged fourteen hours per day, discounting time out for meals.

That meant I was making fourteen dollars per day! I was into big bucks, and Peter was getting his truck paid for. We worked hard and were happy. I lost at least twenty pounds of schoolboy flab and built muscles like I've never had before nor since. We were healthy, tough, and rejoicing in the strength of our youth.

We could hardly drink enough water. We would put a tin one-gallon syrup pail of water into the freezer every night, and every morning we would take a gallon of ice with us. This would melt during the day, and we would stop and refill it with water each time there was not any melted ice left to drink.

One day about ten o'clock in the morning, I lost all my energy, and no amount of water could restore it. I felt like I would faint. I remembered a grade nine health lesson where I learned that sometimes, when people sweat too much, they need to take salt tablets to replenish the salt lost through perspiration. We stopped at a drug store, and sure enough, they had salt tablets! Within an hour, my energy was restored.

Peter was developing a reputation in the community by this time. A rancher said of him, "If that Peter Hansen doesn't become a millionaire before he's forty, he will have died trying!"

One morning very early, we went to Tilly and put one load into our boxcar. When we came with our second load, we found a smaller truck with three men unloading it into their boxcar. They had already unloaded the first two layers. Peter viewed them, with a jaundiced eye, as potential competition. He said, "Let's show them an example that will make them feel so inferior that they will get discouraged and quit!"

We pulled into our place and worked as fast as we could, unloading ours in a few minutes, and when we drove out empty, those three fellows still had two layers of bales left on their little truck. They looked rather pale to us as we sped away, and we laughed with glee while Peter said, "That will teach them!" After that day, we never saw that crew again.

They probably were farmers who had a little surplus hay for sale, or who came to the area to buy hay. I am sure they had no intention of running us out of business. If they did, they soon abandoned that idea.

During that summer, the two of us loaded something like fifty box cars of hay that were shipped to Saskatchewan. Above that, we filled contracts trucking hay to local feedlots or just stacking hay in people's yards.

We built a stack of hay in John Martin's feedlot. We made it twenty-three layers high. That was the highest stack of bales that we ever made. When we were almost done, we met and chatted with our preacher, Paul Martin. He thought the stack was pretty high. Peter sort of sacrilegiously joked, "Yes, it is high enough that, if one fell off, he would have time to get ready before he hit the ground!"

On the very next load we brought in, I climbed up on top, while Peter got on top of the loaded truck, lifting the elevator up to me. As I reached down to grab the elevator, I lost my footing and came tumbling down to the ground below.

I was scratched, bruised, and a whole lot less jovial as I climbed back up and unloaded the truck. I was deeply thankful for God's protection in what could easily have been fatal, or even much worse. Perhaps it was not wise to make such jokes!

Besides hauling hay all day, Peter was seeing various girlfriends now and then in the evenings. Our conversation usually centered around his girls or his business. Then in August, we heard that Ed's girlfriend and mine were coming to see us. That put some spice into a rather bland diet of hay hauling.

We thought for sure that it was about time for our twenty-five-year-old uncle, Ed, to make a proposal. Maybe he had plans? He never told us if he did.

It turned out for his eternal betterment that his girl came with another plan. She did not believe in writing "Dear John" letters. She believed it was better to spring the surprise on him in person, when his hopes were at their peak! Then she could be there, in person, to enjoy the spectacle of how a good man copes with dashed hopes! She about drained out his lifeblood, but because he was a real man, he held himself together and survived the disappointment. After all, there were "other fish in the sea!"

Venturing into the Unfamiliar "Ivy Halls"

I was accepted at the University of Alberta, Edmonton campus, into the pre-med program of the Department of Science. I arranged to share a room in the home of Ike & Mildred Glick with David Lefever, a boy from Eaglesham, whom I had never met.

On September 17, 1961, I returned my bale hook to its owner and turned my back on all that was familiar and dear to me and set out to explore the strange distant world of academia and city life. I hitched a ride with someone else going there.

I was glad to leave my hay-hauling career behind me, and leaving home was not difficult, but facing a world totally strange to me was stressful, to say the least. The campus had eight thousand students and was spread out over a mile square. I missed the orientation for newcomers, and I did not have friends to ask, so it took me a long time to comprehend the ins and outs of campus life. I never did find out if I was assigned a campus mailbox or not. I had a hard time finding out what was going on, as I never understood how information was passed.

David Lefever was another farm boy, like me, fresh from the bush at Eaglesham in the northern Peace River country. He could not help me much. We lived together in Ike Glick's basement apartment on 96th Ave. and 79th St. It was a bare, drab basement with block walls and bare cement floors. It always had the stale odor of musty basements.

In the winter, the floor and the walls radiated the cold inward. Our feet were always cold. Sometimes, I would lay awake for hours waiting for my feet to warm up so I could sleep. The warm air from the furnace went upstairs, and we got an obnoxious blast of stale cool air blown down on us from the ceiling duct above our bed. To our knowledge, the house had no fresh air exchanger, and as the winter wore on, the air became more and more foul. The furnace blower circulated the air but did not improve its quality.

David and I cooked our own food. He was as good a cook as I, so needless to say, our diet was extremely basic, and we did not eat more than necessity demanded. It was instilled in both our homes that frugality was one of the highest virtues, and our aim was to get through university with as little cost as possible. So, we were the thriftiest of shoppers.

Our diet consisted of cooked red beets, carrots, and potatoes, which we brought from our mother's gardens at home; Red River cereal or cracked wheat porridge for breakfast and maybe supper too; fried liver with homemade liver gravy twice or three times a week, if it was on special at the supermarket; several days old bread, if it was not moldy yet, and the cheapest margarine and thin watery grape jelly; fried eggs, poached eggs, boiled eggs, and scrambled eggs if cracked eggs could be found on special; and of course baloney to add variety to our grape jelly sandwiches, just so there would be balance in our lunches that we carried to the University each morning. Occasionally, we had a chunk of chicken, if it could be located at a throw away price.

We became adept at whipping together a meal in a hurry. It obviously could not have been very "balanced," but we had not studied all about nutrition yet. That was why we were at the University! We did not suffer from nutritional deficiency any more than our Russian relatives who thrived on the rations offered in the banqueting halls of the Gulag.

David and I slept in the same bed and had our study desks in the same bedroom. There was no couch or easy chair to spread out on, just two strait backed chairs. There was not much option but to work or sleep. The rent was cheap, so we did not complain.

At first, we took the bus across town to reach the University. It took a good hour to reach one way. Later we made a friend who had a car and was eager to carpool. That made it nicer to get to and back from school, especially when the temperatures dipped to minus forty degrees, where standing at bus stops was no joke.

I was financing my studies at the University with the savings from my summer job and the sale of my sheep. My folks were poor and had many obligations that they were struggling to meet. They could not help.

I was too naive and ignorant to even inquire about financial assistance. I never thought about taking out a student loan, so I was, as usual, doing it on my own. "A penny saved is a penny earned," was my philosophy of monetary management. I would spend as little as possible and squeak by somehow. And I did, even if it meant wearing the same shabby clothes and eating unbalanced meals.

At the university, I took courses in chemistry, zoology, physics, English literature, calculus, and physical education. I enjoyed the English literature and the science courses, but the calculus was complete confusion to me from the start.

The professor was most unhelpful. He may have been a mathematical whiz. I did not have enough expertise to judge, but I do know that he was a pedagogical disaster, and an environmental eyesore. He was about thirty years of age. He dressed in rumpled trousers from the war era, an old brown moth-eaten turtleneck sweater, and scuffed shoes which had never been acquainted with shoe polish, at least not in recent decades. In the morning he looked like he had just crawled out of a sleeping bag backwards, clothes and all. His curly hair was unkempt with lint and other debris clinging to it, and he rarely shaved. He wore thick-lensed glasses, always had stuffed up sinuses, sniffled, snorted, and drew the surplus mucus gobs down into his throat and swallowed them as he went on with his pedagogical monologue explaining calculus. He was no help to most students. One by one we dropped out.

In physical education, I took a lifesaver swimming course that I enjoyed. I immediately became friends with a Ghanaian student, Francis Sam, whom I often assisted in learning to swim. That was the first time I ever talked to an African. I was quite naive and ignorant of Africa. I was surprised that he could speak English since he was new to our country. I had assumed that the British colonialists would have learned his language if they were living in his country. How naïve! Of course, the colonizer, believing his language to be superior to that of the colonized, would insist that the miserable masses must learn his language to become "civilized"! And so, it was.

Francis was on government scholarship and was planning to study medicine, as was I. We had several classes in common. I invited him to our home one evening for supper. I do not know if he ever was invited to dine in any other Canadian home; I certainly hope so, or he will carry an unorthodox view of Canadian cuisine for the rest of his life!

One day, Francis invited me to a "Christian" meeting on campus. He was a Christian from Africa and had a certain idea of what Christianity meant. Here we found only two scholars discussing a topic in philosophical and theological language that we did not relate to at all. Since we were the only students who attended, Francis thought we came to the wrong meeting, but they assured him it was the right meeting, so we stayed for a while, until we could gracefully excuse ourselves. It was an intellectual world for which we were ill prepared.

Our house was close to the Holyrood Mennonite Church, of which Ike Glick was acting pastor. I would often go over there by myself to make bulletins for the church or for some other business. It was a chance for privacy and solitude that I missed since my living quarters and busy schedule did not provide much opportunity. It was a good place to pray and sing and worship God by myself.

I was still feeling God's call to ministry, while waiting for the Church to confirm the call. Up to that time, I had never talked with anyone about my sense of call. And since the Church had not confirmed the call upon graduating from high school, I decided to study to become a medical doctor. I did not really have an interest in medicine as such, but I thought, perhaps, I could serve as a medical missionary. Besides, it was an honorable occupation and afforded an opportunity to be of service to humankind.

My high school social studies teacher, Mr. Tarney, upon hearing me say I wanted to become a medical doctor, had advised me differently. "Carl, you should become a teacher!" Later, life proved that he was more cognizant of my gifts than me. Secretly, I wished that I had gone with my uncle David Friesen to study Bible at the Ontario Mennonite Bible Institute at Kitchener. But I had put my foot forward; I must step ahead.

So, here I was in the university studying for a medical career. My interest was in the church, theology, Bible, and Christianity. I kept thinking of the needs of the church. There would be much need for leadership in the years ahead. Many of our leaders were old and had limited education. Some were ready to retire; others were ill and no longer able. The one young pastor who had the most education seemed more interested in confusing young people than in building them up in the faith, and, therefore, could not be given pastoral responsibilities.

The young people seemed, like me, to be heading in other directions. I heard one boy my age boasting about his call to train for the pastoral ministry. I was appalled. That was considered presumptuous in our church circles. You waited for the confirmation of the church before you talked about your ambitions. He did go for training, but he left such a bad name behind that he was not welcome in that college community anymore, and he never was called by his church.

At church, the young adult Sunday school teacher was trained in sociology and theology and was a bit unconventional in some of his beliefs. He was suspected, as a "liberal," to be "unorthodox." He had a habit of trying to get the young people to doubt the beliefs they were taught by their parents and church, so they could rethink and formulate their own beliefs or unbeliefs.

He would do this by denying or questioning any miracle or supernatural event in the Bible. I was quite challenged by his stance. I would argue with his presuppositions in class. One time I thought I had him cornered. He could not wiggle out, so he simply said, "I would like to discuss this again with you two or three years from now." So, he was indirectly insulting me, implying that I was too ignorant to discuss these things intelligently, but if I stayed in university long enough, then I might be able to see it his way. Actually, I had been reading books on my own, and I did know where he was coming from. I simply did not agree with his presuppositions, and to this day, I do not.

David Lefever's pastor, Loyal Roth, was suffering from a heart condition for years. It got so bad that specialists recommended open-heart surgery to replace a worn-out valve. In those days, open-heart surgery was still relatively new, and they gave him a fifty/fifty chance of survival and no chance of survival without the operation. The time came for the surgery. His wife, Ruth, came to stay in our basement in another room for the duration of the surgery and recovery period.

Loyal Roth meant a lot to me since he had lived and preached in Duchess for a year or more, and his daughter, Olive, had been in my class at school. He was a pioneering type of missionary to the Peace River country in northern Alberta. He and his wife had pastored a church planting effort at Culp before coming to Duchess. Now they were giving leadership to the church at Eaglesham. They were struggling against great odds, pastoring a small church without support, in a poor community divided by cultural and religious differences, and working full time to raise a large family while his health was steadily declining due to a failing heart. Now they were here facing this life and death crisis.

The day came, the operation was performed, and he was still alive. But something went wrong. They had to go back in again. His heart was too weak. It stopped. At age forty-four, this man of God laid down his burdens and went to his eternal rest. He left behind his grieving widow, two almost grown daughters and three young sons, and a struggling young church without a pastor and leader.

There followed a well-attended funeral in Edmonton and one of the largest ever gatherings at his memorial service and burial in Eaglesham. In his three years there, he had impacted that community in a deep and profound way.

Being close to this unfolding drama had a significant impact upon me. More than ever, I felt the challenge of the call to ministry. Who would take up the standard that Loyal left? There were so many challenging needs calling. "Whom shall I send? Who will go for us?"

I tried to concentrate on calculus and chemistry, but my mind kept wandering to the challenge of the church. I was getting behind in my work. Assignments were not getting done. I was getting low scores on tests and quizzes. I tried harder to concentrate. I prayed for God to guide me. If I were to become a doctor, I would have to do much better than that. The more I prayed, the more clouded and disturbed my mind became. I just could not think and concentrate on my lessons. I just was not interested in the subjects I was taking.

My mind and spirit and heart were hopelessly oriented towards the church, rather than the hospital. I began to feel arthritic pains in my lower back and hip region and developed chronic diarrhea, all stress related, but I consulted no one.

Looking back on it, I wonder how much my diet and living conditions contributed to my growing crisis?

Christmas recess finally arrived, and it was wonderful to leave my stuffy cold cave for two weeks and go home to my family, my friends, and my church. I was still corresponding with the lady in Guernsey and hoped that she could visit us at Duchess over the holiday, but she did not come. I was disappointed and upset, so I decided to take out another girl for something to do. Maybe it was for spite; I was not sure. Maybe there were "other fish in the sea"?

Back at the university, we faced end of term examinations in January. I failed calculus, chemistry, and physics. I did fine in the other courses. I knew that it was the policy of the university to accept more students than they intended to keep and that one third of all the first-year students would be weeded out in the first term. But I never ever feared that I would be among those rejected. I had never failed a course in my life before. Now, all my efforts, and all my praying had not helped me over the top. I was failing.

Finally, it dawned on my thick skull that I was asking God to lead me, yet I was pushing as hard as I could in a direction that I never sensed him leading. It was completely my idea to become a medical doctor. Deep in my spirit, I knew that I and God wanted me to become a minister of the Gospel. I was not even interested in medicine. By this time, I was two weeks into the second term. I decided to quit.

In all this inner turmoil, I never sought the counsel of anyone. I do not know why I thought I had to work it all out between God and myself. I was so inexperienced and could have gotten a lot of help if I would have reached out and asked for it. I must have been extremely independent or naïve, probably both.

I told my roommate and my landlord that I was quitting. I withdrew from the University and got a small tuition refund. With that, I went to a used car lot and bought an old 1950 Chevrolet 2-door sedan for $135. It ran okay, but it sure was ugly. It was a faded pale blue with large rusted out places on all fenders and along the lower edges of the doorsills. The tires were almost worn out.

It was the only car on the lot that had a price tag that I could afford, so it became my first car. All cash; no car payments! By the time I got a license and insurance for it, my money supply was down to where I might just have enough to make it home. I never said, "Goodbye!" to my friends nor to my teachers. Like my dream, I just faded away!

It was a cold, bright, sunny morning in February when I loaded all my earthly possessions into the trunk of my faded little "limousine" and headed south from the big city and its University towards home. I had no idea if this car would actually reach that far. I knew that if it did not, I had no money to fix it or to find another means of transportation.

I knew I was going home, and I was happy. It was exciting driving my own car, alone, away from a nightmare and towards a future that was still a complete mystery. It felt good to know that God was ahead making arrangements that would no doubt surprise us all. I felt like a convict who had escaped from maximum security, except I had nothing to hide; no cops were following me! I was free!

The journey went smoothly enough, except, I soon learned that it was an oil burner. Also, only one tire went flat. I had it repaired at a service station.

I arrived home before dark. I had not told my family I was quitting university, nor that I was coming home. Just before supper, I appeared in the doorway. They were totally shocked, especially my mother.

She was quite disappointed that I quit. She must have put quite a bit of hope in me that I would amount to something. I had been the first of all our relatives, along with Uncle David, to graduate from high school. I was the only one of us to enter university, and there was a lot of prestige and respect to go along with a medical degree. People had congratulated her, and she had high hopes.

Now, I had let her down completely. She took it hard. She would have to answer all the questions of her well-wishers, the curious, and the plain nosey. All I could tell her was that I had failed. I could not explain all the agony of spirit and mind that I had been through.

Mom worried about me and what I was going to do with my life now. She remembered her uncle John, and her own father, the one who never started anything, and the other who never could stay with the thing he set out to do. Was this going to be a pattern in Carl's life too? It was a worrisome thought, and a valid question, seeing how I was only the second grandchild. What would the grandchildren of Jacob Friesen turn out to be like anyway?

Post University Training

Dad had sold our farm along the highway in November of 1961 and had bought a half section of land two miles east of Duchess. Ever since we bought that farm from Mr. Skrobot and found out how poor the soil was, we had been trying to sell it again, but there had been no takers.

Now, after we had farmed there for six years, the neighbor, Herman Grossfield, wanted to buy it to add to his operation. He came over and offered Dad $18,000 for the farm. His offer was accepted. We would be moving our cattle over to the new farm in the spring and putting in the crop, then fixing the house during the summer, and moving in the fall.

I soon found odd jobs doing chores for Werner Barg, Mogen Sanders, and Art Eckert for four dollars a day during the months of February and March. All my stress-related symptoms, my arthritic pains and diarrhea faded away after three weeks. Dad offered me a job with pay for the months of April, May, and June. Paul was working in Martin's Garage, and George and Charles were still in school, so Dad could use the help to put in the crop, especially since he would be moving to the new farm in the summer.

The half section or 320 acres that Dad bought had 110 acres of almost virgin soil, forty acres of alkali salts that could only grow weeds, and 170 acres of marginal land that could grow a crop if worked just right. It was a mile long and half a mile wide with the homestead located near the center at the end of a 2000 foot lane.

The homestead consisted of an old, vacant four-roomed CPR house in a yard surrounded by tall poplar and spruce trees providing ample shade. There was a small shed for a barn, an old gray out-house that leaned to one side, and an ancient, dilapidated car garage. The farm had been used for pasture, so there were fences surrounding it.

There was no electricity or telephone or natural gas or running water. Dad ordered electric service to be installed immediately, but a telephone was never installed.

We went to work on the old house, knocked down all the broken plaster, ripped out the slats, and installed new wallboard, which was then painted.

When the land thawed enough, I began to plow the 110-acre dryland field out front. It was rough land, but the soil was good. We got it worked down nice and seeded.

Then to irrigate, Dad bought a hand-move sprinkler system with a seven-inch mainline and a half-mile of four-inch laterals. We were among the first to use a sprinkler system in our area to grow grain. We were happy for that system. It eliminated the need for cutting up the field with ditches. It made the field smoother for harvesting. Today, most farmers use sprinkler systems to irrigate their fields.

That spring, the long-awaited confirmation came in the form of a letter from Stanley Shantz, then Secretary of our Alberta Saskatchewan Mennonite Conference Board. In the letter, he stated that my name had been submitted, along with several others, as a person who may have a sense of calling to Christian service of some kind, and if I did have such a sense of call, and if I wished to discuss it further with him, he would be much obliged.

I made it a point to discuss it with him at the Annual Conference meeting in Guernsey at the end of June. The Conference had no suggestions or assignments for me, just affirmation and encouragement to think of voluntary service, Bible school, or of moving north to help one of the mission churches. I replied that I felt I needed more education and would think about it.

It was good to be back in the fellowship of our young people's Bible study group, but things were not the same. The more radical conservative ones were having their own meetings on the side that involved a few of the middle-aged members of our church who were concerned about the "drift" in our conference and denomination. They were opposed to change of any kind.

Yet, I joined with some of those people to start an outreach Sunday school at the little ranching town of Wardlow, across the Red Deer River. Every Sunday, Ken and Grace Torkelson and family, with one or two others and me, would drive out the twenty miles to Wardlow and hold Sunday school in the schoolhouse there. About fifteen women and children would come to be instructed in the ways of God. I was assigned to teach the youth, which consisted of two fourteen-year-old girls.

The Torkelsons were into the conservative movement so deep that they used a curriculum produced by "Rod and Staff," a conservative Mennonite publishing company. It was not very fitting for mission work. I was a bit embarrassed to use it, but too young to protest.

Those were wonderful days, and the experience in attempting to plant a church where there was none, was preparatory for me. Events in our Church that followed my leaving, forced this work to close – another casualty of church feuds.

Near the end of June 1962, I borrowed Peter's yellow Pontiac and took Connie Spicer and Paulette LaRochelle with me to the annual meeting of the Alberta Saskatchewan Mennonite Conference at Guernsey. On the way, the car broke down near Maple Creek. We had to get it towed into town to a garage. I did not have very much money and had even less experience with these emergencies. The timing chain had broken, and it would take time to fix it. We waited around the garage all afternoon as the mechanic worked on it.

Closing time came, and it was not done. I begged the manager to keep the mechanic working on it until it was complete. He told me to ask the mechanic. The mechanic was not willing at all. He said he wanted to go home to be with his family. I never once thought that we should find a hotel for the night. I just insisted that we had to reach our destination that night. I offered to pay him extra for overtime. He finally accepted, but he was angry about it.

It was eight o'clock when we got back on the road. We arrived before midnight at my uncle's place. Years later, I came to realize how selfish I was and how much we imposed on that poor mechanic. It was as though we were the only ones on the road with problems, and our agenda was more important than the mechanic's.

I stayed at my girlfriend's folks' place that time. They put me up in their chicken house. That sounds awful, but it was so thoroughly cleaned out and decorated that it was more like a bunkhouse. It was customary in those days for the people of the host congregation to host all the Conference visitors in their homes. Young people were sometimes accommodated in such a fashion.

At that Conference, I was assigned to give a speech on the topic "Serving Christ Through Farming." Those who assigned the topic assumed I was going to be a farmer.

When school was out at the end of June, my brothers were free to help Dad. I accepted an offer to work for John Barg for the next two months at ten dollars a day and two dollars extra for irrigating, plus room and board. I would work six days a week.

John Barg, who was born in Russia and knew tough times, was a member of the Mennonite Brethren Church. He was a wise man, a diligent worker, and a careful manager who had prospered.

I learned much from him about management. He told me, "Whenever you do a task, always think about ways to improve how you do that task." He also made me realize the value of punctuality. He told me to leave my work at ten minutes to twelve at noon, so that I would be in the house and washed, so we could start eating at exactly twelve o'clock sharp. Otherwise, I would be forcing the cook and the others to waste their time waiting on me. If we all kept time, all of us would be using our time to the maximum efficiency. The same applied at quitting time. There was to be no overtime.

This was sure different than the way I was brought up. At home, lunch was between twelve and two, and supper between six and eight. The cook never knew when we men would pop in for our nourishment. Sometimes we would waste time waiting for her to get it ready, but more often she wasted her time waiting for us to come and eat it before it got cold. Then, we often worked after supper for several hours.

John Barg had three children. His oldest son, Peter, was a year older than I.

One day in late July, Peter Barg and I were stacking hay bales, and as we worked, we talked. Peter asked me about my future plans, and I expressed my uncertainty about what I wanted to do next. Then he said to me, "Carl, you should go to EMC!"

The suggestion struck me as a word from the Lord. Yes, why not go to Eastern Mennonite College? That was one of our denominational liberal arts colleges in Virginia, U.S.A. During my high school days, I had considered going there, but I had sort of forgotten about it in waiting for a confirmation of my calling through the Church. Peter Barg had gone to EMC for one semester just for a broadening experience and found it very enjoyable and enriching.

"Carl, you should go to EMC!" Why, of course I should go to EMC. Why not?

I sent away for information and an application form. It took a week for the letter to reach Virginia, and another week for the information to be sent, then a few days for me to fill out the form and get the letters of reference lined up, and another week for the completed documents to reach Virginia again.

If I was going to go to Virginia for a year, I needed to make one more trip to Guernsey to say "Goodbye!" to my girl. Last time, I had broken

Peter's car, so this time I resolved to try my own trusty Chevrolet. Its tires were bald, and it was ugly and burned oil, but it ran on most cylinders most of the time. I was not sure the auto would impress her deeply, but I did not want to catch a girl by the kind of vehicle I drove. I could not have chosen one more devoid of impressible qualities!

This time I took David Friesen along for company. The car had a few flat tires, but it got there in one piece. I had a very pleasant visit, except parting was so difficult. By this time, the tires were about finished. We stopped at Uncle Jack Broadfoot's home on the way back. He looked at my tires and said, "I think you better take one of my spares along, just in case." It turned out that he did not have one to fit, but he had a small farm implement tire that fit my rim size; so, he threw that into the trunk. Sure enough, on the way home, we had two more flats that rendered the more than worn out tires totally unusable. We came home the last seventy miles on the farm machine tire. We thanked Jack for that.

I had saved most of my wages, and I arranged for Dad to sell my remaining cows and car during the coming year and forward the money to me. There should be enough to pay the $1,250 tuition and room and board that was required to keep me there for one nine-month term. If I lived frugally, I could make it.

It was time to be leaving on the long journey to Virginia, and I still had not received a reply to my application. James Roth was driving to EMC in his sporty '56 Ford with Marian Martin. Would I like to ride along? But was I accepted into the school? I never thought of phoning. I felt it was God's plan for me to go, so I figured he would pull the strings somehow, so I went.

What do I tell the immigration people at the boarder when I have no documentation of acceptance from a school in the U.S.A.? I asked my pastor, Clarence Ramer, for advice since he often traveled that way. He said, "Just go, and if they ask you, tell them that you are just going along for a visit."

On the day of departure, I put all my earthly treasures into one small suitcase and a cardboard carton and loaded them into James's Ford with Marian and myself, and we started out on the biggest venture of my life. I did not know it then, but I was leaving home for good.

A few hours later, we reached the international boundary at Sweet Grass, past the Canadian Customs, and stopped at the U.S.A. Customs and Immigration. The officer wanted to know where we were headed and looked at James and Marian's F-1 forms. Then he turned to me and asked, "And you?"

My heart was halfway up in my throat, but I blurted out, "I'm just going along for a ride to see the country."

He replied, "And how are you coming back?"

Now, my heart was up three quarters of the way, and I spoke with a slight shade of unbelievability, "I will take the bus back."

The officer fixed his steel-gray eyes on me in the most piercing squint and said, "Are you sure you are not a student that is going to school there too, but you do not have your papers?"

Now it was all the way up, and I could just barely whisper a meek, "Yes."

Then he scolded me harshly, "Do not ever try a trick like that again. I should send you straight back to where you came from."

He paused a second—as I braced to hear my fate—then continued more graciously; "I will let you in under only one condition. We will phone the school you are going to and see if they have accepted you or not. If they have, you will go; but if they have not, we will not let you in. In addition, you will pay for the phone call."

The phone call was made; I was accepted. I paid two dollars and eighty cents, and we were moving ahead. My heart slowly slid back down into its place. We had made it through. I was accepted! We were on our way to EMC!

Somewhere on the way to Great Falls, we picked up two more passengers from Kalispell. Then we drove straight through to Ohio, where we slept at James's relative's place for about two hours. Then we continued to Harrisonburg, Virginia.

NINE

EQUIPPING FOR SERVICE

Eastern Mennonite College

In Harrisonburg, we found the little suburb of Park View, which is dominated by our denomination's second largest liberal arts college. The city of Harrisonburg and Eastern Mennonite College, (now "Eastern Mennonite University") are in the Appalachian Mountain chain in the beautiful historic Shenandoah Valley between the prominent Massanutten Range to the east and the Shenandoah Range and West Virginia to the west.

Pioneer Mennonites had settled there in the 1790's, and during the Civil War, battles were fought up and down the valley. Many stories have been told, and many books have been written about those times. Museums have been built to commemorate them. There are fantastic limestone caves under the mountains that go thousands of feet into the bowels of the earth with spacious rooms and magnificent stalactites and stalagmites as big as giant tree trunks. People have parties or even weddings down in some of those cathedral-like cavernous rooms.

Eastern Mennonite College (EMC) sits on the eastern slope of a long ridge on which all of Park View is built. This gives a fabulous view of the town of Harrisonburg and the Massanutten Range to the east. In September of 1962, the campus consisted of about 107 acres of land sloping from the crown of that hill down to Highway #42.

Near the top of the campus was the administration building, which has since burned down and been replaced with a modern campus center. The basement of the former building was devoted to the science department. The next two floors were the main nerve center of the school, and the top floors served as the men's dormitory.

There was a large women's dormitory called "North Lawn" which included the dining hall on the basement level. South of that was a large chapel that could seat about 1200. There was a new student center and small gymnasium complex, and a small high school was in the process of being built. There were no other buildings of significance. The enrollment numbered over 600 college students.

James introduced me to the dean of men, Alphie Zook. This little man gave me a very warm welcome and assigned me a place to live and gave me all the directions I needed to get involved in the orientation process. What a contrast to the University of Alberta. I felt the Christian spirit and warm atmosphere already. This was like family. I was going to like it here.

There were not enough dorm rooms for the men, so I was put off campus with eight other fellows in "Brunk House." This older structure had been a family residence that was converted into a temporary dormitory. I was given a small room all to myself, which I appreciated very much.

There were several of these older family residences that had been acquired as temporary dorm space for the men. Two men's dormitories were to be constructed during the current year.

We took our meals in the dining hall in the basement of the women's dorm. We were fed "family style" at tables of six. Each student was arbitrarily assigned, usually three men and three women, to eat at the same table for three days. This encouraged us to get to know more of the students. I was such a shy fellow, but I made a conscious effort to get to know as many people as I could. This helped me to overcome my basic shyness.

As a rule, I found the students open and friendly. Many of them came with the same interests that brought me there.

A very pleasant surprise was to find our former childhood friend from Berea Mennonite Church in Ontario. Darrell Jantzi had also made the trek from Canada to advance his knowledge in Bible and theology in preparation for a life of Christian ministry. He introduced us to his wife, Florence, who took a job working in the college business office and later in the historical library while he studied. The couple had been married for about two years and had served in the Red Lake Gospel Mission in Ontario. We quickly renewed our friendship and became prayer partners.

After a few days of orientation, we registered for our courses. I registered for a Bible and history major.

Dean Ira Miller informed me that I, being a Canadian, could be given twelve hours of college credit for some of my Alberta high school courses. If I wanted to take summer school for one year, I could graduate in three years. I was astounded. I was not thinking of graduating. I protested that I had only come for one year, that I only had funds for one year and would have to work during the summer if I wanted to continue.

He promised that, if I kept my grades up, he would arrange for a student loan for me to stay for summer school and continue the following year. I had never once thought of a student loan. I did not know they existed. Rich people helped their children to go for higher education, and poorer people stayed home or worked, scrimped, and saved until they were able to go on their own, like myself, or so I thought. With the dean's encouragement, I decided to go for it.

Shortly after our arrival on campus, we were required to take a battery of aptitude and general knowledge tests. I was quite pleased with my results. My general ability in comparison to other American college first-year students was in the 94-97th percentile. After what I had been through at the University of Alberta, I could hardly believe that, but I was still more surprised when I saw my science score was in the 94-99th percentile. I knew Alberta standards of education were higher, but not that much higher. Somehow, I felt vindicated after my ignominious failure of the previous year. I was not incompetent after all. It was a motivational block. My math score was the lowest at 50th percentile, which is average. I felt much better about myself.

Adjusting

I loved Virginia. I loved the weather, the scenery, the people, EMC, the students, the churches, and I just rejoiced in the privilege of being there. I enjoyed the courses I was taking. I also got involved with the Young

People's Christian Association (YPCA) in cottage meetings with shut-ins, in jail visitation, and in helping small rural churches. It was a new world opening to me, and I loved it. I made many friends among the students.

I often had to think of Jesus' promise to those who left father and mother and brothers and sisters and homes and lands for his sake that they would receive in this life a hundred-fold of brothers and sisters and fathers and mothers. Certainly, my world was expanding.

When the Cuban Missile Crisis occurred in November of 1962, it created a high level of anxiety among the general population and among the student body as well, since our college was located about 120 miles southwest from Washington D.C.

For a generation raised on the propaganda of the cold war, we were led to believe in the ability and the determination of the Soviet Union to eventually defeat and perhaps incinerate the West. We took this crisis with the utmost seriousness. We honestly did not feel too sure if we would wake up the next morning or not. People were quite worried. In our minds, it seemed strange to be faced to face with the possible termination of life here on earth now. Is this the moment? Is this the end? At what moment might we see the flash of brilliance from a mushroom shaped cloud over Washington?

This perception gave us real cause to think deeply about our lives, our relationships with one another, and our relationship with our Creator. This awareness stirred, in some of us, a deeper appreciation for the peace and joy that followers of Jesus can have in such times, a peace and confidence that those in the world, outside faith, can never know.

It made me much more thankful to God for what he had done for me and for his great mercy in providing security for his children. This is the type of security no insurance company nor large bank account nor successful business nor stockpile of nuclear weapons can provide. Material possessions, and even church problems, look insignificant in the illumination of a circle of H-bombs.

Training in Service

My first involvement with the YPCA team doing cottage meetings was to visit Mrs. Shyly and her husband. She was an elderly shut-in, suffering from debilitating arthritis. She and her husband were Pentecostals. She had a deep faith, and we enjoyed visiting her. After knowing her for a few months, she passed away.

The YPCA had a prison ministry group that visited the county jail in Harrisonburg twice a week. This group usually went with a quartet or singing group of men and women and a preacher or two. The male prisoners liked the singing groups the best, especially if there were women along. After the singing and preaching, the men would visit with the male prisoners, and the women would visit the female prisoners.

My involvement started when I was asked to preach there one Sunday afternoon. It was my first sermon, if you could call it that. I spent a great deal of time in preparation and prayer. I had never been in a jail before, and I had never preached a "sermon" before. I was extremely uneasy in this unusual situation.

On November 11th, the hour came. We entered the jail and checked in at the desk. The guard unlocked the gate and let us in, then locked the gate behind us. We were in jail, but we were in a hallway. Where were the prisoners?

Oh, they were in their cells, not just behind bars, but behind a solid steel wall with padlocked steel doors and only a six-inch round glass-covered peep hole, to which one had to get up close to see inside. We could not go inside to mingle with the prisoners but had to get up close to the peephole and talk through a perforated metal plate, built into the wall for talking through. Here was my pulpit, and there was my "captive audience." What an opportunity to preach!

I was not prepared for this. I had imagined a prison chapel setting, where I could mingle with the inmates and see them eyeball to eyeball. I envisioned interacting with them, maybe give an invitation and pray with them or counsel with them individually.

But here I was before this little round, glass, hole. I had to make some fast adaptations to the real situation, so I went up to the wall and delivered my whole sermon at the wall.

I made it to the end of my sermon okay, but there was supposed to be an invitation to repent and accept the Lord at the end of my sermon. I lost my cool at this point and gave the invitation. But there was no altar in there. How should I get them to indicate their response?

I invited them to come forward to the glass window. Then, I noticed that one or two of them were already crowded around the glass window to see the preacher. How could I tell if they, or the rest of them, wanted to respond?

If they did want to respond, how could I help them anyway? The presence of this thick steel wall totally unnerved me.

I said a quick prayer on their behalf, turned and walked out to the next floor where I repeated the performance. I hated walls and locks and steel doors with glass peep holes. I did not like jail ministry. I did not like jails at all.

But there were real people locked away in there, twisted broken people who had lost the way. There were people who did not know that they were loved by God and called by Christ to a new and better level of living of which they knew nothing.

I went back to prison many times, but not always as a preacher. On the third and fourth floor, there were no solid doors, just bars separating me from the prisoners. I could stand the bars because at least we could relate face to face with the inmates.

Gradually, I built a relationship with a few of the men. I would listen to their stories, sympathize with their problems, share my faith with them, hear about theirs, and pray with them. Their lives seemed so hopeless and sad. Some of the older ones were alcoholics. Young ones were in for crimes like killing someone in an accident or under the influence of alcohol, petty theft, rape, reckless driving, or drugs.

Some of them were scared "children." Others were "tough" hardened criminals, their lives warped and twisted, bearing the scars of broken homes, child abuse, discrimination, and a thousand injustices resulting from lives lived at variance with the laws of God and the norms of society. Yet, each human being, bearing some trace of the "image of God" in them, was of infinite worth! So much unrealized potential for good! So sad!

Congregational Support at Bethany

I also joined a group of students that went out about ten miles west to Bethany, a small Mennonite church that needed help on Sunday mornings.

I was asked to teach the older ladies' Sunday school class. These elderly, stable tradition-bound saintly mothers seemed to enjoy having this young "whipper-snapper" teach them, and it was a good experience for me. It was safe for all of us because they could straighten me out when I strayed too far into dangerous thinking or revolutionary ideas. Of course, my radical ideas would never change these seasoned, stable "mothers of the faith."

After getting to know these church people, I became quite critical of them. I saw them as legalistic, bound by the traditions of their past and the control of their elders, unable to introduce anything new lest they be ostracized by their peers. As I saw it, their understanding of God was too limited, and they were bound by their undivided loyalty to the precepts of the church as set forth by the Virginia Conference in the 19th century.

They thought they could win people to come to Christ by zealously inviting them to "Come to Church" when all they offered in church was a Sunday program which consisted of a Sunday school lesson always followed by a standard two songs, scripture reading, bowing for prayer, and concluding with an often ill-prepared, highly opinionated, lengthy sermon, followed by another song. None of the regular attenders had their roots in the nearby community but drove in from the neighboring Bank Mennonite Church.

After church, our group would eat our packed lunches and then scatter out in the community two by two, a man and a woman to visit in homes.

Home visitation was interesting. We got to meet and know the non-church people in the community to whom the Bethany people were directing their invitation: "Come to Church!" I gathered that the community was hardened spiritually. Many of the residents were the descendants of the once flourishing Mennonite Church or the Church of the Brethren, which were now practically dead. They liked to brag about the attendance records and prizes they achieved when they went to Sunday school as children.

But now they were either nominal members of the Brethren, Nazarene, or United Methodist churches, but seldom attended, or they had no church affiliation and did not hesitate to say so. They had no use for the modern soft-spoken preachers but admired the "men of God" who were "not afraid to step on your toes." Yet, they made no effort to attend the church to see if indeed such preachers were preaching there. Although they knew the way, they just did not seem concerned for their own spiritual welfare.

They did not show any interest in surrendering themselves to the lordship of Christ. They wanted to live their own lives as they pleased, without any interference, and were determined to do so regardless of the consequences. It seemed to me it was a waste of time to beg these people to accept Christ, of whom they have already heard, while there are millions going to the grave without hearing the "Good News" even once. Did not Jesus instruct his disciples to leave such communities, shaking the dust off their sandals as a witness against them as they proceed on to a more receptive community?

Congregational Support at Lucas Hollow

Therefore, seeking a different experience the next summer, I was persuaded to go, with a carload of students, forty miles east across the mountains to Lucas Hollow near Stanley. Lucas Hollow was a valley between two faces on a mountain. A narrow road winds up the hollow for about six miles until it comes to a dead end at the upper extremity. The valley is very narrow, sometimes just wide enough for the road and a stream to pass. The road provides access to the many small houses and shacks that are scattered along its length.

The people living there were the "mountain people" or "mountain folk" that you read about. Reputed to be the descendants of the original English settlers that came when Virginia was a penal colony, they had been born and bred in these "hollers," as they called them, for many generations.

They lived in tiny shacks or small houses, usually surrounded with junk and remnants of old car bodies and broken-down appliances in the yard, and an outhouse, and maybe a pigpen or a chicken house. They farmed their tiny garden-sized plots of land cleared on the mountainside with a mule or by hand.

There seemed to be children, dogs, and chickens everywhere. Families tended to be large. Girls tended to begin reproducing when their biological time clocks allowed, not necessarily waiting for matrimonial arrangements to be completed first. There were many children bearing children in the same homes where the mothers were still bearing. Many of the families were on welfare.

Many of the breadwinners commuted out of the hollow to find jobs in the towns and cities that were connected by good roads.

There were other ways to make a living as well. There were nine house fires in the hollow the first year we visited there. One family owned a new car, although no one had a job in that household. We heard they had four houses burn down from the same foundation in the last few years. When it burned down once more, the insurance company cancelled all policies in the Hollow.

Remarkably, the occupants were always away on the night of the fire, and their TVs or finer furniture somehow just happened to be at a neighbor's place. Making and selling "moonshine" was also a valid way to keep self-employed. Hunting bear, deer, coons, or wild turkey supplemented their need for meat. They raised and butchered their own hogs and chickens.

Recreational activities, especially for the many unemployed, included hunting in the mountains, attending cock fights, fixing old cars, drag racing, watching T.V., drinking, sleeping, and just getting together and "spinning the yarn."

It was like a breath of fresh air to leave the work at Bethany and come to Lucas Hollow. Here was a real mission setting and a real mission church. Pastor Mahlon Horst with his wife and family put their lives into the work. They had been there for about fifteen years without pay or significant support. Mahlon earned his living by providing commuter service with his bus for the people of the community. The bus doubled as a church bus ministry on Sundays.

The Horst family lived in a basement apartment in Stanley. They had intentions of building a house on top of the basement, but due to lack of funds, the house was delayed, and they raised their family in that basement.

They had built a small white chapel up the hollow. At that time there were about 35 regular attendees at the church services. Most of them went by the surname "Cubbage." The people were very friendly. They welcomed us warmly, and we got to know many of them by visiting in their homes. We college students helped with the Sunday school.

Pastor Mahlon ran the church his way. People called it "Mahlon's Church." He was the greeter, the program leader, the song leader, the preacher, the church board, made the decisions, made the announcements, and was even the bus driver. I suspect he also paid most of the bills.

This was a good missions training assignment for me. I attended for a full year. During that time, I learned a lot about how to, and how not to do mission work. Mahlon, despite his total commitment and the laudable way he and his family sacrificed themselves, had many faults.

One of them was his dogmatic conservatism. He did not really like me to come after he found out that I was wearing a necktie at college. I did not wear it there out of respect to his convictions, but he would not let me preach in his church, and he favored those who wore the "plain suit." He tried to make the mountain people of Lucas Hollow into "Mennonites" by pushing them to adopt the plain dress customs of the Virginia Conference, at a time when Mennonites themselves were abandoning such customs.

Stretching Ends to Meet

I came to EMC with a small amount of cash and left several cattle at home for my dad to sell when I would need the money. I had calculated that there would be enough to cover the fees, tuition, room, board, and books as estimated in the catalogue: about $1,250. There was nothing left for spending money. I came with almost no clothes that weren't at least three years old and worn out.

From time to time, I took odd jobs like mowing lawns, catching chickens, and de-beaking chickens, which kept me in toothpaste, haircuts, and razor blades. I had no money for non-essentials like sodas, snacks, and entertainment. At Christmas, while everybody else went home and the dormitories were locked, I moved in with Jim Roth and Jim Hackman in their off-campus apartment. I was given a job cleaning the dormitories and waxing the floors, for eighty cents per hour.

I put these substantial earnings towards some clothes. I purchased a new suit whether I needed it or not. I got a good deal at Alfred Neys, one of the quality clothing stores in Harrisonburg at their after-Christmas sale. I got an all-wool gray-black Botany 500 suit priced at seventy dollars for fifty-five dollars and sixty cents. It fit well and was the best suit I ever owned. Of course, a new suit demanded a new shirt, socks, shoes, overshoes, overcoat, and such accessories, so the man did not look like a bum who got a new suit through relief.

By the time I was done, I was over one hundred dollars nearer bankruptcy. I figured I had not spent very much on clothes in the first twenty-one years of my life, and my faithful old fourteen-dollar sports coat was becoming an eyesore on formal dress-up occasions. With this rationale, I salved my conscience.

With the new clothes and other expenses, my total costs for the year were close to $1,500. I was short one hundred dollars, so borrowed that amount from my good brother, Peter. After I had worked for Uncle Chris, in Ontario, during the month of August, I repaid the loan in September. Dad bought my last cows from me. I took out a student loan of $780. EMC gave me a grant of $350 and a Bible major discount of $168. This saw me through summer school as well as the second year of college. However, I had no spending money for necessities like haircuts and toothpaste, let alone for entertaining any of the fairer sex.

Ontario Revisited

For the Easter break of 1963, Darrell and Florence Jantzi offered to take me to Ontario to visit my uncle, Chris, and see all my old friends and neighbors. It was more than seven years since we had seen any of them. Of course, as my habit was, I never thought to notify anyone of my coming.

We drove up to Chris's barn and got out of the car. Chris came out of the barn to see what these strangers wanted. He recognized me immediately, but he was puzzled as to how I got there, seeing that I came in an Ontario car. Chris was surprised but very glad to have me as his guest. I made his place headquarters for most of the week.

Chris was a bachelor and did not see the need to make house cleaning a high priority in his life. Since he did not have company often, it had been quite a few years since someone had slept in his guest bed. The whole house reeked of cigar smoke and stove oil fumes, the two combustible substances that he used to keep himself calm and warm. There was a layer of dead flies from how many previous summers, mixed with an accumulation of straw and dust that followed his socks and shoes in from the barn, over an equal number of years.

He invited me into his house and made some coffee and lunch. Then it was time to do the chores. After the livestock were cared for, Chris noticed that his house keeping had been neglected slightly, so he got out his vacuum cleaner and filled its bag with the flies, the dust, and the straw. It looked much improved. He found some clean sheets somewhere, and he was all ready for his guest. He found some food, and cooked up a nice, tasty meal. Afterwards, he cleaned his kitchen a bit, and then we sat down and talked way into the night. I could tell he missed having his brother and family nearby.

Chris was into raising pigs. He had remodeled his barn and built super strong farrowing pens with concrete walls four feet high and six inches thick with iron bar partitions to protect the piglets from their mother. With this setup, he was weaning an average of twelve piglets per liter.

I visited as many of our former friends and neighbors as I could. I visited the Hubers, Fosters, Cressmans, Bowmans, and Jantzis. But I could not find Carole Davison. She was working in Guelph. When she heard I was in the area, she came looking for me, but could not find me. I also visited my uncle and aunt, Albert and Martha Grove, at Hanover for two days.

Before I left Ontario, Chris invited me to return for the month of August, the free time I had between summer school and fall classes. He would have a paying job for me.

After summer school, I was back in Ontario. I really enjoyed working with Chris that month. Besides haying, cutting, stooking, and threshing, I enjoyed forking and spreading manure, plowing, and even milking his cows. I enjoyed farm work. I also visited old neighbors and went to a boxing match at Fergus with Carole Davison and her sister Ruth.

Our old farm had undergone a radical transformation. Now it was one of the nicest dairy farms in the area. The barn was enlarged and painted, remodeled completely inside. Two big silos were erected outside, a machine shed was added, new trees were planted, the swamp was drained, and most of the land was tile drained. The crop yields were at least three times as great as ours used to be.

The Radstake boys had bought Ira Huber's 200-acre farm and were renting the Johnson farm and the Lloyd Mark farm. They were doing everything we Hansen boys ever dreamed of doing. I felt afresh the pain of being cheated of our birthright by our move to Alberta.

Carl E. Hansen

News From Home

While at EMC, I kept a keen interest in what was going on at home in Alberta. Mother's letters kept me informed. Dad had found an old four-roomed house and moved it to our farm and placed it alongside and joined it to the little house already there. Electricity was brought in and installed. The family moved in on Halloween day. The house was skirted with polythene plastic, and soil was embanked around it to keep out some of the winter draught. Freda and Linda and the boys had a long walk out to the road to catch the school bus, a taxing venture on the many cold days.

Peter had done very well that first year in his trucking business. The November after I left him to go off to the university, he had already purchased his second truck and hired another crew to match. Then, in the fall of 1962, he bought out Martin's cattle trucking business. However, he did not like trucking animals, so he sold the cattle liner to Ralph Siemens and formed Raylor Trucking, of which he was a co-owner.

The demand for hay never let up, so Peter went into using flat deck trailers and tractors. He designed a system of "no-hands" unloading hay bales by dropping the front of the trailer to the ground and then, using a winch to pull the trailer out from under the load. With six hundred bales to a load, each load was a stack in itself. Gone were the days of loading hay into boxcars by hand. With these large trucks, hay could be delivered right to the doorsteps of any rancher or dairy farmer in Saskatchewan or British Columbia just as cheaply and a lot easier than by train.

Peter's business kept expanding. His reputation as a major supplier of hay spread throughout those three provinces. He even had a regular customer on Vancouver Island. He always tried to give fast, dependable service and tried to supply the exact kind and quality of hay that pleased each customer. He put effort into cultivating personal relations and in knowing each customer. His business reached its peak in the mid 1970's when he had a fleet of twenty huge trucks hauling hay for him. By that time, he had expanded to offering chopped hay and round bales to those who preferred it.

Peter was getting tired of flirting with so many girlfriends. When he met Margaret Wiebe, he settled down to some serious courting. They announced their engagement at Christmas, 1963, and were married on May 30, 1964.

A major development that disturbed me immensely was a split in the Duchess Mennonite Church. This was due, at least in part, by the influence of an outsider, a certain dissatisfied bishop from Pennsylvania, who felt it was his duty to interfere in the affairs of our bishop. With his encouragement, the conservative elements in our church were galvanized into a movement to stop the perceived "drift" of cultural change in the church towards "worldliness."

Seven families were united in this movement, and preparations were made. On a given Sunday morning, in the spring of 1963, this group presented an ultimatum to our bishop, C.J. Ramer, which demanded that our congregation withdraw from the Alberta Saskatchewan Mennonite Conference and adopt certain changes, or they would separate themselves from the brotherhood and form their own church.

This was nothing less than an attempted coup d'état. C.J. Ramer was taken by surprise, and there was no time given to discuss nor negotiate together. They demanded a capitulation.

Our bishop was also the moderator of the Conference from which they were asking him to separate. It did not make sense to him. The reasons they gave for this action were not true of our Conference nor of its congregations. The list of grievances was imported from the east and did not reflect the reality that existed in our Conference. To capitulate to their demands would be to abandon, reject, and dishonestly accuse the hundreds of faithful Christians in our other congregations. There was no way out, but to plead with them to reconsider their rash actions.

They were determined, so there was no way out. The seven large families left their brothers and sisters and started their own Bethel Mennonite Church. Now the little town of Duchess with a population of 500 had two large Mennonite churches. I could not imagine that God was very proud of them that day. Was this the proper response to our Lord's desire for unity among his followers as expressed in his prayer in John chapter seventeen?

To my way of thinking, this was completely unnecessary and unchristian. Families were divided, and Christians would not talk to each other. Deep disappointments and hurts divided them. Young people became disillusioned and bitter, and some left the church altogether.

For years after, the critical and stubborn judgmental spirit that spawned this debacle in the first place continued with them and destroyed many of those who participated. Among them, one by one, members were judged unworthy and were disciplined, banned, or excommunicated. Some of them came back to our church in contrition and were reinstated. Others moved out of the community, too proud to repent, or too steeped in tradition to return, yet were unwanted by those who led them or used them. They paid a heavy price.

Searching for a Mate

I had left that sweet girl in Saskatchewan in good standing. I had no complaint against her, but I was restless. I had carried on a courtship largely by correspondence for two and one-half years. I had limited my relationships with the fairer sex to that one person, and mostly through writing. I felt it was unfair to myself and to her. Now was the time for exploring and discovering what possibilities were out there. I needed to know what other girls were like. Here I was amid many excellent candidates, but I was limiting my courtship to a familiar address, when I should be free to explore further.

I wrote to her before Christmas explaining how I felt and asked her to suspend our special relationship for the time being. This suggestion was not very popular with her. It was one of the hardest decisions I ever made, but I felt it was something that I just had to do. After a few more letters, our relationship ended.

There is something about a young man that doesn't make sense. When he gets "free" from a long-standing relationship with a girl, he will celebrate his newfound freedom, and then he will make a new relationship and slip right back into "bondage" to another girl before he realizes it.

Now that I was "free," I determined to date around a bit. I did. However, I found myself taking girls too seriously. Instead of being free to date and concentrate on my studies, I became preoccupied with thoughts about all the choices out there. Which one should I date next? Should I ask this one again? What are my chances with that one? What a bondage and waste of time. There were too many nice girls out there, each one a challenge to get to know. Sometimes it is better to just have one to choose from. Maybe I should have stayed with the one I had?

I prayed a lot about it, asking God to guide me to the right one. I did not feel any answer, so I just went ahead exploring. "God helps those who help themselves!" There was a girl I dated several times. Then the school year ended. Should we stay connected through the summer? I was tired of writing, so I never suggested it, and neither did she.

Summer school started and would last for eight weeks. There were about seventy-two students in all. I took a heavy course of New Testament Greek, Christian evidence, and typing.

There was a Fourth of July watermelon party for staff and students. I decided to solicit the company of the fair damsel, Vera King, whom I had often noticed working at the switchboard in the information office. For today, she was willing to accompany me to the social. We began dating through the remainder of the summer.

Vera was a five-foot four inch, slim, 115 pound, fine, brown-haired, blue-eyed, smiling beauty that dressed well. She was friendly but not gushy, open but not intimate, reserved, well-organized, serious, and responsible. In getting to know her, one sensed that there was more inside that was not going to come out easily. She was from Bellville, Pennsylvania. She had come to EMC to take a one-year business certificate in 1960-61 and was working at the College since that time.

Summer school ended, and I was offered a ride with Clair Widemans, who were going to Ontario. We stopped in at Belleville, PA to attend a Mennonite Youth Fellowship (MYF) Convention. From there I wrote to my family:

> *Belleville is situated in a long, narrow, and extremely pretty Kishacoquillas Valley in central Pennsylvania. Low forested mountains form the valley walls. It is a great farming country. I had the pleasure of staying in the home of Miss King. Vera is a secretary at EMC and was home in Belleville for her two-week holiday. I had been doing a bit of courting with her this summer when there was nothing more important to do, and she extended the invitation to drop in, on our way to Ontario. She seems to be sort of a nice girl, but I did not fall in love yet, at least I do not think I did. Her family is rather nice and very hospitable. Her mother, sister, and brother live*

in a rented apartment in Belleville. Her dad died when she was fourteen.

There is one problem, no, two: indecision and competition. She is writing to a young pre-med student this summer, who is also interested. They weren't going steady though. I guess I sort of intruded, but she seemed quite willing to go with me. The other guy is dating girls at home, too, but apparently wants Vera to come back to next fall.

After the convention, Clair took me on to Ontario where I worked for my uncle Chris for the interim, from August 17 to September 17, 1963. I helped Chris and his neighbors with stooking and threshing and other farm duties. He had some of the finest crops in the community.

When I arrived back at EMC in September, I felt I needed to see Vera again, to see where we stood in our relationship. I phoned her; could I see her? Well, no, she was "busy tonight." "Tomorrow night." I had to patiently wait another day.

The next evening, I went to see her, half expecting to release her to the other guy, if she was so inclined.

Well, good fortune for me, Vera had made up her mind to terminate the relationship with the guy. Vera informed me that she was open to continue with our relationship.

Now the ball was in my court. How should I play it? I could give her a dose of the medicine she gave the other guy, which I had been prepared to receive from her myself. Or since I was the obvious winner, I could claim the winnings and move on into the future with my princess! There was no good reason to quit while I was ahead, so I was pleased to continue the relationship. My next letter home stated:

Vera volunteered to iron my white shirts the other night. She sent the other guy on his way, so I feel honored and yet cornered. She's a sweet girl, but I do not know if it's all worth the heavy price at stake, my independence. The thought of matrimony fills me with sort of an awesome feeling of horror.

Vera further enticed me by offering to do my typing. Although I had learned to type in summer school, I turned all my assignments over to her and did not practice for twenty-eight years. When I bought a computer in the fall of 1991, I took up the challenge of putting my typing skills to practice.

We continued seeing each other once or twice a week on dates and several times at work. I would sneak up to the little development office where she now worked above the men's latrine in the old administration building.

She ran the addressograph, an antique machine that clanked so loudly that one would think it was stamping out auto body parts. She was also responsible for sending out the alumni bulletins and other mailings, including responses to contributors. I could usually steal a few minutes of her time to greet her. I always seemed to be welcome, so there was no good reason to stop coming.

Back at EMC in September, I was given a room in the new men's dorm, which I was to share with Clyde Herr, a young fellow from Pennsylvania. Clyde was a likeable chap. He went with me to Lucas Hollow for church. He was a bit of a contemplative philosopher and loner. He enjoyed reading Henry David Thoreau's "Walden" and Steinbeck's "Travels With Charlie."

At the end of the semester, Clyde quit school to go and live in an eight by ten-foot camper in Lucas Hollow. He wanted to live a simple lifestyle and be free to learn their wisdom and ways from the simple people of the "holler." He also wanted to help them spiritually by befriending them and being with them in their daily lives, not just in the church on Sundays. It went well for him for a while, but then he had a fallout with Pastor Mahlon, who felt Clyde was identifying with the people too much. Clyde could not appreciate the way Mahlon kept himself separate from the people, so he got discouraged and quit.

On the weekend of November 16th, Vera brought me to her home in Belleville for a visit. It was good to get to know her family better. Her mother was a widow and had to work to raise her three children. She had a job as a nursing assistant in the Lewistown hospital.

Vera, at twenty-two years of age, was the eldest. Her brother, Sanford King, was about twenty years old. He was working for a construction company and was engaged to Mildred Byler, a local girl.

Her younger sister, Vernane, was in twelfth grade in Belleville Mennonite High School. She was very popular in school and had a lot of male admirers.

The family was poor and had been through tough times since their father, Norman King, had been injured in a fall from a cherry tree. He had broken his back and remained in a wheelchair, paralyzed from his waist down, for three years until he passed away in 1955.

Christmas 1963, for me, was nothing like that of 1962. Vera had pity on this poor "orphan" and took me home with her for one week. It was a great time for me to get to know her family and more about her as well. They treated me as one of the family.

I noted that Mrs. Elizabeth King was a real gem of a mother. She worked full time to support her children, yet she got all her housework done and a lot besides. She cared for her children, like a mother hen, seeing to every need. She welcomed me and soon treated me as one of them, loading me down with gifts and food to take back to my bachelor quarters. She even invited me to "Come again!"

Vera's whole line of ancestors were poor as well. Her grandmother, Sadie (Cutman) Hartzler, had also lost her husband from pneumonia when he was aged thirty-six. She had raised her three daughters all by herself through the Great Depression. The King family was also poor. Grandfather Ephraim King had been a carpenter, as had been his son, Norman. Hardship and premature death had left the family without lands or accumulated estates.

Vera gave me a beautiful 8" x 10" colored photo of herself for Christmas.

It was a real challenge to get to know Vera. She was very quiet and kept her thoughts and feelings to herself. I had to struggle to get her to open up and reveal her true inner self. Questions would usually get short, superficial answers that sort of closed the subject. One would have to start again from another angle to gradually open her up. Sometimes it was discouraging, and yet it was challenging because, when she did open up just a bit, I always discovered gold inside. It was worth trying.

I spent the remainder of the vacation back at EMC scrubbing and waxing floors for a pittance. I was glad to have work as I had no other source of pocket money.

My brother George had finished high school and was taking his turn at helping Dad on the farm. He had free time during the winter months and decided to attend a Mennonite Bible school run by the "Conservatives" at Carbon Hill, Ohio. He went there with some of the Torkelson boys from Duchess and attended for three weeks before coming to visit me. He was the first family member that I had seen in eighteen months. I was excited.

It was mid-January 1964, on a Saturday morning that I woke up to a knock on the door, and in walked George. Neither of us had the habit of phoning ahead. We talked all day Saturday. We made room for him on the floor, so he stayed with me for six days. He had no plans of how long he would stay, and it was my final exam week, so it was a relief to me when George decided to attend the "Minister's week," an annual gathering of Virginia Conference ministers that was being held on campus. He joined the more than seventy ministers in their activities.

At age eighteen, George was younger than most of them, but he fit right in and enjoyed the input and the fellowship very much. Most of them assumed he was a minister. One person asked me if he worked in a lumber camp or something, judging by his arms. Vera and I set him up with a blind date with her roommate, Grace. It was interesting for us all, even Grace.

George went on to visit a girl at Shippensburg, Pennsylvania. There, the relationship was terminated due to religious-cultural incompatibility, another casualty of the controversy between the churches at Duchess. George was on the wrong side, and the girl's father did not approve. He went on visiting in New York and Ontario before returning home.

Vera and I were getting attached to each other. We were struggling with the question of whether to pursue the relationship to its logical conclusion or to break it off. I really needed my family or someone to talk things over with, someone to ask questions or give advice or affirmation. However, my family was not there. On February 1, I wrote to my folks:

> *I had a real good talk with Vera last night. It's a kind of peculiar situation we're in. It seems to me that quite soon we'll either be getting engaged or be breaking up. I do not know which is the more likely, and I do not think she does either. It seems that each one thinks the other is not his/her type and yet we get along together almost perfectly. … I wish I could bring Vera home for an occasional weekend, so you could get to know her. I think you'd like her.*

On February 14, I scraped the few remaining pennies off my dresser and went and bought the nicest heart-shaped box of candy that it could buy and brought it to Vera that night with a card. She was in a romantic mood that night as well and had prepared a nice chocolate cake. I was overcome by the atmosphere of the occasion and found myself advancing to her a formal proposition of marriage.

She must have been equally enthralled by the sentiments of the evening, for she responded in the affirmative, without even any hesitation or demand for time to think it over. Wow! Now, I had conquered! Or was it her who had conquered?

We wanted to go home to Belleville over Easter and announce our engagement there. However, there was one conflict. My uncle Chris had planned to visit my folks in Duchess over Easter, and I had earlier agreed to come to Ontario and do his chores so that he could be free to go.

Therefore, we decided that I would go to Ontario, Vera would go home, and we would send out our announcements by mail anyway. It was less than ideal, but then many things in our lives were less than ideal. We measured "irregular" when it came to societal conventions.

On Thursday, March 19, 1964, I went to Goshen, Indiana, as a delegate to a Peace Conference. Friday evening, I had dinner with the fellows at Elkhart Seminary and attended a lecture at the University of Notre Dame in South Bend. One of the couples left me off at the South Bend railway station. While waiting, I wrote to my sweetheart:

> *Here I am at 9:30 p.m. seated on a cold, dusty, wooden bench in a cold, concrete, empty railroad station which would, if it were not so dirty, remind one of an ancient medieval cathedral with its immense arched ceiling and the hollow echo of vulgar voices resounding there from. What a painful contrast from our habitual Friday night activities! My train for Ontario is due at 11:16 p.m. I wonder what you are doing.* (There were no mobile phones nor texting messages in those days!)

I boarded the train that night and arrived at Kitchener at 9:00 a.m. Saturday. I tried to phone my friends at the Ontario Mennonite Bible School, but could not make contact, so I walked, carrying my suitcase the full two miles to the First Mennonite Church where the Bible school was held. There, I found friends and acquaintances from Saskatchewan and Alberta including Esther Friesen and several young people from Guernsey and Tofield.

My uncle David was not present. A friend took me to the farmer's market. We were looking around when suddenly a hand grabbed my shoulder from behind. I turned, and there was David chuckling as usual. He was accompanied by his girlfriend, Esther Derstine from Lansdale, Pennsylvania.

We went back to the Institute to have dinner with about ten western friends. David and some of the others would graduate the following week.

Visiting my uncle Chris in his home in Ontario Easter, 1964

In the afternoon, David and his two Esthers took me to Uncle Chris's farm. When we arrived, we found that he had cancelled his ticket reservations that morning. He had decided that he was not going after all. I visited around there a few days.

On Thursday morning, Chris took me to a bus in Arthur, and I set out for Belleville. I could still reach there to be with Vera for Easter. I was excited. I would walk in on her and surprise her completely. I liked to surprise people, especially her.

The bus was slow, stopping so many places and going around via Rochester, New York. It arrived in Harrisburg at 7:00 a.m. on Friday. There would be a seven-hour wait before a bus left for Lewistown. I could wait no longer. Although the ticket was already paid for, I took my little suitcase in hand and walked down to the riverfront, to the main highway. I hitchhiked the eighty miles to Belleville, arriving two- and one-half hours later.

No one was home at the King house, but the door was unlocked, so I went in, shaved, took a bath, changed clothes, and sat down and started reading a book.

You can imagine the shock Vera and her mother suffered when they came in and saw me sitting in the chair! Vera was happy that her wishes were fulfilled after all! We had a happy Easter together.

This was a very unsettled and busy year for Elizabeth King, for she was taking a one-year course in Licensed Practical Nursing in Lebanon, Pennsylvania, which she started in February of 1964. This meant that she was not earning a full salary and was not living at home. Sanford was paying the rent and keeping the apartment while Vernane was finishing grade twelve and graduating without a mother in residence. Sanford and Mildred were getting married in April without his mother to help, and now we were announcing our intention to marry, probably in the same year. It must have been quite a burden for Mother King, but we did not think much of it, and she did not complain. Somehow, she was always there when we needed her.

Suddenly, the nest-building instinct hit us. Vera had been living in the James Bomberger house with four other women for the past year. Now, since Bombergers were returning from a sabbatical abroad and would need their house, she was going to have to find other accommodations. I was very tired of living in the dorm with all the noisy immature freshmen. I was ready for marriage. Why not get married this summer? That would solve the housing problem for both of us. Vera agreed.

She had saved up $600, and she would continue working. I would work as much as I could during the summer. My tuition would be entitled to a fifty percent discount since my spouse was an employee of the school. Looking at our situation, in one way, we could not possibly afford to get married. In another way, we could not afford to not get married. We chose to look at it the latter way!

Vera found a little house belonging to EMC with two bedrooms, a living room, a kitchen-dining room, and a bathroom for forty dollars per month. It was just south of the college behind the E-building, perched up on top of an old garage that was used to store old books. It had a little porch at the back and a storage room big enough for a freezer. There was a small garden patch that they let us use for growing vegetables.

This little house had a bed, a dresser, a couch, a chair, a stove, and a fridge. We picked up a small desk for fifteen dollars and a deep freezer for seventy dollars. Mother King and Uncle Lawrence bought us a dinette set with six chairs. Vera's mother came to help for two weeks near the end of June. They cleaned the house and painted the rooms: the kitchen light green, the living room light gray, and the bedroom a light blue. Vera got drapes for the living room and curtains for the other rooms. Everything was set for housekeeping. In the beginning of August, she and Grace Neer moved in until the wedding. That little box became our first home, our love nest for three happy years, the place where we really learned to know and love each other and where our first two children were conceived.

Our friend, Darrell Jantzi, was a former car salesperson, and he was always dabbling in the used car trade. He approached us with the offer of a good, used, light tan-colored 1960 Plymouth two-door sedan, the kind that had the hugest tailfins ever. This one had gone 70,000 miles but was in excellent condition and had four new tires, and he convinced us that the Lord wanted him to sell it to us for only $650! On the market he could have sold it for at least $1000 or $1200. What else could we do?

Vera agreed with me from the start that, as a rule, we would never buy anything on credit. If we could not pay cash, we did not buy it. In compliance with that principle, our car, our start-up home furnishings, and our wedding were going to be modest, reflecting the reality of our financial condition, our convictions, and our chosen lifestyle. Yet this car was too good a deal to pass up, so we compromised our principle a little. Vera paid $450 cash and borrowed $200 from the bank, which she would pay back during the summer.

I was batching (one could hardly call it "living") in one of Perry Martin's apartments for the summer. It was Jim Roth's apartment, but he went to Ohio for the summer and was getting married as well. Sometimes, Vera, feeling sorry for me, would come over and clean it up a bit and cook me a decent meal. This was much appreciated after a dull diet of pork and beans supplemented with cornflakes for breakfast!

Vera's brother, Sanford, was married to Mildred (Micki) Byler in April. They stopped by to visit us on their way home from their honeymoon trip to South Carolina. Then, back in Alberta, on May 30, my brother Peter married Margaret Wiebe. They made a long honeymoon trip east to see us in Virginia and went on to Ontario. It was very exciting to visit with Peter again after being away for almost two years. They were with us about the same time that EMC recessed for the summer. Peter and Margaret stayed with Vera's household for the few days of their visit.

Vera and I planted a garden in the spring. Vera used her free time to sew dresses, a wedding dress for herself for eighteen dollars, and a bridesmaid dress for her sister. After I got a job, I bought a black summer suit for forty dollars and matching shoes for twenty dollars.

Contributing to the Interstate Highway System

Right up to the end of the school term, I had no idea where I was going to find a job for the summer. I knew that if I failed to find work, there was no way that I was going to be able to get married this summer. However, we had already set the date for August 15. We must have had some faith. I heard there were jobs in Denbigh, and Uncle Chris phoned me, informing me that I could get a job with Arnot's Construction in Ontario for a dollar and twenty-five cents per hour. I felt I needed to be closer to the scene, if there was in fact going to be a wedding in August.

Then, I heard there was an opening where three other college students were employed. There was a plant east of town starting on a contract to make those huge pre-stressed concrete bridge beams that span the overpasses and underpasses of Interstate Highway # 81 that was under construction at that time.

I went to apply and was employed on the spot. Wages were one dollar and thirty-five cents per hour and would be raised to one dollar and fifty cents, if we "did good work." The other workers were Don Bender, Nelson Sakwa, and Eugene Diener from EMC, and three fellows from the Elkton community.

In Virginia, you can fry eggs on the asphalt on a hot day in June or July. Working out in the sun in a huge concrete yard was stressful, to say the least, and working with steel reinforcing rods, wires, cables, and forms in the heat was almost unbearable.

Making those sixty-foot beams is not as simple as it looks. The construction bed was long enough to make four such beams at a time. There were sturdy bulkheads at each end of the bed through which passed from thirty-two to sixty-four one-half inch thick steel cables that were stretched with a hydraulic jack to about four tons stress on each cable.

Some of these cables ran straight through the beams near the bottom. Others were placed at an angle running from top to bottom and back to top in each beam. Around these cables, stretched like a tuned piano, we built a network of reinforcing rods wired together like cages.

When these innards were all in place, a crane was brought that lifted the thick steel forms into place on both sides where they were bolted fast. It would take us about three days to set up the steel infrastructure on the beds in readiness for pouring the concrete.

When all was ready, the ready-mix concrete trucks would line up, and pouring would commence and go non-stop until all the forms were full, the bubbles all vibrated out, and the covers in place, ready for curing. I usually had the privilege of operating a vibrator. That was the heaviest work, pushing the vibrator down and up through five and one-half feet of slushy concrete and a jungle of bars and wires. But one could bear it because it had an end to it. It wouldn't take more than a couple of hours to finish pouring a batch.

After pouring, the concrete-filled forms were covered with polythene plastic, which was fastened down tightly at the bottom on both sides. The curing bed had a row of iron pipes laying in a gutter underneath the beams that were covered with water. An oil-fueled boiler heated boiling oil that was circulated through the pipes. These hot pipes, in turn, made the water in the gutters give off moist, steamy heat. This created a hot, steamy environment under the polythene for the concrete to cure in. This steamy environment was to be maintained at a constant temperature all around the concrete for twenty-four hours as it cured. There were temperature-recording clocks that had to be checked every fifteen minutes throughout that curing period.

That meant that one of us, after a hard day's labor, would get the easy job of staying awake all night checking the temperature every fifteen minutes and making the necessary adjustments as required. I looked forward to that job because it often meant overtime pay.

The job did not go so well. Since it was a government contract, there were two government employed engineer inspectors on site every day to check on the quality of the beams at every stage of their construction. Everything had to be according to specifications. Samples of the concrete had to withstand a certain number of tons of pressure per square inch within a certain number of hours after being poured. We had to discard the whole beam if the samples failed the test. Our samples failed. Something was wrong with the chemistry of the aggregate, sand, water, cement, or the curing process.

The foreman was baffled, the engineers were baffled, and of course so were we. The company owners were not amused. We got no raise. The foreman was under intense stress. Each beam that had to be discarded represented an investment of $800. Out of the first twenty-four beams we produced, only six passed inspection. Things were stressful when I left to attend my wedding. The engineers did solve the problem later, as the highway bridges around Harrisonburg bear testimony. However, the atmosphere at work that summer was rather tense. My earnings reflected the situation. Some days there was no work. Other days we worked seventeen hours.

I learned something more about human beings that summer. The foreman was a hard-hearted, tough, French Canadian who was under the most stress and resorted to strong drink to prop himself up. Three of the crew were local labor, men whose understanding of the world was very limited and whose vocabulary was completely dominated by the extremely unimaginative and distasteful use of less than a dozen four-letter words.

Nelson, one of our EMC fellows, was a Kenyan, so he of course was black. Being from Africa, he had a limited knowledge of the names of, or the uses of, our tools. He spoke good English but with a Kenyan accent. These "mountain folk," as we might call the local labor, could not appreciate having Nelson on the crew. They hated black people. They could not understand his English, and they made fun of his ignorance of our technology.

Nelson was an educated and experienced schoolteacher; these guys never went to school. He understood them in a short time. He patiently and quietly endured their abuse and was kind to them. He emersed himself in the work with integrity and quickly learned the use of the tools. Soon two of the local guys were fired because they were caught smoking in the shade when they thought the boss was not looking.

When Nelson quit to go back to school in the fall, the foreman grieved over his departure, saying to him with regret, "Now you are leaving me with these prodigals."

TEN

DOMESTICATION OF A
NON-CONFORMIST

A Wedding to be Remembered

The day of our wedding was drawing near. Planning and preparations involved all of our off-work hours. Our physical examination was done, and a marriage license was procured. Invitations had been sent to 150 people. The wedding ceremony would take place in the Allensville Mennonite Church, Allensville, Pennsylvania. That was Vera's ancestral church in the "Big Valley," where her family were still members. Bishop Raymond Peachy had consented to officiate at the ceremony. The church building had been reserved for the afternoon of August 15th, 1964. The Allensville town hall was booked for a 6:30 p.m. reception.

A wedding ceremony format was agreed upon. Vernane would be maid of honor, and Grace Neer would be bridesmaid. My brother Paul would be serving as best man and Uncle David as groomsman.

A quartet agreed to sing songs appropriate to the occasion. A photographer was invited to attend and immortalize the occasion with photographs. A few flowers were ordered. The reception meal was all planned and preparations were underway.

My parents could not come due to the distance, poverty, and the priority of getting in the August harvest. Paul and David would be bringing our aunts Hedy and Esther. The four would be the sole representatives from my relatives.

I quit my job on Thursday and went to Belleville with Vera. The group from Alberta arrived on Friday. David, Paul, and I were given a place to stay at Thelma Smith's house. On Friday night, we had a rehearsal at the church. Mother King had everything so organized; I did not have much to worry about. It was soon Saturday.

We men were not allowed to visit at the King house, so there was not much to do except visit with each other. David and Paul were tired from the long journey, and I was tired from a heavy week at work. There were still three hours before the ceremony was to commence, so we decided to relax and sleep a bit. We really slept.

After a while, I woke up and saw that we had less than one hour to get dressed and get to the church! I quickly woke the others and we got bathed, shaved, and dressed in a hurry. Paul flew his 1958 red and white Plymouth Fury the six miles down the narrow, winding #655 highway to Allensville at eighty miles per hour, dodging Amish buggies, and passing sedate Mennonites, leisurely driving their sedans to a wedding! We arrived five minutes before I was to walk in, just enough time to get our boutonnieres installed. How much more time did we need?

All my life I have struggled in making decisions. Perhaps I take life too seriously. True to form, just then the thoughts struck me again, as they had many times over the last six months: Do I really want to be doing this? Am I sure that God was leading to this? Is this what I've been waiting for all these years? Is it really happening to me now? Would I be wise to bolt out the door and run for my life? This is your last chance to reconsider.

After a final review of the alternatives, I got into line and stepped through the door into the front of the church. My course was fixed, my fate sealed! Now, for the formalities.

We had chosen as the theme of our marriage, "Each for the other, and both for the Lord."

Words and music by John Petersen, copyright 1957. It was on our engagement announcements. Now a male quartet was singing

> Darling, the day has come that we've been dreaming of,
> When at the altar white, we'll say our vows of love.

Oh, what a happy time, all gone the doubt and fear,
And with all the promises, we'll add this one so dear.

Chorus:
Each for the other, and both for the Lord,
Oh, darling Sweetheart, let the angels record;
Vows sweetly spoken, that will never be broken,
Each for the other and both for the Lord.

There was no recorded or instrumental music at our wedding, as that was still frowned upon in Mennonite circles. Duets, quartets, and other special arrangements as well as congregational singing were a very adequate substitute. The quartet continued with "God Holds My Hand" and "Jesus, Thou Joy of Loving Hearts," and then as a processional, "Faithful and True."

The two bridesmaids and then the bride, smiling sweetly and a bit nervously in her radiant white gown, stepped slowly forward to the music until she was by my side. She was not "given away;" she just came of her own free will. The wedding party was seated on chairs while Bishop Peachy gave a substantive discourse on "Holy Matrimony." Then we stood to face him as he led us in our vows.

Pastor:

Dearly beloved, we are gathered here in the sight of God, and in the presence of these witnesses, to join together this man and this woman in holy matrimony; which is an honorable estate, instituted of God, and signifying unto us the mystical union which exists between Christ and His Church; which holy estate Christ adorned and beautified with his presence in Cana of Galilee. It is therefore not to be entered into unadvisedly, but reverently, discreetly, and in the fear of God. Into this holy estate these two persons come now to be joined.

I require and charge you both, as you stand in the presence of God, to remember that love and loyalty alone will avail as the foundation of a happy and enduring home. No other human ties are more tender. No other vows more sacred than those you now assume. If these solemn vows be kept inviolate, and if steadfastly you endeavor to do the will of your heavenly Father, your life will be full of joy, and the home which you are establishing will abide in peace.

Carl, will you have this woman to be your wife, and will you pledge your troth to her, in all love and honor, in all duty and service, in all faith and tenderness, to live with her and cherish her, according to the ordinance of God, in the holy bond of marriage?

I heard myself say, "I will."

Pastor:

Vera, will you have this man to be your husband, and will you pledge your troth to him, in all love and honor, in all duty and service, in all faith and tenderness, to live with him and cherish him, according to the ordinance of God, in the holy bond of marriage?

I heard her say, "I will."

Now we turned to each other and made the most sacred promises:

I, Carl, take you, Vera, to be my wedded wife; and I do promise and covenant, before God and these witnesses, to be your loving and faithful husband; in plenty and in want; in joy and in sorrow; in sickness and in health as long as we both shall live.

I, Vera, take you, Carl, to be my wedded husband, and I do promise and covenant, before God and these witnesses, to be your loving and faithful wife; in plenty and in want; in joy and in sorrow; in sickness and in health as long as we both shall live.

Then the pastor turned to us both and said:

> As you now recall your personal commitment to Christ at
> the time of your baptism and consecration to Him and to
> His service, do you now renew this pledge and endeavor
> by the grace of God to establish a home in which Christ
> shall be the head, in which his love shall be practiced, his
> Word shall be read, and his Church shall be honored and
> upheld? If you are willing to assume this obligation, then
> answer with one heart and one mind.

And we both heartily replied, "We do." After this the pastor announced
to the congregation:

> For as much as Carl Hansen and Vera King have
> consented together in holy wedlock and have witnessed
> the same before God and this company, and have thereto
> pledged their faith to each other, and have declared the
> same by joining hands, I as a minister of the Gospel and
> as authorized by the state of Pennsylvania, pronounce that
> they are husband and wife together, in the name of the
> Father, the Son and the Holy Spirit. Those whom God
> hath joined together let not man put asunder.

Then we knelt, and the pastor prayed for us.

After that the quartet sang, "O God of Wisdom." Then we stood
and a duet sang, "Since first my soul was knit to thine." Then we were
introduced to the people as "Mr. and Mrs. Carl Hansen." We marched out
as the quartet sang, "May the Grace of Christ Our Savior."

Then followed the usual congratulations in the receiving line and some
photo opportunities. After that we made our way to the community hall
for a light supper reception. The guests were served sandwiches, cake, and
ice cream, and punch.

Vera and I were married on August 15, 1964. The wedding party, L. to R.:
Marvin Peachy, usher, Grace Leichty, Vernane (King) Stutzman, Vera, Bishop
Raymond Peachy, Carl, Paul Hansen, David Friesen, and Sanford King, usher

A Honeymoon Like no Other

According to the prevailing custom of the times, the bride's family would provide and pay for the wedding celebrations, and the groom was responsible for arranging and paying for the honeymoon. Vera paid most of the wedding expenses. I would pay from my summer earnings for the wedding trip.

I had no experience with arranging honeymoons, so I did what I knew. We had packed for a trip to Canada beforehand. Our plan was, after the first night in a nearby motel, to go to Niagara, spend a night at a hotel, visit the Falls, go on to Ontario, visit our uncle Chris and other relatives, spend a night with him, then take the CPR Flyer (a Canadian Pacific Railroad luxury passenger train) to Brooks, Alberta, visit for two weeks, then return to Ontario and drive home. But I had made no reservations, not even for the motel for the first night.

In finishing all the business details, we weren't able to set out for our wedding trip until after ten o'clock p.m. We were already tired when we started west towards Highway #219. We began looking for a motel right away. It is interesting how motels are scattered everywhere along highways, until you need one. Then of course, they are invisible. We kept going on from hamlet to hamlet, slowing down to look for motels, but no luck. One or two were found but were decorated with flashing neon "No Vacancy" signs.

Our growing despair was relieved as we approached Philipsburg, where we found one that had a room for us. By then, it was near midnight, and we were very tired. We were just happy for anything that we could crawl into.

The next day, we got up at a more relaxed and leisurely pace. We had breakfast and then set out for Niagara Falls.

We took a guided tour of the Falls from the American side. Our American tour guide kept pointing out the inferiorities of the Canadian side. He said the gasoline over there was more expensive, and the quality of the premium was the equivalent of America's regular, and the regular was so bad it would hardly burn. Canadian roads were bad or non-existent, except for the Queen Elizabeth Way, which was not too bad. His degradation of Canada went on and on.

If it had not been our honeymoon, I would have made a fool of myself by seriously challenging him in front of all the other tourists. Considering the festivity of our occasion and the sensitivities of my new American bride, I managed to restrain my nastier impulses.

We found a motel near Niagara Falls with a swimming pool. Vera did not know how to swim, so I decided that I would take this opportunity to teach her.

How naïve a man can be! On my first day of marriage, I learned lesson number one: A husband should never undertake to teach his wife. Period. After fifty-eight years of marriage, Vera still does not swim. We had a nice evening there anyway.

On Monday we crossed the border into Canada. We spent some time visiting historical Fort Erie and some other places like Queenstown Heights.

An essential component of my honeymoon scheme was that Vera and I would experience our uncle Chris's hospitality together, including staying one night in his "honeymoon suite," his guest room!

When we reached his place, we found Paul, David, Esther, and Hedy had already preceded us and were visiting our uncle Chris, and we had a nice visit.

Paul was to hurry back to Alberta to be "best man" in Fred & Eileen Barg's wedding the next Saturday. He would be leaving on Wednesday.

Would we like to ride along back with him and the other three? We would save train tickets for two, and we would drive straight through, getting there in good time!

To an economy-minded student, a child of poverty, Paul's offer was very tempting, too good to turn down, even if we were on our honeymoon. Vera reluctantly agreed to accept her new brother-in-law's generous offer.

Vera had heard me talk about Chris and his living conditions, but she was not prepared for the real thing. The outhouse had not been used nor cleaned since Mrs. French had moved off the place. Chris did vacuum the latest crop of dead flies off the bedroom floor, and he did produce some clean sheets for the ancient, squeaky, sagging bed. It was not exactly Vera's idea of an ideal honeymoon accommodation, but it was cheap!

The next morning, we parked our car at Chris's place and set out on a never-to-be-forgotten journey west, a honeymoon like no other!

Vera was not exactly thrilled about this sudden change in plans. She was looking forward to the luxurious train ride aboard CPR's world famous "Flyer." But here she was, stuffed in between a bunch of five newly acquired relatives whom she hardly knew, in a car that burned more oil than gasoline, and that was being driven by a new brother-in-law who never heard of a speed limit, let alone a defensive driving course. To know that we would be driving non-stop, the full 2050 miles from Ontario to Duchess, Alberta, squeezed in this car, without any place to stretch out and rest was a test!

The farther we went, the more she knew it was a terrible mistake to commit her life to be a member of this family! What other unknown horrors awaited her at the western end of her journey of destiny? What kind of a monster had she married that would bring her to such a place? Why had she not insisted on an investigative trip to meet his family before making such an irrevocable lifetime commitment? "Until death do us part!" What does that mean? The inexperienced thoughtless reckless daring of youth!

We made that trip in about forty hours, arriving at my folks' place around midnight or early Friday morning, August 21. We really surprised Mom and Dad. There was no telephone in the house. Of course, they had no idea that Paul would be bringing Vera and me. They expected us to come by train as planned.

We came into the kitchen and made a lot of noise, so Mom came out of the adjoining bedroom to investigate, and there we were. She was happy to see us and welcomed Vera. It was a bit embarrassing to welcome a new daughter-in-law at that hour, in her night attire, but what else could she do?

We were shown to an empty bedroom and were soon asleep. It was a long journey, one leg of a different sort of honeymoon.

We spent seventeen wonderful days in Alberta visiting and introducing my lovely bride to my family and friends. So much had changed in two years. The church had changed a lot through its troubles. My family had moved to the new farm. My brother Peter was now married and was living with Margaret in a house trailer on the yard of his business premise. Edward had married Faye Roth and had moved to Eaglesham.

I helped Dad with the harvest for a few days. I particularly enjoyed driving his brand new International 610 tractor. He must have hit good times on the farm. I borrowed Dad's old red car and took Vera around to all the famous and not-so-famous tourist points of interest in the Eastern Irrigation District (EID).

I wanted to show her the John Ware Coolie. I lost the way and got into a slough. I saw the water on the trail too late, so instead of stopping and backing out, I made a bad decision and floored the accelerator, hoping to slide through to the other side. However, I did not know that there was no dry "other side," so we got in as deep as we could!

We tried to back out of the brown, watery goo but were in up to the frame. Paul, who was along, walked several miles home to get the tractor. Sadly, the chain was too short, and the tractor could not help us either.

Finally, he had to go borrow the tow truck from the Duchess Garage where he worked. Vera was not very impressed with my driving after that. She was a no-nonsense girl and failed to see much humor in standing around in an alkali slough swatting mosquitoes for several hours on an otherwise pleasant sunny afternoon. Even decades later, whenever my driving becomes a reference in discussion, I am reminded of my dismal record. She does have a way of keeping me humble, at times!

Vera helped my mother with the housework, washing clothes and canning the produce of the garden. Mother was impressed with her ability to work fast and efficiently. I think any fears she might have had about entrusting the health and welfare of her little boy to the care of a strange

Pennsylvanian woman vanished completely. Mom confided in her diary, "We think Vera will make a good wife."

The church people decided to put on a joint reception for us and Fred and Eileen Barg. This was a pleasant surprise. Vera had brought her wedding dress along to show the family, so that was an advantage. The members gave us gifts of money that came close to $200.

Hansen family welcomed us home on our honeymoon: Back l to r: Charles, Peter, Carl, Paul, George. Middle: Linda, Margaret, Vera. Front: Elizabeth, Freda, & Jens—August 1964

Too soon, it was time to head back east to get settled into our new home before the fall semester of college began. I went to the CPR station in Brooks and asked to book two one-way tickets to Arthur, Ontario, for Monday morning, September 7th.

Imagine my horror when the ticket agent looked at me incredulously and informed me that the train was full. Such tickets had to be booked at least three months in advance! The beautiful promotional pamphlets had not mentioned that.

Now what could I do? We must get back next week. There was only one thing left to do, and it was the least desirable thing to do on a honeymoon journey, which was to go by Greyhound! Maybe they would have a waiting list too?

To my deep relief, at the Greyhound bus station, the clerk responded positively to my inquiry: "Yes, there is still room on the Monday bus, and a one-way ticket costs only a money-saving sixty dollars per person!"

Monday morning found us saying, "Goodbye!" and boarding a bus heading east.

The bus was quite full, and in those days, there was no "non-smoking" section, so we were about smoked enough to be "smoke-cured" by the time we arrived in Arthur two days later.

The bus ride was not bad the first day, but by the end of the second night, it was getting mighty slow and painful. It seemed to stop at every hamlet along the way. Vera's feet were swollen and hurting. Her enthusiasm for our "honeymoon" reached an all-time low about then.

But every negative has a positive side to it. The good side of this tortuous journey was that even the prospect of sleeping another night at Uncle Chris's "bridal suite" was welcome!

We arrived at Chris's place at noon on Wednesday, slept there that night, and drove to Belleville the next day. There, we loaded our car with the wedding gifts and several boxes of frozen food prepared by our concerned mother. We settled into our own new nest on Friday, September 11, 1964, at 8:00 p.m.

For a poor student who had nothing, and a poor girl who had very little, we had had a "honeymoon" like no other! We had been gone one day short of four weeks, had traveled over 5,000 miles, and came back with money left over in our pocket! That has been sort of symbolic of the story of our lives ever since.

Marriage: The Challenge of Domestication

Our marriage got off to a good start. There were a lot of things that I, a rather unrefined specimen of the male gender, had to learn about treating a woman properly. I provoked tears more often than necessary. Then, I would have to repent and apologize, and usually the making up was worth the agony that necessitated the making up. Gradually, we learned to understand, accept, and respect each other for what and who we were.

From the very beginning, Vera was a first-rate homemaker. She always wanted things neat and tidy and done on time. No spider webs nor dust stood a chance in Vera's house. She also was the best cook. She spoiled me with her pies and desserts. We started to gain weight.

I had no excuse, but soon learned there was another reason Vera was gaining weight. I wrote home in January:

> *The way things look now, a stork may be coming through these parts. He is tentatively scheduled to arrive on June 28, 1965. The shipment we ordered should be a strapping big masculine nine-pounder with blue eyes and blond hair, but if otherwise, we will be happy anyway.*

A Year of Change

I began my senior year in college, this time as a married man. It was great to be out of the dormitory, where I found the immaturity of the boys there increasingly annoying. Also, as a senior working on a double major in Bible and history, I found the courses more mature and interesting.

As to extra curriculars, I served as president of the Mennonite Historical Society. Since I stopped going to Lucas Hollow on Sundays, Vera and I decided to attend the Park View congregation where I served as assistant to Darrell Jantzi as teacher of the college class. I continued visiting in the jail on some Sunday afternoons.

Vera's sister, Vernane, enrolled as a freshman at EMC.

For Christmas, we visited Vera's home in Belleville. This time we went to spend Christmas day with the family of Vera's aunt, Lena Cashman. It was the one time that I actually was able to talk a little to her husband, Sidney, who was seldom home with his family. He had some stories to tell about the time, in a previous era, he spent at EMC. He used to run around with youthful and fun-loving Paul Martin, now the dissenting preacher at Duchess, and he remembered my uncle Jake Friesen who had been there for a Winter Bible school.

After Christmas, I worked for George Swick, a bricklayer, for a week, mixing mortar and keeping the four bricklayers supplied with bricks and mortar. That made us a few extra dollars that delayed economic collapse. The man offered me part-time work whenever I wanted it.

Vera's mother graduated in February as a certified Licensed Practical Nurse (LPN), but there was no job in Lewistown for her, so she got a job doing homecare for a while. Eventually, she got a job in the Huntington Hospital where she worked until her retirement some twenty years later.

Responding to the Changing Times

Having been founded in 1917 by the Virginia Mennonite Conference, Eastern Mennonite College had always been owned by and operated under the control of the Conference. As such, it had always been a conservative institution reflecting the theological and cultural values of its supporting constituency.

However, in the 1960s, the winds of change were sweeping across the nation, challenging the status quo. The church and its college were not exempt. Changes were taking place at EMC, albeit on a very modest scale. I wrote:

> *EMC is turning "liberal," I guess. This summer Virginia Conference made it permissible for EMC faculty members to wear ties if they are not ordained men. Now it's a lot easier to identify the "rebels." One, the most rebellious, doesn't stop with a modest tie, but wears a bright stripped one with a big, oversized gold pin. Even professors are human, I guess.*

Another first, the Conference granted the college permission to allow the wearing of caps and gowns for the first time, convenient for my 1965 graduation. It seemed they are letting up on one restriction after another. Critics were becoming alarmed at the question of where this trend is going to stop. Others questioned, "Should it stop?" Progressives questioned, "Why is change taking so long?"

Eastern Mennonite College was actually still a very conservative Mennonite institution. Women were required to wear "prayer veils" and dresses. Shorts, slacks, and pants suits were taboo. Theologically, the stance of EMC was evolving from a simple Mennonite fundamentalist view, re-discovering the deeper faith and implications of its historic Anabaptist roots, and figuring out how to relate to the newer Evangelicalism that was replacing the older Fundamentalism in America in that era. Its motto was "Thy Word Is Truth." I reassured my mother:

> *At this point EMC is no haven for the liberal professor. The opposition is too strong, and the pay is too small. It takes a certain amount of self-sacrifice to work here. Many of our professors could get two or three times as much salary elsewhere. Sometimes poverty helps preserve purity. Much of the heresy stories you hear about our educational institutions ... are the products of ignorance, vivid imagination, and malicious gossip ...*
>
> *Vera works for our two public relations men. They bring home the most fantastic reports and complaints from the constituency. One of our most conservative Bible professors has enough counts against him to merit his "burning at the stake." It is too bad that these reports are always eagerly told, eagerly believed, and eagerly passed on (with minor embellishments). People are always prone to believe the worst. Why is it so difficult to believe the best?*

Unidentified Flying Objects

Professor Earnest G. Gehman and a group of interested students formed an "Unidentified Flying Objects Investigating Club." It got quite a bit of publicity on campus and in the community through the press and local radio.

Late in December, a man reported to the club that he had been driving down a road near Staunton, when suddenly, he saw a thing come down from the sky and land in the field a few hundred yards from the road. At the same time his car stalled, as if it had run out of gas or the ignition had been switched off.

He said this object was about one hundred and twenty-five feet in diameter, about seventy-five feet high, and circular in shape, built in receding layers, somewhat like the old round beehives.

The poor man said he was scared, but he got out of his car to get a better look. The thing rose straight up off the ground silently, then with a swooshing sound, it veered out at an angle and was gone in a few seconds. He said there was a ring of green flame around the whole bottom. When he got back in his car, it started right up, and he drove home. He said he was too afraid to tell anyone, thinking he would never be believed.

A week later, he heard over the radio of the UFO Club and decided to call Professor Gehman. The professor went out to the field with a Geiger counter and reported that the field was "hot" with radioactivity, just in a circle of about 125 feet in diameter! That convinced him.

There had been other reports earlier of such an object landing and burning off the grass where it landed, so Professor Gehman, EMC, the UFO, and the man got good media coverage!

This provoked more reports from others who claimed to have sighted the same. One guy reported that he was out in his field when two of these machines landed beside him. Three little green men, about thirty-seven inches tall, came out and walked towards him. He said they came within twelve yards of him and stopped, stood, and looked at him for thirty-five minutes. Then they went back to their machines and were gone. Another boy reported he saw the three green men in his field too.

Some of the men of the community began to carry guns with them, hoping to shoot one of them. It got so bad, the police issued a warning that they would be checking the area for men carrying firearms and would prosecute any who did not have a good excuse.

I wrote home, rather facetiously: "We are living in expectancy of an invasion by intelligent beings from outer space. So long for now. If you do not hear from us again, you can be sure the green fellows have taken control."

Reflecting upon the hysteria of that time from the vantage point of fifty-five years later, we can dismiss so much of this as "conspiracy theories" or "fake news" or simply "yarn-spinning." Yet, sightings of "UFOs" are back in the news today, and personally, I have not heard that anyone has explained the readings of the now late Professor Ernest Gehman's Geiger counter, indicating the radioactivity of the circle in the field mentioned above. Those of us who knew this honest professor know that he would rather die than lie! The mystery remains for those who wish to speculate.

Celebrating Graduation

The school year slipped by very quickly. Marriage might have had something to do with my getting on the honor roll for the first time. I loved school and could have become a professional student if there had been any employers. The month of May brought exam week and the end of the school year. June 6th was the day of our class graduation. My brother Peter and his wife, Margaret, drove from Alberta to help us celebrate this special occasion. Along with my mother and sister, Freda, they brought their little two-month-old daughter, Kathy. I was delighted to have my family present for this historic event.

Peter had driven the full 2400 miles from Alberta, couped up with a carload of women including the fussy baby. Being tired, he suggested that he and I escape for a day or two to see the sights of Washington, leaving the women behind. I, in good conscience, could not do that, leaving my mother and sister who had travelled equal distance to see us. I replied that it wouldn't be right for the rest of them. Later, Peter congratulated Vera on her successful job in "domesticating Carl."

Earning a Living

I was offered a summer job for one dollar and fifty cents per hour and promised fifty-one hours per week if I wanted to work for Mr. George Swick, the bricklayer. I was glad to accept.

I sweated the whole summer, mixing mortar and carrying bricks or blocks for the three brick layers, George, Caroll, and Allen. I was to keep all three of them busy laying, and they were fast. I could not always keep up, especially when we were doing the two or three-story jobs that involved scaffold work. Then, one of them would help me a bit. We could lay up a block basement in one day or brick a three-bedroom house in five days.

On Saturdays, I was given the extra job of washing the bricks down with hydrochloric acid. This involved wetting the bricks with a garden hose, then scrubbing them with an acid solution of one part 4% HCl mixed with ten parts of water. I would have to work at this, often from a ladder or a scaffold, with a short-handled brush in one hand and a scrapper in the other hand. Then when the excess mortar was all loosened, it would be hosed down again until the bricks were clean.

It was a very dirty job, and the acid was dangerous. The wind would blow the spray from the brush in my face. It burned holes in my clothes until I found some indestructible old nylon trousers that were even immune to acid. That was okay for a while until the acid contacted the threads that held the trousers together. The thread was not immune to the corrosive substance. When my pants started to fall apart, I did have a problem. I still have scars on my knuckles from acid burns.

When Peter came for my graduation, he helped me clean one house. He said he was glad he was in the hay business!

I started a second job of a different nature, a business, actually. I would try my luck as an all-American, self-employed, capitalist, businessman: a Fuller Brush salesman, to be exact. My friend was making up to fifty dollars a day, so why not me?

I got the start-up kit and went out for two hours one evening after work. I made no sales. The next night I went out again and sold a couple of cans of polish. After that, I was too tired and discouraged to go out anymore. I hated going door-to-door, meeting strangers, and representing a company and product I did not believe in myself. I would never be a salesperson. I reported home: "*My Fuller Brush business has come to a standstill. I haven't got the heart nor the conscience to cajole people into buying something they do not need nor want.*" I packed up my start-up kit and sent it back to the company.

Adjusting to Parenthood

About a week after Peter and company left, on Wednesday, June 16, 1965, Vera woke me up about three-thirty a.m. and said she was feeling pains. We tried to rest a bit more but were too concerned, so I took her to the Rockingham Memorial Hospital at five o'clock. I thought it would not take very long, so I stayed in the waiting room like a "domesticated" husband. It was a rainy day anyway, and there would not be any work. I waited all day, until about 5:00 p.m. before they brought me the good news that I was the father of "a healthy baby daughter." Then they let me in to see Vera. She was worn out by her hard work and was crying because she figured I would be disappointed in her for not producing a son! Well, I had no reason to expect a son, so I tried to comfort her.

I sent a telegram to my parents the next day:

Cynthia Marie Hansen arrived on the scene of action swelling our family population by fifty percent. This eighteen-and-a-half-inch tall beauty presented her six pounds and twelve ounces of glamour at five p.m., June sixteenth. Mother and daughter are fine. A toothless grin for Grandma.

A few days later I followed this news with a letter:

Our normal pattern of living has suffered another upheaval. It appears that this disruption will be permanent. The weighty responsibilities of fatherhood are crushing down upon me. Cynthia Marie is being bathed at the moment. Both of the ladies came home yesterday afternoon. Vera's mom and sister came from Belleville yesterday also. They brought Vera from the hospital since I was working about forty miles away.

Vera's mother had come with Vernane on Saturday while I was cleaning a house in Edinburg. She went home on Monday, but Vernane stayed and helped Vera for a week.

Cynthia was a very good baby. Vera began feeding her cereal at four weeks of age. She ate a lot, grew very quickly, slept well, and hardly cried at all. She developed into a pretty and happy baby. We were very proud of her and took her along to show her off at David Friesen's wedding at Lansdale, Pennsylvania when she was about five weeks old.

In December I wrote to my folks:

We had Cindy in for inspection ... The Doctor says that for size she is in the top 10% both in length and weigh, so she must have a few Hansen genes in her body somewhere. She is getting her first tooth now. ... She sure is a happy baby, never sick or complaining. She howls only as a last resort to gain the attentions necessary for the sustenance of life. For this we are exceedingly grateful.

Four generations: L. to R.: Grandmother Elizabeth King, Mother Vera holding Cindy, and great grandmother, Sadie Hartzler - 1965

On to Seminary

In September 1965, I was found back in the familiar classrooms at EMC. Only this time, I was enrolled as a first-year student in the Master of Divinity program at Eastern Mennonite Seminary.

As the Seminary was in its early developmental stage, I was one of only seven students in the whole three-year program. Since a separate facility had not yet been built, classes were held in the same old classroom with which we students were so familiar.

Vera and I had debated as to whether we should move to Goshen Biblical Seminary in Elkhart, Indiana, to carry out my seminary studies, but in light of the logistical and monetary challenges of moving our family to a new setting, we chose to stay in our home place where we had scholarship support and a part-time brick cleaning business to keep us alive while studying. It was easier to stay than to uproot and move to unfamiliar territory.

I enjoyed the first-year classes as a whole, except for Greek. The weakness of this infant seminary was that its teaching faculty were the same persons who had been teaching in the Bible department of EMC's bachelor's degree program. As such, I was already familiar with most of the professors' views, their jokes, and their stories. Most of them were old, conservative, and unimaginative.

J. P. Jacobzoon was a guest lecturer that year from the Mennonites in the Netherlands. He added a remarkably interesting slant to the Mennonite history and theology classes. He espoused Neo-orthodoxy, which brought a breath of fresh air to our institution, which had been holding to the conservative position that Neo-orthodoxy was, in fact, a dangerous heresy.

It was interesting to me, in my stay those years at EMC and EMS, to cross paths with the high and famous of our denomination, especially persons who had stirred my imagination during my adolescent years.

Of particular note was Myron Augsburger. I remembered him as that dynamic, twenty-two-year-old, super-preacher, holding us spell-bound in his tent crusade in Ontario. Now, he was my teacher, a theology professor, as well as a nationally known communicator in North America. He completed his PhD while carrying on his active ministry in the years I was there. After my graduation from college, he was installed as the new president of Eastern Mennonite College and Seminary, a position which he held for the next fourteen years.

Another of those men who had caught my attention in my early adolescent years was George Brunk. After a long career of revival preaching all over North America, he re-tooled by enrolling in the Union Presbyterian Seminary in Richmond and was finishing up his dissertation to receive his PhD when he was installed as Dean of the Eastern Mennonite Seminary during my second year there.

One of the requirements of the seminary program was that each student should get supervised practical experience in a church. I chose to go to the Ridgeway Mennonite Church and help as an assistant pastor. This was a small mission church located on the east side of Harrisonburg in a residential area that had been rather run-down, but was undergoing urban renewal, with low-cost housing developments replacing the slums. The church was meeting in a small cinder block building along Reservoir Street, and a new building was under construction. Vera, Cindy, and

I made this our home church for the remaining two years we lived in Harrisonburg.

I soon got the impression that cooperating as a supervisor to a seminary student was a new challenge for the pastor, Dan Smucker. At that time, he was a middle-aged family man, one of those saints who, despite the lack of advanced training, served the Lord by founding and pastoring a mission church without pay for many years and supported his family by running "Dan's Auto Body," a shop just north of Park View. Vera and I attended for a whole semester before he recognized that he was supposed to be supervising me in the role of pastoral ministry.

My first chance to preach at Ridgeway finally came on January 16, 1966. At 2:00 p.m. on Saturday afternoon, Pastor Dan Smucker called me and asked me if I could preach tomorrow since he had a bad cold. It was short notice, but I had some things ready from Homiletics class. I spoke on "The Christian's Warfare" from Ephesians 6:10-20.

I agonized about the mystery and the calling to preaching. Can God use something I say to help someone else? It seems incredible. If he can't, then I have no business saying anything in that capacity. Yet, it is through his Word and/or through his Spirit-filled messenger that the Holy Spirit does speak. The whole revelation of God came to us through human instruments, some of them rather imperfect.

The questions then came to me: Who is a spokesperson for God? What makes a person qualified to speak? Is it the amount of training and understanding one has, or is it the arbitrary decision of the ecclesiastical officials (like Pastor Dan asking me to preach) that makes one ready to speak for God? Is it a special gift of the Holy Spirit that comes upon a person and empowers him/her to such a degree that he/she cannot be silent even if the "powers that be," in the church, try to shut him/her down like Jeremiah? Or perhaps there are times when every Christian is a spokesperson for God?

In the seminary, students worked as "assistant pastors" in various congregations. We were assigned this responsibility without having to undergo extensive examination on doctrine or the like. For me, I was given only one request: "Please, do not wear your necktie in the pulpit." Quite rigorous screening for so sacred a task! Of course, young preachers need practice, but unless this is more than practice, aren't the people who came expectant being cheated?

I can work up, on my own strength, a fairly neat little outline. That's the bone. However, the people want and need meat, juicy meat loaded with vitamins and minerals. This takes more than a homiletics student to produce. This is where I needed God desperately. My life had been so empty of God, that now, when I came to draw on the accumulations, I found so little there.

For the remaining year and a half, Vera and I and Cindy attended Ridgeway. I preached about once a month and taught a Sunday school class.

That fall, after leaving my summer employment with George Swick and company, I bought a ladder, a jug of acid, a box of brushes, some gloves, a scrapper, and a garden hose, and cleaned houses for him by contract on Saturdays. He gave me thirty-five dollars per house, and I could usually finish a house in a single day. That was a nice supplement to our income.

Vera was only working half time since Cindy was born. Vernane and I helped out with babysitting when she was at work. With my contract work, and a $300 grant from the Alberta-Saskatchewan Conference, we managed to get through the year without borrowing.

My brother Paul and Aunt Esther paid us a visit in February. Esther was graduating from Ontario Mennonite Bible School in a few weeks. Paul had left his job in Alberta and gone to the Bible School also. He was enjoying the social aspects of it the most. He was very restless and was exploring the possibilities of settling in Ontario.

In March, all the seminary students went on a tour to meet church leaders and to give a few programs in selected churches. We visited church centers in Lancaster, Franconia, and New York City, having very interesting dialogue with church leaders at each location.

The day after I got home from the tour, Vera and I started out on a journey to Ontario. We wanted to attend Esther's graduation. We stopped at Belleville and took Mother King along. We showed her the Niagara Falls and other highlights. We stayed nights at Dan Jantzis and met westerners such as Fred Bargs and Paul Martins at the graduation.

The next day we introduced our mother to another style of housekeeping at Chris Hansen's place. Chris was happy to see us.

He had done a lot of remodeling in his barn, including installing a barn cleaner. His house was changed, almost beyond recognition. Outside, he covered the bricks with a layer of white stucco and painted the perma-stone base and the roof black, and the wood trim green, and put on new aluminum storm doors and windows. Inside, he had fixed up the kitchen with a new ceiling, wall paneling, and linoleum on the floor.

He had bought an old 1960 Chevrolet, which he did not like. While he was showing the car to me and saying that it was quite rusty, he gave the fender a kick. His foot went right through the fender. "Oh." he said, "It's worse than I thought!" The back seat floor had a hole in it due to the rust, so he mixed a batch of concrete, and poured about four inches on the floor. "That should take care of that problem!"

That evening, we stopped in to see Clarence Hubers for a while. The next day we visited the museum home of William Lyon McKenzie King, one of Canada's greatest prime ministers, in Waterloo. Then we visited the Elora Gorge on the Grand River and went on to Hanover. Sunday, we drove back to Virginia.

A Brief Foray into a Penitentiary

In late April, I got a temporary job of a different sort. A new penitentiary was built about seven miles north of Harrisonburg. The convicts worked on highway projects in "chain gangs." They did not wear chains, but they had armed guards with rifles to prevent their escape. I was asked to teach a class there for two hours, two nights per week. I had two classes: fourteen in the nonreaders up to grade five group, and seven in a higher group.

This was a new and unique experience for me. Going through all the steel gates and hearing the locks going shut behind me as we went in, and then being alone and mingling with the "dangerous criminals" took some getting used to.

It took me a while to find out what each person could do. Some had intellectual challenges, and some had been out of school for too long. They were all black, victims of poor schooling opportunities and poor homes. Each one really needed a tutor. The authorities did not supply enough books, either. Some of them were real nice guys and tried hard. Others were so troubled that it was a rather hopeless and thankless task to help them.

A Summer to Remember

The summer of 1966, I got involved in brick cleaning full time. I loaded the ladder and a barrel of acid into the trunk of our Plymouth and went around to the various builders and offered my professional services. I lined up enough work to keep me busy most of the summer. I took two weeks off to attend an Evangelism Institute at EMC in late June. Since I was self-employed, I experienced a new freedom of managing my own schedule. Apart from houses, I got contracts to clean a medical center, a new elementary school, the Ridgeway Church, and a new dormitory for Madison College. By the end of the summer, I had averaged four dollars an hour after expenses were deducted.

Cleaning the dormitory was a big bite for me. It was at least forty feet high and had 140,000 bricks in it. I was to get four dollars per thousand. I went to start, but my twenty-foot ladder was inadequate, so the builder loaned me his fifty-foot wooden extension ladder.

I was not used to working on the top of a forty-foot, shaky, wooden ladder. The wind blew water and acid into my face, as I, clinging desperately close to the ladder and acid bucket with one hand, reached out my other timid hand with the brush or scraper. As I dismounted, I noticed that one side of the wooden ladder had a bad split in the middle. Amazingly, it had not broken!

I got another one, but I did not fully trust it. I worked all day and came home a nervous wreck. I could not sleep that night. I was climbing and falling off ladders all night. I had no insurance and decided it was not worth it. I would drop the contract.

I went back and told the builder that I could not finish it. He understood my problem but asked me to get help and use a swinging scaffold instead. Well, I was not about to look for someone to hire, and I had no experience on a swinging scaffold, so I turned the offer down. There were other jobs waiting that better fit my mode of operations.

Within a day or two, my good college friend, Leroy Berry, came along to see me. He was looking for a job for a month or so before going off to start graduate school. No, I did not know where he could find a job! Then it dawned on me; here is my answer to the dormitory challenge. Therefore, I went back and took up the challenge.

Leroy and I learned to fasten the "sky hooks" over the tops of the walls, then winch ourselves up to the top on this swinging scaffold. We would clean all we could reach from one position, then winch ourselves down about seven feet and clean another patch. At first it was scary for both of us, but we got used to working swinging thirty-five feet in the air as if we were on the ground.

Leroy had a good sense of humor, so we had a lot of fun. We were like brothers. We both were graduates with BA degrees, both loved history, theology, and politics. We argued, discussed, and joked as we worked. Leroy boarded with us during those few weeks he worked.

Leroy Berry Jr. was a poor boy from Sarasota, Florida, before he came to EMC. He was an African American who remembered how it was in the deep south before the civil rights movement made its impact upon America, when a black man could not even use the same toilet facility as a white man or eat in certain restaurants where a sign was posted "Dogs and Black people not allowed." He was the oldest of eleven children, and at age fifteen, felt the deep pain of his mother and family when his father abandoned them in the fall with only fifteen dollars to their name.

He had felt the deep joy of learning about God's love for him personally at a little mission Sunday school in Sarasota, and then, the rude reminder that he lived in a world of sin and hate and prejudice, when he was fired from his job because he waved and said "Hi!" to his Sunday school teacher, just because she was white and female.

He knew the humiliation of being accepted into Eastern Mennonite College "on probation" even though he had been valedictorian at his black "separate-but-equal" high school. He felt gratitude to the depths of his being for the gifts of his newfound spiritual family, a church that believed in him enough that they sponsored him as a student at EMC.

Leroy Berry Jr. was a bright fellow and worked his way up to high honors in college. Eventually, he earned a master's degree and a PhD, and was a professor at Goshen College in Indiana and worked as a lawyer. He married and became the father of two children. He was involved in church affairs, and was the founder of "High Aim," an organization to assist young people from disadvantaged homes to get a good education.

We completed washing the dormitory in good time and washed a few other houses before Leroy had to go. Vera and I weren't busy and had a little money, so we decided to take a quick trip to Alberta to show off our daughter.

It was late August when Darrell took us to the train station in Staunton. We took the day coach, which was cheaper, and brought our own food, but forgot a cake in Darrell's car. The train took us straight through to Havre, Montana, where my brother and sister-in-law, Peter and Margaret, met us at the station and brought us to Duchess.

We had a "short but sweet" visit with our family and friends and proudly showed off our daughter.

All too soon, the time came to return. Peter, with Margaret, Kathy, Mom, and Dad, accompanied us in Peter's 1962 Pontiac back to Havre. We left in good time so as not to miss the train.

The trip went fine until we had a flat tire. We changed it and proceeded on our way. About ten miles from the boarder, a second tire went flat. Now we had no spare tire and no means to repair it as we were travelling through a desolate stretch of the vast prairie. Peter decided to keep going until we would reach a farm where we could get some help.

In that prairie wasteland of southeastern Alberta, there were no farms. Peter kept driving faster and faster, until we were going at least fifty miles per hour on the flat tire.

Can you imagine, the nice 1962 Pontiac, loaded to the gills with six adults, two one-year-old children, and our luggage, (no car seats in those days) speeding down the gravel road, stones and dust flying, on a flat rear tire! I do not know why the tire never came off the rim, but it did not. Eventually it began to disintegrate, bit by bit. Pieces of rubber were banging against the fender in the wheel well. A cloud of smoke from burning rubber trailed us.

By the time we reached the USA boarder, the tire had disintegrated completely, and we were driving on the steel rim.

The customs officer thought we had not noticed that we had a flat tire. We explained our predicament. He warned us that it was against the law to damage the pavement (The USA side was paved) and waved us on. We drove on and the rim began to disintegrate.

Finally, after going a couple more miles, when that rim was about down to the hub, we came to a farm. The man was not home, but the sympathetic wife let us into the tool shed. There, we found a new inner tube that fit the other flat tire. We put it together and soon were rushing madly down to Havre hoping the train would be late. For once it was not. It had gone three quarters of an hour ago!

What do we do now? Another train would come by tomorrow at the same time. What else could we do except wait? We found a cheap hotel near the tracks and booked their cheapest room with a single cot.

Then, we went with Peter to look for another rim and tire for a spare. In that little prairie town, we were fortunate. We all had something to eat; then they said goodbye and went home.

Vera, Cindy, and I turned to spend a lonely night in a strange town in the dingy little western hotel. We bedded Cindy in a dresser drawer, and Vera and I slept fitfully on our single bed. Soon it was morning, then an eight-hour wait, and then we got back on track. To us "Havre" will always be a boring little town.

Riding on a train was relaxing and fun. This train had a dome car where passengers could go and sit to enjoy the scenery. We arrived back in Staunton at one o'clock p.m. on Thursday. We phoned to James Roth who came and brought us home. By three thirty I was back at work, cleaning bricks. I had a few more houses to clean before school opened.

Sometime later, Cindy developed a boil under the point of her chin. The doctor put her in the hospital and made an incision and a drain. It was heart wrenching to leave this little one-year-old there alone for two days. She was too young to understand that we could not stay there with her or that we were not abandoning her forever.

Special Friends

Among our special friends were Darrell and Florence Jantzi. We visited together often on Sundays, going for afternoon drives in the mountains, visiting parks and famous sights, or just enjoying the countryside. Several times, we bought a half a beef together and had it cut, packaged, and frozen. Darrell had grown up with me in Ontario; his sister had married Werner Barg and lived on a farm across the road from us in Alberta. Now we found each other in Virginia. He was older than I and had married earlier, so he was, in many ways, my mentor as I went through the rocky wilderness of courtship. We both were interested in preparation for pastoral ministry, had attended many of the same classes, and had graduated in the same year. Florence worked at EMC in the offices and later in the Historical Library while her husband went to school.

While I went to seminary, Darrell worked for the Mennonite Hour Broadcasts as business manager. He was also taking some seminary classes on the side. Darrell and Florence did not have any natural children, so they adopted a daughter, whom they named "Christine," shortly after our daughter, Cynthia, was born. Later they adopted a boy and another girl and raised a nice family.

Some of our other special friends were James and Ann Marie Roth and Clair and Katie Schumm. James was from Duchess and was my friend from birth since our parents were the best of friends. We also shared a bit of the same childhood Ontario experience. Now they had Kevin, a baby boy four days younger than our daughter.

The Schumms were from Ontario. Clair was also a Bible major interested in the ministry. They had a daughter, Darla, who also was Cindy's age, so we had a lot in common with these friends. Besides these, we had many other friends with whom we spent time doing things or going places. Those were good and happy years.

When we came to register for the fall semester of 1966, we were surprised and very pleased to find that Alfred and Noreen Polzin had moved to the area from Saskatchewan. I had met them in my various visits to Guernsey. Alfred was an immigrant from East Germany, a Catholic who had met the Mennonites in Saskatchewan and married one of them, Noreen Cressman. Now, he had come to train for the pastoral ministry. They quickly were added to our list of special friends. They had a daughter, Maria, about a year younger than Cindy.

George Volunteers to Serve in India

News came from home that my brother George had agreed to go to India under the Voluntary Service program of the Mennonite Board of Missions, Elkhart, Indiana. He would be going to Dhamtari, Mahadre Pradesh to serve as a maintenance person at the Shantipur Leprosy Hospital for a term of three years. He would be leaving home in October 1965, making a journey to Ontario, Pennsylvania, and Virginia before going to Elkhart for orientation. We were excited about seeing him again.

After visiting in Ontario, George got a ride with Clarence Huber to Pennsylvania. From there he hitchhiked to Winchester, Virginia, where he bought a good camera before he caught a bus to Harrisonburg, arriving on Tuesday at seven o'clock, p.m., November 2nd. We were not home, so he phoned James Roth who picked him up and brought him to their place.

We had a wonderful time visiting over the next several days. He helped Vernane babysit Cindy while we went about our duties. Friday evening, we took him to Darrell Jantzi's for supper. The next day our uncle David Friesen and his wife came from Lansdale for a visit. They went with us to see the Endless Caverns, a unique experience. They took George with them back to their home in Pennsylvania. From there, he took a bus to Elkhart.

George had reported that back on the farm near Duchess, Dad was building a modern pig barn complete with slatted floors and manure pits to eliminate cleaning. It was to be a farrow to finish building for about 250 pigs. It was to have no windows, only electrical lights and forced air vents. It was to be sanitary, efficient, and make big profits. It would need to be profitable if the farmer was to pay back the $8,000 that was borrowed to finance it.

An Accident

On an early December Sunday afternoon, Vera, Cindy, and I were out driving around in the beautiful countryside, west of town, enjoying the scenery. We were on one of those narrow, winding, hilly, bumpy, country trails common in rural Virginia. We were leisurely driving along, enjoying the ride, and gawking at the scenery.

There was a new house I was admiring, when suddenly, as we came up a little knoll, there emerged a shiny new Pontiac, hurtling fast out of the dip on the other side towards us. I, leisurely straddling the center of the narrow road, was startled. Too late to get our right wheel entirely into the ditch, I failed to avoid contact. There was a horrible collision and, it seemed, parts flew in every direction!

After the dust settled, we were happy to discover that we were all still alive. In fact, there weren't even any injuries that we could detect. Finally, we crawled out of the wreckage to survey the damage. The Pontiac had only one bruised fender, but our Plymouth was in sad shape. It had badly bruised front and rear left fenders, a twisted bumper, a torn taillight, a dislocated tailfin, as well as a fractured chrome strip. The sight was enough to make a man shed tears, but I did not. I was exceedingly happy that the injuries weren't any worse! After calling the police and answering enough questions to make a lengthy report for a dangerous criminal case, we drove home.

No, the policeman did not arrest me, but he did give me a summons to court. Sometime later I complained bitterly as I self-righteously reported to my parents:

> *American justice hauled me into court on account of that accident and extracted $43.75 from me for failure to drive right of center on the road. They did not even give me a chance to plead guilty, just slapped me with a fine. It made me angry... You know what those roads are like, back in the country. Everybody drives on the center. Well, that's what a guy gets for being normal. On top of the fine, the insurance rate goes up for the next three years, and I still have the car to fix.*

About fixing the car, the damage was estimated at $190.00, which of course I did not have. Later, when my mechanic brother, Paul, visited us, he suggested I fix it myself. I had never thought of such a thing. I got out my simple set of tools and began. I hammered out the tailfin to a similitude of its original shape. Then I bolted the taillight into place. I bent the bumper straight and screwed the chrome strip into place. Finally, I smeared some paint on the scratched places, and the result was amazing indeed. From a distance it looked fine. A close-up inspection revealed a few scratches and minor dents. It did not cost me anything after all, only the less-than just, but uncontested, fine!

ELEVEN

FINDING DIRECTION

Seeking Direction

The fall of 1966 found me back for a fifth year of studies and a second year of seminary. This drive to be useful, call it a sense of destiny or a "call of the Lord" was giving me no rest. Five years in higher learning were enough. I felt it was time to be moving on, to put some of the theory into practice. I expressed myself in a letter:

> *I believe this is the last semester for me for a while. If we go abroad, I would like to finish when we come back after three years. If we do not go abroad, I've got to get out anyway for financial reasons and perhaps for my own good, although the advisors all advise me to stay one more year and finish. I'm amazed that I've been able to stay in school as long as I have. I'm sure it has been of the Lord. Another year looks to me as impossible, yet I've said the same thing every spring for the last several years. Do not ask me how, but by hooks or by crooks I've been able to stick with the books!*

The Ridgeway Church building was nearing its completion, and the congregation moved in that fall and had a dedication service in early

November. I had been doing quite a bit of the preaching that summer since Dan Smuckers had taken a four-week vacation to California. Then he had been hospitalized for some time after they returned. By this time, we were feeling comfortable being a part of the congregational community.

Vera had quit her part-time job at EMC in June when I went to work full time. She began babysitting Debbie Showalter in our house for forty dollars per month. This paid our rent. In the fall, I continued with brick cleaning on Saturdays when there was work and the weather cooperated. Mostly, we depended upon that to meet all our other needs. It was a lean year.

We had decided this would be our last year of seminary for now. I was eager to get out of school for a change and get to work and felt that it would be good to interrupt my scholastic career at this point, and, perhaps, get my final year sometime later at a different seminary. We were open to explore possibilities.

The thought of entering the pastoral ministry, even with five years of training, sort of scared me. I felt I was still too young and immature to be a pastor to the older people. Therefore, when the recruiters from the various mission and service agencies visited campus, I paid close attention.

One of those recruiters was Chester Wenger, representing the Eastern Mennonite Board of Missions and Charities (Now "Eastern Mennonite Missions" or "EMM"). I had made his acquaintance years back when he and his family were missionaries in Ethiopia. When he visited the EMC campus that fall of 1966, he greeted me in the hallway and asked, "You are still here?" I replied that I did not want to be much longer. Then, he asked me about future plans.

When I shared my uncertainty, he said, "I think we have a place for you as a Bible teacher at the Nazareth Bible Academy in Ethiopia." He figured I might be just the person they were looking for to start the next fall. That started a conversation that led to an agreement to consider the matter further and to pray about it.

When I reported this conversation to Vera, her first response was rather hesitant, "Ethiopia? Where is that?"

Dorsa Mishler, representing the Mennonite Board of Missions in Elkhart, IN, contacted us about a great need for seminary-trained men to go to India to give pastoral help to the struggling churches there. He told us they needed a dozen missionary couples there. The problem was, at that time, India would not grant US citizens work permits to be missionaries. But Canadians could be given work permits. Since I was a Canadian, they were asking me to give this need thoughtful consideration.

This assignment would be more difficult, since it would immediately involve language study, and one should have some pastoral experience before undertaking that role in a foreign culture. Now my problem was not "Is there any work to do?" but rather "Lord, where shall we start?"

Over the next months, we gave thought and prayer to the subject of our future. Increasingly, I found myself pulling away from the India challenge.

I reasoned that the Indian church was already seventy years old and should have Indian nationals as pastors. Just before independence, in 1948, there were over thirty missionaries in India. They had enough time to train and install pastors. Who was I to think that I could do the job better than them? How could an inexperienced youth, such as myself, go into a strange culture and function as a pastor and a trainer of pastoral candidates that were twice my age and native to that culture? It just did not make sense to me.

I tended to favor the Ethiopian challenge. At least, I would be a young adult teaching younger students. I believed that I could feel comfortable in that role. On the other hand, Vera was not convinced that she was called to be a missionary anywhere. She did not even want to talk about it.

Interruptions

In January 1967, we got a message that my grandmother, Justina Friesen, was hospitalized and was very sick. Her youngest son, David, was happily married and living with his wife, Esther, in Evanston, Illinois, where he was doing his alternative to military service at a hospital. In late January, he called us in Virginia and invited us to join them on a trip to Alberta to visit his mother. In response, we took some time off and drove to Martinsburg, West Virginia, where we parked our car and took a train to Chicago, where David met us. From there, we set out together in David's car, driving the 1700 wintry miles straight through to Duchess, Alberta, without resting.

We found Grandmother resting in the Brooks General Hospital. She was not well, but she was not in a critical condition either. The doctors were very vague about the nature of her illness, what it was, what could be done to treat it, or what we could expect to come of it.

Finally, they indicated there was nothing they could do for her, except to keep her as comfortable as possible and warned the family that we should not expect her to recover. Much later, the doctors admitted that they thought she was full of cancer, including cancer of the bones.

We visited her several times and spent the rest of the time with our family. On one of our visits, Grandmother gave me words of advice I could never forget, "Carl, be faithful!" She was never one to give advice or to interfere in our lives, so when she said something as brief as that, it was to be taken to heart. She did not elaborate on what she had in mind, but I took her words as a final charge to keep, a passing on of the legacy and the vision. She was passing on to her children and grandchildren that which motivated her and drove her: her faith and sense of call to faithfulness in discipleship. I sensed she was affirming what she had seen in me and was urging me on.

She was a saint, an example, and a role model. She was a woman of character and strength and deep faith. I know she upheld her children and grandchildren in prayer. As done throughout all her life, she still found her strength and solace in her faith, which she nourished from her Bible and her prayers and her church.

I will never forget my grandmother's encouraging words: "Carl, be faithful!" January 1967

David took Grandmother home from the hospital at her request. She wanted to die at home without "heroic measures" to prolong her sufferings. Grandpa would care for her at home.

We stayed as long as we could; then we had to head back east to our work and our studies. Again, we drove straight through without stopping to sleep. This time, we found Chicago digging out of one of its biggest blizzards. Hundreds of cars were abandoned in the snow drifts, roads were nearly impassable, but the clearing crews were out, and the main arteries were being opened, so we got to David's place okay before Saturday noon.

After having lunch there, they took us to the train station. Driving the twenty-five miles through Chicago took a good two hours, most of the streets still being closed. The train left at six p.m., two hours behind schedule and overloaded, but we found seats. We picked up our car at Martinsburg the next morning and arrived home before noon.

A few weeks after our return home, in February, my grandfather, Jacob Friesen, suffered a stroke and was hospitalized. The stroke left him permanently paralyzed on one side and with reduced mental capacities. He would never live at home nor help himself again. He was sixty-eight years of age.

Little did we know that he would live under nursing care for the next eighteen years. Grandmother was able to go visit him at the hospital only once. That was the last time they were together on this earth.

My aunt Melita Grove cared for her mother until Esther returned from the Ontario Mennonite Bible Institute to give full time nursing care at home. During that spring and summer, Grandmother's condition declined ever so slowly and painfully.

Shortly after we arrived back in Virginia, my brother Charles surprised us with a visit for a few days. He had been attending a Bible school at Carbon Hill in Ohio with his Torkelson friends for a few weeks. They brought him to EMC at seven-fifteen p.m. on a Saturday night. He could not find our place and could not reach us by phone because the line was busy. He was about ready to give up and hunt for a motel, but one last attempt on the phone at nine-fifteen p.m. got through, and we met him in front of the chapel. We only lived about 1000 feet from the administration building, but on a Saturday night, no one could tell him where we lived.

Another Accident

The Intervarsity Peace Fellowship was holding a meeting in New York City from March 2nd to the 4th, 1967. About a hundred students representing ten "peace colleges" would be attending. Three of us students from EMS decided to attend. Eugene Shelly drove his late model Ford, and Milton Zehr and I made up the rest of the group. We set out for New York on Thursday at two a.m. and arrived at the Church Center in the National Council of Churches (NCC) building across from the U.N. headquarters in time for the meeting to start. There were special speakers from the UN. We visited the UN and sat in on some of the sessions. We were to spend the nights at the local YMCA.

After the last session on Friday, someone from the YMCA led twenty-two of us on a walking tour of the city at seven p.m. We walked, and walked, and walked, and walked, and rode the subway, and walked some more, then rode the ferry and rode a subway again, then walked, and walked, and walked some more. We saw huge cathedrals that were dark, cold, and empty, huge impersonal buildings, skyscrapers, and cultural centers such as the fabulous Lincoln Center where the Metropolitan Opera Palace is located. We strolled around in Greenwich Village where the "beatniks" lived. This was the center of the "counterculture" where the artists and poets hung out. There was a lot of activity going on.

I'll never forget the strange enticement of a straggly-haired young girl standing down in an open basement stairwell where there was obviously a party going on, calling up to us passers-by in a carefree almost cynical invitational voice, "Come on down and join us, and put some fun into your miserable lives!" We got back to the YMCA well past midnight.

Our meeting was to end at noon the next day, but the important agenda was covered by Friday night. We weren't very sleepy yet, when we got the idea, "Wouldn't it be a nice surprise for our lonely wives, if we would walk in on them for breakfast tomorrow morning?" A great idea! Instead of turning into our waiting beds for a good night's sleep, one o'clock, a.m. found us climbing into the Ford and moving out into the night traffic, heading south.

We took turns driving while the other two were sleeping. Everything went fine, and we made good progress. We were just reaching Winchester,

Virginia, around six a.m., only one hour from our homes and our surprised wives preparing their lonely Saturday morning breakfasts! However, arriving then was not to be so.

Eugene was sleeping on the back seat, and I was sleeping in the front passenger's seat. Apparently, Milton also was beginning to sleep in the driver's seat, for the car went over to the left edge of the road and struck a guardrail, bounced back onto the highway, skidded across a bridge, struck the concrete bridge railing on the left side, which flipped the car over on its right side.

I woke up seeing the asphalt whizzing by the windshield, inches from my right elbow. Only the glass between it and the asphalt kept it from being ground up like hamburger. The car came to a rest, still on its side, at the far end of the bridge. We were all sort of stunned. What a rude awakening! What happened anyway? Are we all okay? Might the car catch fire?

But wake up we did! That was something for which to be thankful. Milton was on top of me. He seemed okay and slowly crawled up out the driver's broken window above us. The door was jammed. Then Eugene crawled out. They were okay. I waited a few minutes. It was drizzling and cold outside and my neck hurt.

They helped pull me up and out too. Was I okay? I had a very sore neck and parts of my face were bloody and numb. At least I could walk.

We could not have chosen a more convenient place to have an accident if we must have one. It was about a hundred yards from the exit that leads right to the hospital. Somebody called the rescue squad, and it was there in no time to pick us up. Although I was walking, they made me lie down on a stretcher and put me in the ambulance and whisked us off to the hospital.

We were examined and x-rayed. Eugene had a very sore whiplash, nothing more. Milton was okay. I had a fractured vertebrae and a crushed disc in my neck. They admitted me in the hospital. Instead of surprising our wives with a visit, we surprised them with a phone call. They had to find someone to come and get the other two.

Some hours later, when Vera came to see me, the doctor had me stretched out on the bed with my head in a harness fastened to the front and a fifteen-pound weight dangling from the back of the bed by a cord that was connected through a pully to my feet, keeping me stretched to the maximum. The attendants explained that this was to protect my spinal cord from any possible jolt that might endanger it from the cracked vertebrae or crushed discs.

After some hours, that became real torture. I felt a new level of sympathy for the Anabaptist martyrs stretched out on the rack. As the hours and then the nights and days went by, the muscles tensed up tighter and tighter until I was in sheer agony. As I was laying on my back strapped in place the whole time, I could not turn over on one side nor the other. The irritation became more and more intense. I began to understand how bedsores come and how awful they must be.

Finally, when the treatment was becoming unbearable, two days later, the harness was removed. I was fitted with a thick stiff neck collar and allowed to get up and move about. Ever since, I have much empathy for any patient or prisoner that is strung up with any kind of harness or stretched on the rack.

It was a week later that I was discharged and allowed to complete my journey home.

Traveling all night after a busy day is not always the fastest way to reach home! The car was totaled. Had we gone off the road twenty feet sooner, we would have landed in a twenty-five-foot-deep gully. This was before seatbelts or air bags were mandatory. What would the results have been then?

We were very grateful for guardrails and thankful that I could go home having only a yellow bicep, a yellow eye, a few scratches, and a very stiff neck to remind me, from time to time, to count my blessings. All I can say is that in the innocence of sweet sleep, a hand that is mightier than ours guided that wheel to a softer landing.

I had to wear a stiff collar to protect myself against any possible jolts for the next six weeks. I had to miss the annual seminary tour that took place a week later in order to catch up on missed studies.

People were very kind to us. I received many cards, flowers, and visitors in the hospital. The insurance adjuster came to visit me and assured me that the company would pay the hospital bill. Friends and family sent thoughtful cards, well wishes, and flowers. The college students took a collection of money that totaled about one hundred and forty dollars to help us out. That sure was a help since we were down to our last fifty dollars and depended upon my part-time brick cleaning for survival. I wrote home, "He takes care of us sparrows in the oddest ways." I never had so much attention in my life before and never knew I had so many friends.

I could not wash bricks for about two months. I got around that by becoming an exploiting capitalist, hiring other students to work for me. I would bring my books along to study, while they did the work. I still made a good profit.

During my time of recovery, I reflected a lot on the meaning and purpose of life, and I was impressed most with its fragility. Dying can be so easy and instantaneous. In my accident, when I awoke from sleep, the damage was already done. I had not noticed a thing. I had to think, what a nice way to go when it comes time to die—in one's sleep, no pain, no fear, and no prolonged agony—only instantaneous eternity. What a blessing to be ready!

Then I thought, how selfish of me, how escapist. I have responsibilities here on this earth to fulfill. I have a young wife and a child, and a yet unborn child that need me. I, who always up to now had been a receiver, have a debt to pay, to be a giver, to pass on to others the blessings I have received, to help others on the way to a better, fuller life. In the words of a song writer, "Still undone things I long to do. Lord, give me grace and strength renew!" Or to borrow from Robert Frost:

The woods are lovely, dark, and deep.
But I have promises to keep,
And miles to go before I sleep.
And miles to go before I sleep.

Preparing for a "Safari" in Africa

The Eastern Mennonite Board of Missions stayed connected with us about a possible assignment to Ethiopia. On March 22nd, we had an interview with Paul Kraybill and Harold Stauffer at their headquarters in Salunga, Pennsylvania. They discussed the Ethiopia assignment and needs in Somalia and Tanzania. They promised to issue a formal "call" in a few weeks. We would have to make up our minds soon.

Vera had been reluctant to think about going to Africa. She had never thought of herself as the "missionary type." She was a mother and a homemaker, and that was all the challenge she craved. Besides, she found out that a second child was to be expected in October. Why would anyone, in his or her right mind, want to go wandering off to some remote part of the earth in that condition?

She thought and prayed a lot about it. We could not stay at the seminary forever. We did have to make a move to a place where I could work at some kind of ministry that we could feel was where God wanted us. Slowly, her horizons stretched, and she could see us doing a useful ministry in a needy country, although she had no idea what Ethiopia was like. She finally came to see it as a challenge that the Lord was putting before us.

One day Vera, who always gives attention to the details, said something like, "When we go to Ethiopia, I want to take … (she named some things) along." I was surprised, and responded, "Oh, so we are going to Ethiopia then?" From then on, we knew the decision was made; we would be going to Ethiopia. What a life-changing turning point that came to be!

We notified the Board of our decision and began to plan all the details that we would need to consider. Besides finishing the final term of seminary and carrying on with the brick cleaning business on the side to keep us in bread and butter, there would be application forms and doctrinal questionnaires to fill out, interviews, and appointment procedures to go through. We would have to have physical examinations and vaccinations. There would be passports and visas to get.

Beyond that, there would be all the shopping for and packing of all the necessities that our growing family would need for the next three years. The final preparations would also include breaking up housekeeping, selling, giving away, or storing all our possessions that we were not squeezing into the four steel drums that we were allotted to be shipped to Ethiopia.

We were summoned to appear before the examining committee of the Bishop Board on Saturday, May 13th. I gave an account of the ordeal to my folks:

> *Before this austere and august body of five gray-haired and black-clad Lancaster Conference bishops, we were carefully examined as to doctrinal orthodoxy. We had to answer questions that arose from a 12-page doctrinal questionnaire*

> *that we had filled out previously. Since we were not from Lancaster Conference and since we expressed minor "heretical" views on some issues, it took them an hour to get us through.*
>
> *It was kind of amusing, if not pathetic, that they weren't as concerned about our views on marriage and divorce, life insurance, or the three-fold ministry, as they were concerned about our views on, and willingness to conform to, their standards of dress. The right garments apparently can cover up a multitude of heresies. After promising not to embarrass them within their constituency, they appointed us as "Missionary Associates" to a three-year teaching assignment in the Bible Academy at Nazareth, Ethiopia.*

The Board wanted us to stay on at EMC for a two-week Missions Institute in June before we moved out of Virginia. Additionally, there would be orientation and commissioning at Salunga, Pennsylvania in July. We would then say our farewells in the east and travel west to spend August with our family in Alberta before flying to Ethiopia.

I disposed of my acid barrel, brushes, hoses, ladder, and business by selling them to our friend, Clayton Kipfer, a fellow student from Ontario. He had been helping me and learned the trade. We sold our furniture to EMC to remain in the apartment. The remaining things that we could not squeeze into our four barrels or into our cheap suitcases for trans-Atlantic shipment were stored in Vera's mother's attic in Belleville.

We said our "Farewell!" to our friends in Virginia and departed on the third of July. The next few weeks were spent in Pennsylvania attending missionary orientation at Salunga from the fourth to the tenth of July, being commissioned, finishing all related business, and saying "Farewell!" to Vera's family and friends in Belleville.

During those weeks, we got wind that a certain lonely, widowed gentleman was clandestinely courting Vera's widowed mother. Being a prudent woman with a strong distaste for being the subject of local gossip, Mother Elizabeth King did her best to disguise their comings and goings together from the prying eyes of the neighborhood by smuggling him into her upstairs apartment through the basement door at the back of her house.

This was going on for some time, and, while Mother King vacillated between continuing and terminating the relationship, a more aggressive Jacob B. Yoder, recently widowed, cast his lonely eyes on the virtuous King widow. At first, he did not seem to know that a secret competitor had staked out the ground ahead of him. When he did find out, he refused to be smuggled in through the back cellar door. He insisted on coming in openly at the front door, in full public view, thus compelled the vacillating widow to make up her mind about who was the better man. It did not take the admiring Elizabeth long to be persuaded.

Since these things were just in process as we were preparing to leave for three years, she thought it prudent and right to introduce us to Jacob prior to our leaving, just in case the romance would lead to a more permanent relationship in our absence. She arranged for a family picnic in the mountains, to which she brought the lucky man for official introduction and thorough family inspection. She was very pleased that her children were not opposed.

We decided to drive our battered and bruised Plymouth to Alberta and leave it there. We ordered our tickets for August 30 to fly to Ethiopia from Calgary, Alberta. Then, we drove up to Fort Erie, Ontario, where Vera registered herself and Cindy as landed immigrants in Canada on July 26, 1967.

We visited our relatives and friends while there. My brother Paul was living and working in Ontario by then. We met his fiancée, Irene Ropp of Wallenstein. They were planning their wedding, which we would miss, in Ontario on October 21. We decided to drive through Michigan on our way to Alberta. There we visited Vera's cousin, Elaine Swartz, her husband, Olen, and her family as well as Lena Roth and her children.

We took the long way to Alberta via Chicago so we could visit David Friesen's in Evanston, Illinois. They entertained us well, showing us the city. We were impressed with the Bahai temple and the gardens surrounding it.

Then we headed west, stopping to sleep at St. Paul, Minnesota. The next day, we planned to stop around Regina, Saskatchewan, but drove past all the motels. By the time we reached Swift Current, it was getting late, and the motels were all filled, so we went on towards Watrous.

We phoned ahead to warn our uncle and aunt, Jack and Neta Broadfoot, that we were coming. It was about one o'clock a.m. when we finally arrived. They had to move some of their boys from the comfort of their beds to give us a warm welcome. We felt a bit like intruders, but after being on the road for seventeen hours, we appreciated the bed.

That was my first visit in Saskatchewan in five years, and a lot had changed. A huge potash industry had been established with a big mine near Guernsey. The company had bought many farms, and a lot of people had moved out of the area.

A few days later, on August 8, we arrived at home in Duchess. It was harvest time, and I was able to get involved in helping a bit. Grandma was still living, so we visited her quite often, and she appreciated that. She was bedfast and in constant pain with cancer of the bone. Marian Martin, a nurse, came in twice a day to give her shots of painkiller. There was no other medication that could help.

We were waiting for our visas to be approved so our flight dates could be finalized, and our tickets issued. We were wanted in Ethiopia by early September. Now it was early September, and there was still no word about visas. The Board told us to just be patient; it could be approved at any time, including a month or two later than we liked.

We enjoyed the extra time with my family and friends. We visited the mountains in the Waterton Park area and saw the Japanese Gardens in Lethbridge. However, we were getting anxious about Vera's condition. We were told that the airlines would not allow a woman more than seven months pregnant to board an overseas flight. She had already reached that point by the end of August.

Grandmother's Departure

As we waited, Grandmother's condition slowly worsened. She could no longer walk, and then she could no longer sit. The cancer was in her spine and made it very painful. Esther had to get up almost every hour of the night to tend to her. She ate a little soft food and soup and drank coffee, yet she remained cheerful and thankful. Marian came faithfully twice a day to give her the injection of morphine or another strong painkiller. Towards the end, nothing could kill the pain. Visitors came and went every day. They brought cheer and comfort and showed that they cared.

The last week of her life, Grandmother was in and out of a coma. On September 23, seventy-one years and one day after her birth, she passed away quietly in peace, just as she had lived.

I was helping dig her grave when a phone call came from the Mission Board, notifying us that the visas had been granted. They wondered what date we preferred to fly. We asked for the day after the funeral. It seemed to us that we could see the hand of God in arranging the timing of the issuing of the visas to make it possible for us to be present at this awesome occasion!

All her fourteen children attended her funeral. She had twenty-eight grandsons, thirteen granddaughters, and three great granddaughters at the time of her passing.

Grandmother had planned her funeral. Her pastor, Clarence Ramer, conducted it according to her wishes. She chose scripture and songs that expressed her faith and deepest longings: "Psalms 121," "Safe In The Arms Of Jesus," "Rock of Ages," "Only A Sinner Saved By Grace," "Going Down The Valley," "How Beautiful Heaven Must Be," "Take Thou My Hand, O Father" (the song sung at their farewell when they left their home in Russia forty-three years earlier), "Will The Circle Be Unbroken?" "I Need No Mansion Here Below," and "There Is Sweet Rest In Heaven."

Her body was laid to rest in the Duchess Cemetery. It was a holy moment. Yes, her body was laid to rest, but her spirit joined "the cloud of witnesses" in the heavenlies, and I can still hear her quiet encouragement, "Carl, Be faithful!"

After the funeral, Vera and I and some others drove to Medicine Hat to say, "Goodbye!" to Grandfather who lay in a nursing home there.

The next day, September 28th, 1967, my folks and family members escorted Vera and Cindy and me, with our suitcases, to the International Airport in Calgary.

> "Go and make disciples of all nations, baptizing them in the name of the Father and of the Son and of the Holy Spirit, and teaching them to obey everything I have commanded you. And surely, I will be with you always, to the very end of the age." – Jesus (Matthew 28:19, 20 NIV)

Printed in the United States
by Baker & Taylor Publisher Services